Campaigns &

Campaigns & Elections
Contemporary Case Studies

Edited by Michael A. Bailey, Ronald A. Faucheux,
Paul S. Herrnson, and Clyde Wilcox

A Division of Congressional Quarterly Inc.
Washington, D.C.

CQ Press
A Division of Congressional Quarterly Inc.
1414 22nd St. N.W.
Washington, DC 20037

(202) 822-1475; (800) 638-1710

http://books.cq.com

Printed in the United States of America

03 02 01 00 99   5 4 3 2 1

Photo credits and acknowledgments: All photographs of candidates courtesy *CQ Weekly*, except Mark Neumann (p. 46) and Jim McGreevey (p. 152), courtesy Reuters; Tammy Baldwin (p. 84) and Jesse Ventura (p. 123), courtesy *Campaigns & Elections* magazine; and Josephine Musser (p. 84), courtesy Josephine Musser's campaign. All screen shots from TV spots and direct mail pieces courtesy *Campaigns & Elections* magazine.

Library of Congress Cataloging-in-Publication Data
Campaigns & elections : contemporary case studies / Michael Bailey . . . [et al.], editors.
    p.   cm.
    ISBN 1-56802-495-9 (pbk.)
    1. Electioneering—United States Case studies.   2. Elections—United States Case studies.   I. Bailey, Michael A., 1969–   .   II. Campaigns & elections.   III. Title: Campaigns and elections.
JK2281.C33   1999
324.7′0973′09049—dc21   99-38502

Contents

Preface   ix

Contributors   xi

Contemporary American Elections: An Overview   1
Michael A. Bailey, Ronald A. Faucheux, Paul S. Herrson, and Clyde Wilcox

Part I. Senate Races

1
So Close and Yet So Far   31
Two Unpopular Incumbents Meet with Different Fates in
California and New York in 1998
SEN. BARBARA BOXER (D) VS. MATT FONG (R) AND
SEN. AL D'AMATO (R) VS. REP. CHARLES SCHUMER (D)
Michael A. Bailey

2
They Did It Their Way   45
Campaign Finance Principles and Realities Clash in
Wisconsin in 1998
SEN. RUSSELL FEINGOLD (D) VS. REP. MARK NEUMANN (R)
Clyde Wilcox

3
Cornhusker Upset   55
Underdog Defeats Nebraska's Popular Governor in 1996 Senate Race
CHUCK HAGEL (R) VS. GOV. BEN NELSON (D) IN AN OPEN SEAT RACE
Doug McAuliffe

4
How to Beat an Incumbent   62
The Hard-Fought Senate Race in South Dakota in 1996
SEN. LARRY PRESSLER (R) VS. TIM JOHNSON (D)
Karl Struble

5

The Senator from Central Casting   71
How Fred Thompson Turned Tennessee Politics Upside Down in 1994
FRED THOMPSON (R) VS. JIM COOPER (D) IN AN OPEN SEAT RACE
David Beiler

Part II. House Races

6

Professionalism, Progressivism, and People Power   83
Baldwin's Victory Blends All Three in Wisconsin's 2nd District in 1998
TAMMY BALDWIN (D) VS. JO MUSSER (R) IN AN OPEN SEAT RACE
David T. Canon and Paul S. Herrnson

7

Winning in Unfriendly Territory   93
A Republican Victory in New Mexico's 3rd District in 1998
BILL REDMOND (R), ERIC SERNA (D), AND CAROL MILLER (GREEN PARTY) IN
A SPECIAL ELECTION
Chris Wilson and Mike Burita

8

Beating B-1 Bob   100
Underdog Ends Conservative's Congressional Career in California's 46th
District in 1996
REP. BOB DORNAN (R) VS. LORETTA SANCHEZ (D)
Bill Wachob and Andrew Kennedy

9

Incumbency and Base   106
How a Black Incumbent Won Renomination in a New Majority-White
District in Georgia in 1996
REP. CYNTHIA MCKINNEY (D) DEFEATS SEVERAL OPPONENTS IN PRIMARY
John Rowley

10

Coming On Strong Down the Stretch   112
Republican Leaves Democrats in the Dust in Kentucky's 2nd District
in 1994
RON LEWIS (R) VS. JOE PRATHER (D) IN AN OPEN SEAT RACE
Al Cross

Part III. State and Local Races

11
The Body Politic Registers a Protest   **121**
Jesse Ventura's Stunning Victory for Governor of Minnesota in 1998
JESSE VENTURA (REFORM PARTY), NORM COLEMAN (R), AND SKIP HUMPHREY (D)
IN AN OPEN SEAT RACE
David Beiler

12
'Bama Bash   **137**
Endorsement Backlash Saves a Governor from Primary Defeat in
Alabama in 1998
GOV. FOB JAMES (R) VS. WINTON BLOUNT (R)
David Beiler

13
The Squeaky Wheel(s) Make It Interesting   **150**
A GOP Star Barely Survives New Jersey Governor's Race in 1997
GOV. CHRISTINE TODD WHITMAN (R) VS. JIM McGREEVEY (D)
Peter Wendel

14
Only in Louisiana?   **156**
Populist Message Propels Republican to Governor's Mansion in Louisiana
in 1995
MIKE FOSTER (R) DEFEATS SEVERAL OPPONENTS IN AN OPEN SEAT RACE
Ronald A. Faucheux

15
The Unsinkable Willie Brown   **166**
Local Forces Elect Controversial Politician Mayor of San Francisco in 1995
WILLIE BROWN (D) BEATS MAYOR FRANK JORDAN (D) AND
ROBERTA ACHTENBERG (D)
David Beiler

Part IV. Referenda and Initiatives

16
Gun Play   **177**
How the NRA Defeated Initiative 676 in Washington State in 1997
Ronald A. Faucheux

17
Political Football   189
How the San Francisco 49ers Won a New Stadium and Shopping Mall in 1997
Noah Wepman

18
Using Conservative Values to Support Gay Rights   196
How Opponents Defeated Oregon's Anti–Gay Rights Referendum in 1994
Bob Meadow, Dawn Laguens, Heidi Von Szeliski, and Michael Terris

19
Bay State Class Warfare   201
How a "Guaranteed" Income Tax Cut Proposition Was Defeated in Massachusetts in 1994
Phyliss Johnston

Index   207

Preface

Campaigns and elections are central to democratic politics. Campaigns present voters with information they can use to decide among potential officeholders and policies. Elections provide voters with a level of control over officeholders who make the rules under which all citizens live.

To understand these aspects of American politics, campaign insiders have long turned to the insightful case studies found in *Campaigns & Elections* magazine. These cases, from federal, state, and local elections, show that each campaign is unique, with its own critical decisions and turning points.

The *Campaigns & Elections* case studies reprinted in this book represent the most interesting of these studies, yet they also have a significance beyond the specific races they cover. They teach us about the cast of modern politics: the candidates who seek public office and the consultants and activists who help them. They teach us about the techniques of modern politics, on both a tactical and strategic level. They also teach us about the factors outside a specific race that can influence the outcome, about the underlying trends that benefit some candidates and causes.

The goal of this book is to bring knowledge gained from the study of individual races together with an understanding of broad trends and the national context. The cases—some written especially for this book but all appearing in *Campaigns & Elections*—provide the specifics, while an introduction outlines general issues from a political science perspective, which is necessary for appreciating the patterns underlying the individual examples. This format allows us to present the full array of colorful characters, innovative tactics, and varied coalitions that contribute to election outcomes, while also providing an academic framework.

We believe that this approach serves several communities. First, it is ideal for the classroom. The engaging and consequential case studies put names and faces on abstract themes. They will appeal to "political junkies" who love learning about real politics and to reluctant students who find textbook politics distant and lifeless. At the same time, the links to general trends provide all students with a framework that they can apply to other elections.

This volume will also be useful to campaign professionals. The case studies provide accounts of what works—and what does not—in a variety of political environments. Particularly helpful are the discussions that show what key players knew and expected when they made pivotal decisions. Instead of Monday morning quarterbacking, the case studies give a sense of the uncertainty facing decision makers and the criteria they used to set their courses.

Finally, the book will be of interest to general readers. Nowhere can you find such a comprehensive sample of real campaigns, as told by the people who know them best. At the same time, we help readers understand them in the context of the broader national electoral experience.

We selected the cases carefully. First, we cover a variety of election types, picking roughly equal numbers of cases for the U.S. Senate, U.S. House, state and local offices, and referenda. Second, we balance the cases according to party, with a similar number of Republican and Democratic winners. Third, we represent all regions of the country, from New York to California, Louisiana to Minnesota.

Some types of campaigns and elections are not represented in the book. We do not cover presidential races, which are so well known that they do not need coverage here. To emphasize recent trends, we also do not cover races from before 1994.

This book has benefited greatly from the help of many individuals. We are particularly grateful for the valuable assistance of Brenda Carter and Gwenda Larsen at CQ Press.

Contributors

Michael A. Bailey is an assistant professor of government at Georgetown University.

David Beiler is a freelance writer and political analyst. He is also an elected member of the Stafford County, Virginia, Board of Supervisors.

Mike Burita was Bill Redmond's campaign manager. He is an account executive at Creative Response Concepts in Alexandria, Virginia.

David T. Canon is a professor of political science at the University of Wisconsin—Madison.

Al Cross is the political writer for the *Courier-Journal* in Louisville, Kentucky.

Ronald A. Faucheux is editor in chief of *Campaigns & Elections* magazine.

Paul S. Herrnson is a professor of government and politics at the University of Maryland, College Park.

Phyliss Johnston is an independent consultant who has worked on a number of ballot question campaigns.

Andrew Kennedy serves as principal of Kennedy Communications, a political consulting firm specializing in direct mail and opposition research. He formerly served as senior vice president for M&R Strategic Services.

Dawn Laguens is a partner in the media consulting firm Seder/Laguens.

Doug McAuliffe is chairman of McAuliffe Message Media, a strategic communications and media consulting company in Alexandria, Virginia.

Bob Meadow is president of the polling firm Decision Research.

John Rowley is a partner in the Nashville-based media consulting firm of Fletcher and Rowley Consulting, Inc.

Karl Struble is a Democratic media consultant. His Washington-based firm, Struble, Oppel, Donovan, handled Tim Johnson's campaign.

Michael Terris is a partner in the direct mail firm of Terris Jaye & Barnes.

Heidi Von Szeliski is vice president of the polling firm Decision Research.

Bill Wachob directs the West Coast operations of the Campaign Group, Inc., a Democratic political media consulting firm.

Peter Wendel is managing editor of *Campaigns & Elections* magazine.

Noah Wepman was formerly associate editor of *Campaigns & Elections* magazine.

Clyde Wilcox is a professor of government at Georgetown University.

Chris Wilson is president of Wilson Research Strategies, a Republican polling and strategy firm that worked for Bill Redmond.

Contemporary American Elections

An Overview

Michael A. Bailey, Ronald A. Faucheux,
Paul S. Herrnson, and Clyde Wilcox

American democracy is a complex phenomenon. It has many pockets of power: 1 in the White House, 435 in the House, 100 in the Senate, 50 in governor's mansions, and thousands more in statehouses and city halls across the country. The individuals who hold these diverse offices cooperate and compete in a complex, and sometimes obscure, manner to make policy in the federal system.

But one thing is clear: campaigns and elections are fundamental to this process. Public policies, whether enacted at the national, state, or local level, are ultimately subject to voter approval. Usually policies require the assent of elected officials, although increasingly voters decide policies directly in "elections without candidates"—referenda and initiatives. Even policies decided by courts or agencies are indirectly tied to campaigns and elections, as judges, cabinet members, and civil servants are either chosen by or must respond to officials who have passed the bar of getting elected.

Therefore, study of campaigns and elections can provide important insight into American politics and policy. Practically, this insight helps us see why and how our government does specific things. More philosophically, it helps us judge the democratic process. If campaigns and elections are vigorous and engaging, popular control is enhanced; if they are anemic and stultifying, private interests will more likely prevail in backroom deals and horse-trading.

There are additional reasons campaigns and elections are interesting. First, they are interesting from a technical standpoint. How can political consultants and activists help elect candidates who share their goals? Faced with a given electoral environment, how can a candidate maximize his or her

1

votes? There are no easy answers, as what works in one election may not work the next year in the next district over.

Second, campaigns are a source of great drama. They bring together some of the most interesting people in the country: some are smart, some are colorful, some are ruthless, and some are simply lucky. These people compete intensely in an arena with clear time and money constraints. The results can be fascinating: some candidates self-destruct early from over-confidence, others hold on until they finally get a break late in the campaign. Other races are slugfests from the opening bell, with one candidate barely standing as the final bell rings on election day.

This book seeks insight into this multifaceted phenomenon by looking directly at real people running real campaigns. The cases speak for themselves, revealing the actors who were important, the environment they faced, the information they had, and the choices they made. They cover national elections for the U.S. Senate and House, state elections for governorships and other state offices, state legislative races, and referenda. We have chosen races in years such as 1994, where national trends helped Republican candidates, and good Democratic years, such as 1998.

Taken together, the cases provide insights into a larger whole. In order to provide some context for this whole, this introduction surveys the major influences on election outcomes, focusing on issues, national trends, money, party, incumbency, candidate quality, campaign techniques, and referenda. By identifying patterns and trends, we hope to enable readers to recognize the broad forces, as well as the idiosyncratic factors, that influence how campaigns are conducted and who prevails in them.

Issues and National Trends

Many students of American politics believe that elections should focus on issues. Candidates should present different policy choices, and voters, after a period of reasonable deliberation, should choose which set of policies is more consistent with their values.[1] In this way, the public would have a direct influence on the major policy decisions that face government. In reality, however, campaigns often stray from such an ideal. Instead, the process whereby issues affect elections is often convoluted.

One reason that issues do not play as large a role as some would like is that candidates often adopt similar positions. Candidates from rural areas, regardless of their party, support agricultural programs, and candidates from conservative districts usually favor a balanced budget. Candidates from poor urban areas favor social spending. Those who do not are not viable. The lack of debate on these issues does not mean these issues are unimportant, only that they are uncontroversial in the district. The result may be tweedledee, tweedle-dum politics, but tweedle-anything-else politics often gets most candidates in trouble.

A second reason campaigns may not address the major topics of our times is that politicians face strong incentives to emphasize local issues over national issues. Most voters care more about local issues. National issues may dominate the *New York Times* and the *Washington Post,* but they seldom make it to kitchen table conversations about politics. Most voters simply do not have the time or interest to care, for example, whether the International Monetary Fund is re-authorized or not. As Democratic pollster Peter Hart puts it, "Most voters think about politics only two minutes a year—and resent the intrusion!"[2]

National issues have another strike against them: it is unlikely that a typical member of Congress, governor, or state representative can do much about them.[3] For federal legislation to pass, it must go through committee, be approved by the House leadership, pass the House floor, avoid a filibuster in the Senate, and pass the Senate as a whole. Differences between the House and Senate versions must be reconciled, and the compromise must pass both the House and Senate again. Then, it must be signed by the president and avoid court challenges by disgruntled opponents. State legislation must run a similar gauntlet.

Voters may reasonably think that a single elected official can do little to affect national or state policy and may look for more tangible benefits. That is, they may ask their representatives for material benefits, such as federal projects that bring jobs to the area. Candidates, then, must focus attention on the local demands for services, and incumbents must find ways to claim credit for new programs that affect the area. Hence former Speaker of the House Tip O'Neill's famous aphorism: "All politics is local."[4]

Local issues thus often become the center of campaigns. Nevada politicians battle over who is most effective in blocking nuclear waste dumping in the state. House races in southwest Georgia center on who can do more for peanut farmers. Candidates in Washington state discuss efforts to protect the Columbia River. Races in rural areas of Illinois, South Dakota, Colorado, and North Carolina feature heated debate over the regulation of hog farms.

That is not to say that larger national issues do not play a prominent role. Sometimes they directly influence an election's outcome. In 1998, for example, exit polls showed that the top concern of 20 percent of voters was education; of these people, 66 percent voted for Democrats.[5] Health care and taxes routinely play a prominent role in the national debate. Gun control, the environment, and education were major issues in 1998, and the role of government was a major issue in 1994. National issues become potent weapons when candidates tie them to voters' immediate circumstances, such as the cost of getting a physical checkup in Los Angeles, the tax burden borne by Manhattan residents, or the number of incidents of crime and violence in neighborhood schools.

These issues need not be significant to all voters. In fact, the most effective issues are usually important to only a subset of voters. Seniors have responded strongly to Medicare issues, whereas many women have responded to the abortion rights debate. In 1994, men were particularly opposed to "big government" and moved strongly toward the Republicans. The percentage of men voting Republican rose from 47 percent in 1992 to 57 percent in 1994; among men whose highest level of education was high school, the swing was from 38 percent to 56 percent.[6] When candidates take opposing positions on such issues, they become "voting issues," or issues that determine who will win many individuals' votes.[7]

More important than the direct role of national issues is their indirect role. Most voters do not have perfect—or even extensive—political information. To make decisions, they must rely on information and judgment shortcuts that help them figure out where they stand and for whom they will vote.[8] Public policy concerns thus often get wrapped up in specific symbols, or identified with particular personalities and groups, sometimes to the point even of obscuring major policy issues. This occurred at the presidential level in 1988, when George Bush campaigned on the Pledge of Allegiance and had a photo session in a flag factory. The substance of the issue was negligible—Michael Dukakis had vetoed a bill that would have mandated flag salutes in classrooms in Massachusetts, because his attorney general had advised him that the bill was unconstitutional. But the symbolism of the issue—to ally Bush with mainstream pride and patriotism, and to portray Dukakis as opposed to these values—was powerful. In cases like this, general issue concerns may manifest themselves in the form of national themes that wash over individual campaigns.[9] These themes provide a "bump" for candidates of one party across the whole country, a bump only the most competent campaigns are able to counter.

National trends, while sometimes affecting state and local elections, have their most direct influence on national elections. The most famous recent example is the 1994 Republican revolution. Many voters, especially white men, saw Clinton's national health care proposal as an excessive government intrusion into private matters. Many conservative white men were also angry with Clinton because of his proposal to allow gays and lesbians to serve openly in the armed forces and because of his support for gun control. Picking up on this discontent, Republican party leaders created a "Contract with America" that listed ten Republican priorities, including a balanced budget, welfare reform and congressional term limits.

The contract set the tone for the campaign, but as a practical matter the results of 1994 elections were primarily an expression of displeasure with

Bill Clinton. By election day, only one-third of voters had heard of the contract, but almost all were informed about the president and his unpopularity.[10] Republicans therefore associated national displeasure with the government with the persona of the president, morphing their Democratic opponents into grotesque versions of him.

In such an environment, few Democrats did as well as usual, and many were unable to withstand the tide, whatever their strengths or their opponents' weaknesses. Republicans picked up an extraordinary fifty-two seats in the House and eight in the Senate, taking unified control of Congress for the first time since 1954. Democratic losers included the Speaker of the House, Tom Foley, and the Chairman of the House Ways and Means Committee, Dan Rostenkowski.

While seldom so strong, such national tides are common. In 1996 the Democrats tried to turn the tables on the Republicans, arguing that Republican extremists had taken over the Congress, shut down the government, cut planned Medicare expenditures, and rolled back environmental protections. By election day, the Democrats had used these issues to create a fierce-sounding beast, a "Dole-Gingrich," who threatened to dismantle the government in behalf of the wealthy. In contrast to 1994, many Republican candidates had to run away from their leaders and core issues.

The bump in this election was modest, however. One impediment was retirements. Thirty Democrats retired from the House and eight retired from the Senate, many from the South, where the Democrats would have trouble winning open seats.[11] Another impediment was the late-breaking campaign-finance scandal. It sapped energy from many Democrats and drove President Clinton's support somewhat lower than the pre-election polls had predicted. Even as President Clinton rolled to reelection, the Democrats achieved only a nine-seat gain in the House and actually lost two seats in the Senate.

In 1998 national issues played an unusual and surprising role. As the nation sank deeper into the seamy details of the Lewinsky scandal in the late summer, many political pundits anticipated that Democratic voters would be demoralized, and therefore less likely to vote in November, while angry Republicans would flock to the polls. At a minimum, most pundits thought that the Republicans would gain ten seats in the House and a couple of seats in the Senate; some analysts, such as former Clinton advisor Dick Morris, spoke of Republican gains of more than twenty-five seats in the House and five in the Senate.

Both parties believed the conventional wisdom, although to starkly different effect. Congressional Republicans, basking in confidence months before the election, were so focused on impeaching Clinton that they neglected to pass essential budget legislation. That meant that in the final weeks of the session, they had to make considerable concessions to Clinton on a host of issues, lest they be blamed for another government shutdown. Conservatives lamented their lack of backbone, and moderates and liberals worried that they were more intent on destroying the president than addressing the nation's problems. For the Democrats, on the other hand, their belief in the conventional wisdom was a blessing. They were so fearful of an implosion of Democratic turnout that they poured resources into a "ground war" aimed at ensuring that Democratic voters would show up at the polls, meaning that they were able to turn people out in large numbers on election day.

Republicans made a bad situation worse in the final days of the campaign. Their core problem was that they had few issues to run on. A *Wall Street Journal* poll days before the election found that more than 40 percent of respondents thought Democrats could best handle health care, education, and Social Security issues, and that only 20 percent thought Republicans could best handle these issues. The issues on which Republicans had advantages, such as taxes and crime, were less salient due to the booming economy and improving crime situation. In desperation, House Speaker Newt Gingrich authorized $10 million to be spent on TV spots in targeted districts criticizing President Clinton's ethics. The idea was to jump-start conservative turnout, but the plan backfired as the national media picked up the ads, with an unintended consequence of making the Republicans appear obsessed with Clinton's personal life. Throughout the year polls had consistently shown that the public wanted Congress to drop the impeachment inquiry, by a margin of two to one. The Republicans seemed to many to be flaunting the desires of their constituents en route to a personal and partisan vendetta.[12]

On election day, the Democrats picked up five seats in the House and stayed even in the Senate. These gains were modest in an absolute sense but extraordinary in light of the fact that, historically, the president's party had lost seats in the House in every midterm election since 1934, losing an average of 32.2 seats.

In state and local elections, national trends do matter, but they are heavily mediated by local issues and institutions. First, not all states have elections at the same time as the federal elections, meaning that the environment of state elections may differ dramatically from that of congressional and presidential elections. Second, economic and social conditions can vary dramatically from state to state. California's economy, for example, slogged through the early nineties as parts of the Midwest boomed. Third, because the federal government and state governments have primary jurisdiction over different issues, the politics differ. States are more concerned with education, for example, whereas the federal government sets tariffs. Finally, states have their own political history; sometimes a state will simply tire of a politician who

has been in power too long, and that incumbent may be d‹
national trends.

The 1996 and 1998 state elections were typical. In 199‹ eleven gubernatorial races. In seven of them, popular incur.   ‿oin both parties won handily. The others were decided based on local issues and personalities, with no obvious trend. In state legislative races, Democrats gained control over eight chambers, while Republicans gained control over four, again with no obvious trends.[13]

In the 1998 state elections, a nation-wide pattern was visible but muted. Democrats had a good year in state legislatures, bolstered no doubt by voters' concerns with typically Democratic issues such as education, the environment, and gun control. The process was not uniformly pro-Democratic, however; even as Democrats made net gains, Republicans won control of some state legislatures.

The national pattern was even less clear at the gubernatorial level, as there was only a small change in partisan control. Moderate conservatives did well, especially Republicans such as George and Jeb Bush in Texas and Florida. Democrats picked up gubernatorial victories in traditionally hostile territory of the Deep South. In these races, Democratic challengers beat Republican incumbents by pushing for state lotteries that would fund education improvements.

Sometimes the influence of national trends on state and local elections is much more pronounced. This occurred in 1994, when Republicans picked up eleven governorships and gained control of both chambers in eleven legislatures (bringing their totals to thirty governorships and nineteen unified legislatures).[14] Prominent Democratic governors such as Ann Richards in Texas and Mario Cuomo in New York were among the many to fall from power.

Overall, then, issues do matter, but in complex and varied ways. Issues matter most if candidates articulate them to the public through effective messages. This process requires political advertising, which is generally quite expensive. We turn next to the importance of money.

Money

While the influence of issues has ebbed and flowed, the role of money in elections has increased steadily. The amount spent by candidates goes up every election cycle. Perhaps more importantly, the variety of ways that money enters elections has increased in recent years, making it increasingly difficult to account for and trace the source of political money.

Adding to the chaos, the rules that regulate campaign money continue to change, as federal and state regulations are challenged in the courts. Moreover, regulations on the funding of state and local races differ dramatically, with some states providing public funds, others imposing some limits and disclosure, and still others offering candidates a virtually unregulated environment in which to raise and spend money. Campaign finance is a regulated environment, but regulations are complex and ever changing, and they vary by type of election and by state.

Money in all types of elections comes primarily from four sources: individuals, interest groups, political parties, and the candidates' own funds. The ultimate source of most political money is individuals, giving directly to candidates, to political action committees (PACs), and to parties. For each election, federal law limits individual contributions to $1,000 per House or Senate candidate, $5,000 per PAC, and $20,000 to party committees. Individuals can also give unlimited amounts to the parties in "soft money," or spend unlimited amounts to independently advocate the election or defeat of a candidate, or to advocate an issue associated with a candidate. State laws cover individual contributions to state and local candidates; in some states there are strict limits, in others, none.

PACs are committees that raise money from individuals and spend it in federal or state elections. Most PACs are sponsored by interest groups, such as AT&T, the NRA, or the AFL-CIO, but some are independent groups whose members are simply those people who contribute to the organization. PACs can contribute up to $5,000 per congressional candidate per election, give to other PACs or party committees, and spend unlimited amounts as "independent expenditures" advocating the election or defeat of a candidate. PAC receipts and spending must be disclosed to the Federal Election Commission (FEC) and are therefore transparent to the public and the media.

Interest groups and individuals can also make "soft money" contributions to parties. These contributions go to party building activities such as voter registration, get-out-the-vote drives, and advertising efforts. They are not limited, but they must be disclosed. They can come directly from group treasuries, meaning that corporations can contribute funds generated by their business activity.

Another source of campaign spending, which is totally unregulated, is called "issue advocacy." Issue advocacy ads can mention candidates by name and even feature their pictures, but they cannot directly call for voters to vote for or against that candidate. The sources of such ads and the amount spent on them need not be disclosed. Labor unions, environmental groups, business groups, and conservative Christian groups have spent large amounts of money on such ads. In addition, dozens of groups have formed solely to develop and air issue advertising, a troubling development for those who want to know the sources of funding for these groups and their motives.

Another major source of election money is the political parties. To help specific candidates, parties can contribute directly to congressional candidates or spend money in coordination with the candidate's campaign. Both of these types of spending are limited by law. Parties can also spend unlimited amounts in generic party advertising, in issue advertising, and in voter mobilization efforts. Much of this latter spending is done with the soft money that parties raise from individuals and interest groups. Once again, state laws regulating parties vary by state.

A final source of campaign money is the candidates themselves. Few incumbents finance their campaigns from personal resources, but challengers and open-seat contestants often take out loans and dip into their personal savings to ensure that they have sufficient funds to get their message out. Candidate contributions often provide early seed money that the campaigns use to raise additional funds.[15]

To raise money, candidates assess their resources and develop a strategy to appeal to individuals, groups, and party committees. Ideological candidates often raise money from individuals through direct mail appeals, while moderate candidates are more likely to hold special events and in many cases to build networks of larger donors. Candidates also attempt to find networks of interest groups that will support their campaigns. This is relatively easy for incumbents, who regularly solicit the PACs of groups with business before the committees on which they serve. Non-incumbents do best by appealing to groups—whether business groups, labor groups, social conservative groups, or women's groups—that have an affinity with their stance on particular issues. Finally, candidates in close races attempt to persuade party committees to fully support their campaigns by showing that they have a real chance to win election.

A candidate's lack of money can mean defeat, especially for those who face well-financed opponents or incumbents. Money buys access to political consultants, who can help a candidate develop a viable campaign. Money buys polls that can help candidates assess their own and their opponents' weaknesses, test and hone messages, track changes in public opinion, and identify sets of voters who can be targeted with ads that will likely sway their votes. It buys access to media specialists who can develop sophisticated television spots, radio ads, and direct mail pieces. And, most importantly, it pays the cost of airing those spots at times when targeted voters are watching or listening.

Some of these resources can be gained without money. Candidates with strong ideological appeal can sometimes enlist sufficient numbers of volunteers to mount door-to-door voter contact. Linda Smith, who ran for the Senate in Washington in 1998 against incumbent Patty Murray, had an army of Christian conservative volunteers who met in churches and carried her message through the state. In some kinds of elections—state legislative races in large, expensive media markets, for example—buying television time may be unrealistic, and networks of volunteers may be an extremely valuable substitute.

Nevertheless, it is rare for candidates to win major competitive elections without raising significant sums of money.[16] Incumbents usually raise enough money to mount a competitive campaign, but non-incumbent candidates face a far more difficult task. In U.S. House races, few non-incumbents can be competitive unless they raise $500,000–$600,000.[17] In Senate races the amount needed to be competitive differs state by state, because some large states, such as California, have expensive contests, while in other less populous states, such as Wyoming, elections cost far less. State and local races differ in their costs as well. But in each of them there is a threshold of spending that is necessary to make a candidate competitive.

Interest groups and parties recognize this threshold, and they often insist that any non-incumbent candidate who they support raise a certain sum early in the campaign before they will contribute additional funds. Early fundraising is often referred to as "seed money" because it enables a campaign to grow. Early money buys a benchmark poll, a consultation with a consultant, and the professional help to create a "PAC kit," which can then be used to help persuade institutional actors that the candidate is viable. Some interest groups specialize in helping candidates with seed money. EMILY's List helps raise early money for pro-choice, Democratic women candidates by encouraging their members to contribute to candidates whom they have endorsed. The name of this PAC—Early Money Is Like Yeast—embodies the logic of early money, the ingredient that "makes dough rise." Many non-incumbent candidates launch their campaigns by loaning the campaign some of their personal funds, but institutional actors are far more impressed by money that is raised from individuals in the district, since this suggests that the candidate has a viable base of electoral support.[18]

It has become necessary to raise serious money to compete, not only for national offices, but for state and local offices as well. Elections for governor in large states are increasingly expensive, although in some states it is easier to raise money, because there are no limits to the amounts that individuals and groups can give. State legislatures differ enormously: some are professional bodies with great influence in their states and large staffs, while others are more amateur chambers in states dominated by governors. State legislative elections therefore likewise differ in their competitiveness and in the amount of money needed to run a successful campaign.[19]

Regardless of the office, one of the most consistent patterns in campaign finance is that incumbents raise far more money than their challengers. The average House incumbent raises more than 250 percent of the revenues of the average House challenger. Of course, most House races are not competitive, and many challengers in these races raise very little. Yet even in competitive contests, when parties and interest groups rally to aid the challenger, incumbents in House races usually outspend their opponents by two-thirds.[20]

In Senate races, incumbents also have an advantage, although some challengers are able to raise as much as incumbents and in rare occasions to outspend them. This is because many Senate challengers are House incumbents who have an established fundraising base, or because they are current or former governors or other state officials with strong in-state financial support. In recent years, party committees have increasingly sought to recruit for Senate races candidates who are wealthy and are willing to spend parts of their personal fortunes on their races. Yet generally Senate incumbents are able to outspend their opponents by a substantial margin.

Incumbents also enjoy advantages in state and local races. In the California state legislative races in 1994, for example, incumbents had nearly four times the resources available to their challengers. In Missouri in 1992 the advantage was more than two to one.

The fundraising advantage of incumbents is often cumulative. Many incumbents do not spend all of their available money in any given election and are able to invest it and build up a sizable "war chest." Potential candidates considering a challenge to the incumbent may be deterred by significant funds in an incumbent's account before the race even begins.[21]

As a consequence of the fundraising advantages that incumbents enjoy, interest groups, parties, and individuals who wish to change the composition of Congress usually focus on open seats, created by the retirement of an incumbent. Such open seat elections can be quite competitive, and they attract considerable campaign money. In general, open seat candidates raise less than incumbents but far more than most challengers. In a few races, especially highly competitive Senate contests, open seat candidates raise and spend even more than typical incumbents.

Party affiliation also influences the amounts that candidates can raise. Whether a candidate's party has control of a legislative chamber can make an important difference. Interest groups and individuals who seek access to government give to incumbents, especially those who chair key committees, and to party leaders of the majority party, because these members can affect the content and fate of legislation. In 1992, when Democrats controlled the House and Senate, corporate PACs gave half of their money to Republican candidates for Congress. In 1996, when Republicans controlled the chamber, corporate PACs gave 73 percent to Republicans. Trade association PACs made a similar change, from 37 percent to Republicans in 1992 to 60 percent in 1996.[22] By 1998, Republican candidates and party committees collected significantly more PAC money than their Democratic counterparts.

A candidate's party affiliation will also influence the amount received from individual donors, who tend to be wealthy, conservative, and Republican.[23] Republican party committees in 1998 received twice the total individual contributions of Democratic committees. Overall, Republican party committees have a substantial advantage at the national level in both soft and hard money. In 1998, the Republican party committees enjoyed a $285 million to $160 million advantage in hard money, collected under the contribution limits discussed above, and a $132 million to $93 million advantage in soft money.

This advantage means that Republicans in close races can often count on the party to spend money in late October for voter mobilization, issue advertising, and other activities designed to boost their candidacies. Democratic candidates cannot count on their party committees for as much aid but often receive similar assistance from friendly labor unions to offset GOP party funding. Of course, parties are important for reasons other than their money, as the next section demonstrates.

Party

No one doubts that issues and money matter in campaigns, but issues and money have little direct impact on many individual voters. Instead, these individuals vote based on party: Democrats choose Democratic candidates and Republicans choose Republican candidates. In House races in 1996, for example, 87 percent of strong Democratic partisans voted for Democratic House candidates and 98 percent of strong Republican partisans voted for Republicans.[24]

One reason for this is that the sense of self of many voters "may include a feeling of personal identity" with a political party.[25] These individuals have been socialized into party loyalty and use their party affiliations as a cue for assessments about what is good and what is bad in politics. Their party affiliations are stable over time and predict their votes and attitudes better than any other single predictor.

Despite the importance of political parties for most voters, party identification has declined in recent years. The decline of partisanship is the product of many forces. Reduced immigration, increased geographic and social mobility, suburbanization, and improved education have deprived party politicians of their traditional bases of support.[26] The introduction of new issues that cut across each party's original core policy positions left many voters feeling that their party had abandoned their concerns. Staunch partisans with a vivid recollection of New Deal politics have been replaced by younger independent voters who cannot fathom the centrality of the Democratic and Republican parties to American politics during that tumultuous time.[27] The demise of the old-fashioned political machines that connected neighborhood residents to politics, and the rise of modern, money-driven, media-oriented campaigns, have further weakened the associational and emotional ties that voters once had with political parties.[28]

As a result of changes in American society and in the conduct of political campaigns, the number and intensity of party identifiers have fallen precipitously since the middle of the twentieth century. In 1952, 35 percent of all voters identified themselves as strong Democrats or Republicans, another 39 percent considered themselves weak partisans, and 17 percent identified themselves as independents but were just as likely to consistently vote for one party's candidates as were the weak partisans. Thus almost three-fourths of all voters considered themselves Democrats or Republicans and more than nine out of ten voters behaved like partisans.[29] By 1998, the percentage of strong partisans had shrunk to 31 percent, the percentage considering themselves weak partisans had shrunk to 35 percent, and the percentage of independents had grown to 26 percent. Moreover, the number of pure non-partisans—who had no fealty to either party—increased to 6 percent.[30]

The rise of independent voters and candidate-centered politics has injected greater uncertainty into electoral politics. In this new environment, campaigns play a more important role in determining election outcomes. Many campaigns focus as much attention on persuading independents and weakly identified partisans to support their candidate as they do on mobilizing core party supporters, using complicated targeting strategies based on geographic, demographic, and occupational variables.[31]

The increased complexities associated with campaigning have created major challenges for many candidates, especially non-incumbents running for congressional and statehouse seats. Some of the best candidates lack the technical know-how or strategic expertise needed to wage a contemporary campaign. They also lack the political experience or contacts needed to hire political consultants or raise money.

Contemporary party organizations, particularly those located in Washington, D.C., and in some state capitals, have sought to meet some of the needs of these candidates. The Democratic and Republican congressional and senatorial campaign committees assist candidates with strategic advice, polling, issue and opposition research, mass media communications, and other areas of campaigning requiring technical expertise or in-depth research. They also provide candidates with transactional assistance designed to help them raise money and other resources from PACs, political consultants, and other groups that are active in elections.[32] State legislative campaign committees play similar roles for candidates in many states.[33]

The parties' congressional and legislative campaign committees and the parties' national committees, state central committees, and local committees often cooperate with one another in coordinated campaigns designed to boost voter registration and turnout among their supporters.[34] The 1996 elections ushered in a new era of national party activity, in which so-called "issue advocacy" ads are used to help the campaign of specific candidates for federal office, without expressly calling for their election.

Despite the best efforts of party organizations, some voters consciously split their ballots between candidates of both parties. Split-ticket voters often play a pivotal role in elections. Some deliberately vote for candidates of different parties, recognizing that, for example, if they put Democrats in control of both Congress and the presidency, they are more likely to see liberal policies enacted. Conversely, if they vote for Republicans for offices in both branches, they are more likely to see conservative policies enacted. However, if they vote for one party to control Congress and the other to control the presidency, then the liberal tendencies of one will be offset by the conservative tendencies of the other, and moderate policy may be most likely.[35] Republicans in 1996 specifically sought to capitalize on this trend, running ads stating that voters should vote for Republicans for Congress to hold President Clinton in check.[36] This phenomenon may carry over to the state level, as twenty-four states now have divided governments.[37]

Another sign of voters' ambivalence toward the two major parties is their occasional willingness to support minor-party and independent candidates. These candidates usually fare better under conditions of economic adversity, or when the two major parties either fail to address voters' concerns or select lackluster nominees.[38] Minor-party and independent candidates are not as disadvantaged in the current candidate-centered election system as they were when political machines enjoyed a near-monopoly over the resources needed to mount campaigns. As the successful election efforts of Independent Rep. Bernard Sanders of Vermont, Connecticut Party Gov. Lowell Weicker, and, most recently, Reform Party Gov. Jesse Ventura of Minnesota demonstrate, minor-party candidates can occasionally win enough votes to capture major offices. Green Party candidates have also enjoyed a modicum of success at the local level, especially in environmentally conscious California.

Minor-party and independent candidates raise issues that have been ignored by the major parties, give voice to voter discontent with the two major parties, participate in the realignment from one era of partisan politics to another, and introduce innovations into the political system. It is in these roles—rather than the power they wield as occasional officeholders—that their influence on American politics is most deeply felt. Ross Perot is an example of an independent or minor-party candidate who performed a number of these functions. Perot forced the major parties to confront the federal budget deficit, gave voters who were dissatisfied with presidential candidates George Bush and Bill Clinton in 1992 and Clinton and Robert Dole in 1996 a voting alternative, aired the first political infomercials in 1992, and was selected in the first national presidential nominating primary in 1996. Nevertheless, Perot came nowhere close to winning, a fate shared by most independent and minor-party candidates. These candidates sometimes alter the dynamics of the political debate, act as spoilers for candidates representing the dominant party, and introduce innovations into the campaign process, but very few of them get elected to public office.[39]

Incumbency

Not all races are decided based on issues, money, and party. Candidates often win on "candidate-centered" campaigns in which they run based on their individual reputations and organizations. The candidates with the most advantages in such an environment are incumbents, as they have established records and access to resources that other candidates do not have.

The effectiveness of incumbent campaigns is awesome. In Congress, incumbents who choose to run again are returned to office at extraordinary rates. Figure I-1 indicates this for recent times, showing that even in the "revolution" of 1994, House incumbents were still reelected at 90 percent.

There are many reasons behind the success of incumbents. Many incumbents win because they are good matches for their districts. They have experience, are familiar faces, work hard, and pursue the policies favored by a majority of voters in their districts. Those that do not fit their district are more likely to be defeated or, more commonly, to retire or run for higher office. This means that in any given election, most incumbents will be skilled, experienced politicians who fit their districts well.

But there are more tangible advantages to being an incumbent. Many come with the office. Members of Congress, for example, have large staffs that answer letters and work on constituency problems with the government. In addition, members are able to "frank" millions of pieces of mail to their constituents. These mailings build name recognition and laud the member of Congress's achievements; they would be quite expensive if mailed by a campaign. In addition, members have access to studios for taping TV and radio shows and are able to fly home to the district at the public's expense.

Other advantages require some work but are generally available. First is the ability to guide government spending toward the district. As we discussed earlier, candidates often seek to run on local issues. Few local issues are as compelling as building a new highway, funding research at a local university, or cleaning up a local river. The modern master at this is Sen. Robert Byrd of West Virginia. In one year alone he was able to bring to West

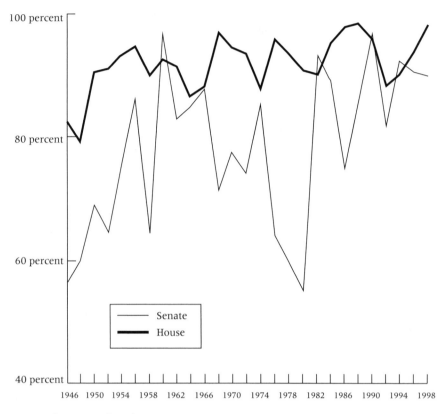

100 percent

80 percent

60 percent

┌─────────────────────┐
│ ────── Senate   │
│ ━━━━━━ House   │
└─────────────────────┘

40 percent

1946 1950 1954 1958 1962 1966 1970 1974 1978 1982 1986 1990 1994 1998

Incumbent Reelection Rates, 1946–1998

SOURCES: Norman J. Ornstein, Thomas E. Mann, and Michael J. Malbin, *Vital Statistics on Congress, 1997–1998* (Washington, D.C.: Congressional Quarterly, 1998); *CQ Weekly,* selected issues.

Virginia $165 million for a highway demonstration project, $32 million to move CIA offices to West Virginia, $48 million to install an automated fingerprint identification system at the new FBI headquarters, $9 million for construction of a dam, $14 million for upgraded radar at Eastern West Virginia Airport, $22 million for a technology center at Wheeling Jesuit College, and much more.[40] A challenger running against such a record would be hard pressed to convince local voters that he or she could do more for them.

In addition, incumbents have an easier time raising money. They have established networks of contributors and experience in tapping them. They are especially well positioned to appeal to individuals and groups who contribute to campaigns in return for access to officeholders, and who view making a contribution as laying the groundwork for later lobbying efforts. These contributors care relatively little about which candidate wins but just want to make sure that they are on friendly terms with whoever does win.

PACs tend to be such contributors. In 1996, for example, PACs gave an average of $294,000 to incumbent campaigns versus an average of $53,000 to challenger campaigns. Even in competitive races, PACs give almost three times as much on average to incumbents as to challengers.[41]

Many of these incumbency advantages carry over to the state and local level. Officeholders at these levels often are good fits for their constituencies and have access to resources and opportunities that are not available to challengers. However, there is an additional factor that limits the power of incumbency: term limits. Forty-four states have term limits on their governors, more than twenty states have limits on state legislators, and nearly three thousand local government offices have term limits. This means that whatever the advantages of state and local incumbents, many will reap them only a few times. Turnover can increase dramatically, and the very concept of incumbency advantage becomes less relevant. In Michigan in 1998, for example, term limits meant that 64 of the state's 110 House races had no incumbents.[42]

Incumbents often win because the candidates who run against them lack the skills and experience to mount credible campaigns. In fact, some incumbents face no opponent at all. In a typical election cycle, sixty-three U.S. House incumbents and one U.S. Senator face no challenger. Unopposed candidates are even more common at the state and local level—in fact, occasionally small towns can find no candidate from either party to seek a particular office.

Those incumbents who do face challengers are often opposed by candidates with little experience and few campaign skills. The best challengers are usually candidates who have previously held elected office. Typically between a quarter and a third of challengers to U.S. House incumbents have previously held elected office, usually in a state legislature or a city or county government. A few others are skilled amateurs, perhaps a House staffer, a local media celebrity, a prominent business leader. This means that in most elections, fewer than a hundred House incumbents face a challenge that is at all credible. Senate incumbents are more likely to face stiff challenges from members of the House or from state officials, but many of them face amateurs who run ineffective campaigns. State and local candidates are of course even less likely to face experienced challengers.

Why are so few incumbents faced with experienced, skilled opponents? The best challenger for a given race is an officeholder at a lower level: a state representative challenging for the U.S. House, a U.S. House incumbent for the U.S. Senate. For these potential candidates, a run for higher office may mean giving up their current job.

With such long odds and high costs, most potential candidates carefully weigh the timing of their candidacy. If possible, skilled politicians prefer to wait until the incumbent has retired, for their odds are better in an open seat race than in a challenge of an incumbent. Yet some potential candidates are impatient, or find themselves in districts or states where the incumbent appears likely to remain in office for a long time. Moreover, many state legislators now face term limits, increasing the number of open seats.

Quality candidates who choose to challenge incumbents try to do so during electoral cycles that benefit their party. When a popular president seeks reelection and the economy is strong, potential candidates of the president's party are more likely to challenge incumbents, while potential candidates of the other party are more likely to sit tight. When the president is unpopular, the economy is poor, and in off-year elections, the out-party often has a good recruiting year. Because candidacy decisions are generally made more than a year in advance, parties often find themselves unable to capitalize on late-breaking trends. In 1998, for example, Democrats had failed to recruit large numbers of quality challengers, and so were unable to capitalize on the anger with the impeachment proceedings that developed in the fall. Conversely, Republicans in 1982 recruited many quality challengers, only to see them lose as the nation plunged into a deep recession.

It is worth remembering that incumbents almost always have experience, political skills, a great deal of knowledge of their district, and the ability to raise significant amounts of resources. Potential challengers often size up the incumbent with a benchmark poll, eye the incumbent's cash on hand, and simply decide not to run for election.

Campaign Strategy and Tactics

Even after one accounts for all the above factors, many elections are still up in the air. It is in these elections that campaign strategies and tactics matter the most. Candidates and campaigns that can create and implement an effective strategic and tactical plan usually win; those who do not typically lose.

There are many keys to a winning plan. Some of them are old standbys that have held since the earliest days of democracy; others emerge suddenly and apply for only a few election cycles. One timeless key is having the right message.[43] The candidate's reason for running must be packaged into one coherent theme that can be repeated until most voters know it and, if the message is any good, approve of it.

Another essential key is money. Only the most exceptional campaign gets by on energy and ideas alone. No one will know who the candidate is, what good things he or she will do, or what terrible things the opponent has done unless the candidate has the resources to advertise these things. Usually, the resource most needed is money to pay for TV, radio, or newspaper ads or to pay for phone banks, direct mail, or lawn signs. To raise it, candidates have to commit—psychologically difficult as many find it—to countless hours of pleading for contributions.

Some candidates become so convinced of this last point, however, that they lose sight of the first. This may be the worst of all mistakes. Money must always be in service of message. That is, all the money in the world does little good if you use it to present an unappealing candidate and theme. The races in California in 1998 provided great examples of this. Al Checchi spent $40 million running in the Democratic gubernatorial primary, but he garnered only 13 percent of the vote in the blanket primary. Republican Bob Dornan spent almost $4 million running for the House seat he lost to Loretta Sanchez in 1996, but his style and views no longer matched the district, and he received only 39 percent of the vote.[44]

The best way to marry message and money changes over time. In the late eighties and early nineties, Republicans developed a simple yet powerful combination: throw money at calling your opponent a liberal. Voters, who were increasingly hostile toward large government, responded favorably and elected hundreds of additional Republicans across the country.

However, after the Republicans took control of Congress in 1994 and voter concern about a growing government lessened, the approach lost its punch. For example, a master of the strategy, consultant Arthur Finkelstein, suffered a series of embarrassing losses in Senate races in Minnesota, New Jersey, South Dakota, New York, and North Carolina in 1996 and 1998. In each, his candidate concentrated on tarring his opponent as a liberal, and yet none could get enough momentum to carry them to victory, even when the opponent did not contest the label, as in Minnesota.

One way to make sure that messages have their intended effect is to target them. If a campaign obtains accurate information about potential voters and identifies the issues that are important to them, it can ensure that these voters only get information about its candidate that they are likely to view favorably. A pro-life candidate gains nothing, and is likely hurt, by informing a pro-choice voter of his or her position on abortion rights. The most effective campaigns tailor their messages to specific groups.[45] The more candidates can do to target their messages, by using direct mail, phone lists, and the internet, the greater the likelihood that they will be able to turn out their voters without spurring more opposition voters as well.

Another key to effective communication is establishing credibility. Candidates who think that it is sufficient to bludgeon their opponents with accusations and half-truths often turn off voters and turn well-informed opinion against themselves. Hence, candidates have to ensure that their messages are believable—or, if their messages will be initially surprising, to document them to such an overwhelming extent that voters cannot tune them out as partisan hyperbole. Media consultant Jim Margolis, for example, once held back an attack ad because the transgression it attacked, even though clearly true, was so egregious that voters would not believe it.

Whatever their messages, all candidates must begin campaigning early, at least in the planning aspects.[46] Raising money, establishing a record, avoiding blunders, and engaging citizens who have few ties to parties or organizations has become so demanding that candidates must continually be aware of and promoting their campaigns. This dynamic could not have been clearer in 1998. The day after the election, House Minority Leader Dick Gephardt declared, "Today is day one of campaign 2000. The days of the Republican majority are numbered." The next day, Dennis Moore, who had just narrowly upset incumbent Republican Vince Snowbarger in the 3rd Congressional District of Kansas, was already polling voters, preparing for an election two years away.[47]

Referenda and Initiatives

The above factors provide substantial guidance about who wins and why. However, they may not always explain which government policies prevail. First, of course, elected officials interact in specific institutional contexts, contexts that can do much to affect which policies emerge.[48] Second, voters directly decide an increasing share of government decisions through referenda and initiatives. These direct votes on specific proposals have a long history and growing role in American politics. Progressives, seeking to reduce the power of parties and special interests, pushed twenty states to adopt some form of referenda process between 1904 and 1918.[49] Currently, twenty-five states have referenda processes on the books and some, such as Oregon, California, North Dakota, and Colorado, have used them extensively. In addition, other states ask voters to approve a range of statewide, local, and regional ballot propositions, constitutional amendments, charter changes, and bond issues. These elections often entail extensive public campaigns, too.

The scope of citizen-sponsored referenda is astounding. Once they were limited to school bonds and constitutional amendments, but now they cover almost every aspect of American life. In 1996, for example, there were over ninety nationwide; Californians alone voted on initiatives that would end affirmative action, reform campaign finance, limit lawsuit awards, allow medical use of marijuana, increase the minimum wage, and restrict tax increases.[50] Sometimes voters have to make very specific decisions. In 1994, voters in Washington made it illegal for anyone but a dentist to make and sell false teeth; Oregon voters banned the hunting of cougars with dogs.[51]

The emergence of citizen-sponsored referenda has meant that elected representatives make fewer important decisions. In California, for example, many important political issues have been decided directly by voters with relatively little involvement by elected officials. In 1978, Californians approved Proposition 13, which reduced and permanently limited local property taxes, an action that spurred a nationwide anti-tax movement. In 1996, they approved an initiative that ended racial and gender preferences in public hiring, contracting, and college admissions decisions.

The Case Studies

Generalizations developed by political scientists elucidate discernible patterns but cannot fully prepare a person for the frontlines of campaigns and elections. An experienced incumbent can call his opponent "putzhead" and then deny that he said it. A muscle-bound former professional wrestler can wrench a governorship from two strong traditional candidates who have the backing of the two major parties. A sitting governor can dance around like a monkey and call his opponent fat—and win! A staid mayor jumps in the shower with shock jocks (literally!) and loses. Campaigns are anything but predictable and dull. The case studies that follow were selected to help readers fully appreciate how issues, money, parties, incumbency, and campaign techniques matter across a wide variety of races.

U.S. Senate Elections

The first five case studies are of Senate elections. Senate contests are more likely to be competitive than are contests for other legislatures. Indeed, Senate incumbents seeking reelection had a success rate of only 80 percent between 1950 and 1998, as compared to the 93 percent success rate enjoyed by House incumbents.[52] There are many reasons for the relative competitiveness of Senate elections. Most Senate challengers and open-seat candidates are more formidable opponents. Many have previously served in the House, as governor, or in some other prominent position. As such, they enjoy high levels of name recognition among voters, have substantial political experience, and are able to raise large amounts of campaign money. They are also able to attract significant media coverage and assemble professional campaign organizations. Most members of the Senate face greater difficulties staying in touch with voters than do their counterparts in the House, state legislators, or municipal governments. With the exception of a few House members from sparsely populated states, senators represent larger and more diverse constituencies than do other legislators, making it easier for them to anger substantial portions of their constituencies while carrying out their legislative duties. They represent large constituencies, serve six-year terms, and face heavy demands on their time, and in consequence they cannot develop the same personal ties that other legislators have with voters.[53]

The Senate elections included in this book illustrate many of the important themes in contemporary elections for the upper chamber. The first contest compares the efforts of two relatively unpopular incumbents, California Democrat Sen. Barbara Boxer and New York Republican Sen. Al D'Amato. Partly by design and partly by the luck of a national "bump," Boxer was on the same side on salient issues as the voters, and she won; D'Amato was not and lost. These races also show the importance of disciplined campaigning and show how candidates' mistakes can make their tasks all the more difficult.

The second case highlights the central role that campaign spending and interest groups play in modern elections, even when the incumbent is a committed campaign finance reformer. Incumbent Democrat Russell Feingold of Wisconsin faced a gut-wrenching decision: should he stick to his principles and limit his campaign expenditures, or should he raise and spend as much as possible in order to counter a vigorous challenge? Feingold chose the former path and won, although his election was complicated by independent and issue-advocacy spending on his behalf by parties and interest groups.

The third case shows the importance of ideological fit and a clear message. Republican underdog Chuck Hagel beat a popular former governor in Nebraska by emphasizing the issues Nebraskans hold dear and using them to highlight the weaknesses of his opponent.

In the fourth Senate contest, South Dakota Democrat Tim Johnson reached the pinnacle of campaign achievement: he knocked off an incumbent in a hard-fought race. The case also shows the importance of a clear message that resonates with voters, as he pounded away at an out-of-touch incumbent. His opponent and his opponent's national party committee, on the other hand, relied heavily on the tired approach of spending vast amounts of money to attack Johnson as "liberal."

In the fifth case, Hollywood movie star and a real life lawyer/lobbyist Fred Thompson presented an powerful image by touring Tennessee in a plaid shirt and pickup truck, evoking his folksy roots as opposed to the Washington feel of his opponent. In this election, attacking an opponent as a liberal proved effective, as did relying on the NRA to get a boost in turnout.

U.S. House Elections

The next set of case studies analyzes some of the more interesting House elections in recent years. House races are less likely to be hotly contested, as many districts routinely support one party. However, the competition in House races can become intense, if two well-funded candidates are aided by party committees and by interest groups. In most election cycles there are between twenty-five and fifty close House races, and many political actors concentrate their resources on those competitive races.

In the first case study, Democrat Tammy Baldwin shows how the mobilization of new constituencies can mean the difference between victory and defeat. She enlisted a large number of students at the University of Wisconsin at Madison as volunteers in her field organization, which helped generate a record turnout in many precincts. Her professional campaign and clear message contrasted with the campaign of her opponent, which was disorganized and ineffective. Baldwin became the first openly gay woman elected to the House.

The second case shows the impact that independent candidates can have on close elections, especially low-turnout special elections. New Mexico Republican Bill Redmond ran a solid campaign, establishing a clear message and targeting the right voters, while Democrat Eric Serna was vulnerable to attacks on his ethics. Redmond was helped by Green Party candidate Carol Miller, who siphoned off critical votes from Serna. Indeed, the GOP campaign even produced a mailing that favorably compared the Green Party candidate to Serna, to encourage Democratic defections.

The third case depicts a classic upset. Although longtime incumbents usually fit their districts well, House districts sometimes undergo demographic change, dramatically altering their composition and voting tendencies. In this case, challenger Democrat Loretta Sanchez of California mobilized the Latino community to defeat Republican Bob Dornan, a longtime incumbent with a reputation of pugnacious conservatism. Sanchez linked Dornan with Newt Gingrich, a symbol of unpopular Republican policies.

Changing demographics do not always doom an incumbent, however. In the fourth case, Cynthia McKinney, one of the relatively few African American women in the House, was re-districted into a majority white district, but she easily won a Democratic primary in which she was the underdog. McKinney won by carefully targeting her messages to key groups—especially African Americans and older voters. Her targeted voter mobilization effort dramatically increased turnout in African American precincts, but she won significant numbers of white votes as well.

The fifth case shows an example of how the "Republican Revolution" worked in practice. Kentucky Republican Ron Lewis, a Baptist minister and owner of a Christian bookstore, won a special election in the summer before the Republican tidal wave of 1994. The case shows the role of party leaders and organizations. Sen. Mitch McConnell met with the candidate and suggested that Lewis turn the race into a referendum on Bill Clinton, and polling by the National Republican Congressional Committee (NRCC) showed that this strategy had great potential. One Lewis spot showed an image of Democratic candidate Joe Prather "morphing" into a picture of President Clinton, thereby creating the impression that the socially conservative Democratic candidate was in fact liberal.

State and Local Elections

The third section of the book covers state and local elections. Although the national government receives the lion's share of media attention, state and local governments have substantial influence over voters' everyday lives—for example, with policies affecting schools, roads, garbage collection, sewage, parks, libraries, regulation of business, and zoning. Moreover, the federal government is increasingly devolving policies to the state and local level, so that states, for example, are taking the lead in designing welfare policies to benefit the poor.

State and local governments differ widely among themselves. In some states governors dominate the political scene, in others their power is quite limited. Some states have powerful, professional legislatures, others have amateur bodies. In some states supreme court justices are elected, in others they are appointed. Moreover, states have widely different political cultures.

The first case study in this section is Reform Party candidate Jesse "The Body" Ventura's improbable, but decisive, victory over strong Democratic and Republican opponents in the gubernatorial race in Minnesota. It shows that links between voters and their parties can be severed and that minor-party access to money and media can generate startling results. Independent and third-party candidates have done best in gubernatorial races, in part because governors can affect state policy in ways that a handful of legislators cannot. Ventura ran his campaign in a manner contrary to professional advice, and used unconventional tactics, such as web-based fundraising. Meanwhile, the two major-party nominees refrained from attacking him in an effort to appeal to his supporters. Minnesota's same-day registration law allowed for a massive late surge that carried Ventura to victory.

The second election shows the importance of mobilizing one's base, especially in primary elections. Alabama's colorful and controversial former governor Fob James resorted to unusual, even Machiavellian, tactics to make sure that his voters came out in force in a hotly contested primary. Over the years James has transformed himself from a moderate southern governor to a populist social conservative, and for this race he signed on former Christian Coalition director Ralph Reed to direct his campaign. The freewheeling campaign, decided in a Republican primary runoff, may have hinged on white backlash against the endorsement of James's opponent by a prominent black mayor.

The third case illustrates a point that politicians have had to learn again and again: be careful of local issues. In it, nationally prominent and seemingly successful Gov. Christine Whitman is almost undone by state automobile insurance rates. After her challenger had successfully exploited this issue to draw close in the race, Whitman aired an ad that claimed to have "heard you loud and clear," but she barely survived in a photo finish. The fourth case moves us to the unique world of Louisiana politics. The state has open elections, in which Republicans and Democrats run against one another in a combined field; if no candidate gets more than 50 percent of the vote, the top two candidates run in a general election, regardless of their party. Such open contests attract many candidates and provide an opportunity for national interest groups to play an important role in mobilizing voters. Republican Mike Foster came from behind in the 1995 primary election in part because of the support of the Christian Coalition, the NRA, and other national groups.

The final case features the mayoral election of Willie Brown in San Francisco. Long a fixture in the California state legislature, Brown saw his career plans altered when California adopted term limits for state representatives. To continue his political career, he ran for mayor of San Francisco in 1995. Brown's flamboyant style, extensive ties with monied interests, and substantial income all provided targets for his opponents, but his campaign was able to mobilize African Americans, Asians, gays, and lesbians behind a platform that promised effective government. Mayoral races often hinge on issues such as whether garbage is being collected and buses run on time, as this case demonstrates.

Referenda and Initiatives

The final section of the book analyzes several referenda campaigns. The first case shows the NRA defeating a gun control measure in the state of Washington. Gun control has been a frequent topic of referenda at the state and local level, and in most cases the NRA has poured considerable resources into the campaigns. This statewide referendum became the focus of nationwide media. In it, the NRA outspent the gun control forces by a margin of at least two to one, and used the grassroots resources of the state NRA to muster support. The case also shows the power of endorsements by key groups, in this case by the police and sheriffs in the state.

The second case discusses the efforts of the San Francisco 49ers to get the public to foot the bill for a new football stadium. Such issues are a major part of local politics, as cities balance their distaste for giving public money to tycoons and millionaire athletes against the possibility that their teams will leave town. This referendum involved local personalities, but it also created unusual political coalitions. Environmental groups opposed the deal, while other liberal groups, including the National Organization of Women, endorsed it. The franchise spent millions of dollars on ads carefully targeted to women, African Americans, Republicans, and other groups.

The third case focuses on an anti–gay rights referendum in Oregon, the third in a series of statewide referenda on this issue. Supporters of the measure called it the "Minority Status and Child Protection Act" and attempted to portray it as more moderate than the one that Oregon voters had defeated just two years ago. Much of the struggle was over how to frame this issue, with the supporters arguing that the measure would prevent "special rights" for gays and lesbians, and opponents countering that the measure would legalize discrimination. Because the measure would have banned teaching about homosexuality in public schools, both campaigns focused on women with school-aged children—the voters who were most likely to be concerned with curricular issues. The opponents of the measure ran advertisements featuring mothers, portrayed by actresses, who argued that teaching children discrimination was wrong, and that any school curriculum problems should be taken up with the local school board. The ads managed to shore up opposition among Democratic and independent women and to decrease support among GOP women.

In the fourth case, opponents of progressive state income tax measures in Massachusetts mobilized themselves behind a focused campaign arguing that the progressive tax law would raise taxes for everyone. They achieved a suprising victory, as they were able to rally many lower income citizens to vote against a measure that people with a low income would normally have been expected to support.

Notes

1. Committee on Political Parties, "Toward a More Responsible Two-Party System," in *American Political Science Association,* supp. 44 (1950).

2. Cited by Gary Nordlinger at CQ's Special Congressional Forecast Conference, *Election '98: What It Means to You,* Washington, D.C., November 5, 1998.

3. David Mayhew, *Congress: The Electoral Connection* (New Haven: Yale University Press, 1974).

4. Tip O'Neill, *Man of the House* (New York: Random House, 1987).

5. Everett Carll Ladd, ed., *America at the Polls 1998* (Storrs, Ct.: The Roper Center for Public Opinion Research, 1999), 33.

6. Ladd, ed., *America at the Polls 1998,* 70.

7. Samuel Popkin, *The Reasoning Voter* (University of Chicago Press, 1991).

8. Paul Sniderman, Richard Brody, and Philip Tetlock, *Reasoning and Choice* (New York: Cambridge University Press, 1991).

9. James Stimson, *Public Opinion in America* (Boulder, Colo.: Westview Press, 1991).

10. James G. Gimpel, *Fulfilling the Contract: The First 100 Days* (Boston: Allyn and Bacon, 1996).

11. David Brady, John Cogan, and Doug Rivers, "The 1996 House Elections: Reaffirming the Conservative Trend," in *Hoover Institution Essays on Public Policy* (Stanford, Calif.: Hoover Institution, 1997).

12. Molly Sonner and Clyde Wilcox, "The Paradoxes of Popularity: Public Support for Bill Clinton during the Lewinsky Scandal," in Mark J. Rozell and Clyde Wilcox,

eds., *The Clinton Scandal and the Future of American Government* (Washington, D.C.: Georgetown University Press, 2000).

13. Thad Beyle, "The State Elections of '96," in *Toward the New Millenium: The Elections of 1996*, Larry Sabato, ed. (Boston: Allyn and Bacon, 1997), 199.

14. Beyle, "The State Elections of '96," 194.

15. Clyde Wilcox, "I Owe It All to Me: Candidates' Investments in Their Own Campaigns," in *American Politics Quarterly* 16 (1988): 266–279.

16. Historically the most interesting exception is William Proxmire, who retired from the U.S. Senate in the 1980s without ever having spent $5,000 in a Senate race.

17. Of course, this figure changes over time.

18. Clyde Wilcox, "I Owe It All to Me"; Robert Biersack, Paul S. Herrnson, and Clyde Wilcox, "Seeds for Success: Early Money in Congressional Elections," in *Legislative Studies Quarterly* 18 (1993): 535–552; Paul S. Herrnson, *Congressional Elections: Campaigning at Home and in Washington*, 2d ed. (Washington, D.C.: CQ Press, 1998).

19. For the most comprehensive account of the financing of these races to date, see Joel A. Thompson and Gary F. Moncrief, eds., *Campaign Finance in State Legislative Elections* (Washington, D.C.: CQ Press, 1998).

20. See Herrnson, *Congressional Elections*, 128–156.

21. Janet M. Box-Steffensmeier, "A Dynamic Analysis of the Role of War Chests in Campaign Strategy," in *American Journal of Political Science* 40 (May 1996): 352–371.

22. Mark Rozell and Clyde Wilcox, *Interest Groups in American Campaigns: The New Face of Electioneering* (Washington, D.C.: CQ Press, 1998).

23. For a detailed look at individual donors, see Robert Biersack, John Green, Paul Herrnson, Lynda Powell, and Clyde Wilcox, *Ideologues, Industrialists, and Intimates: Individual Donors to Congressional Campaigns* (New York: Columbia University Press, 2000).

24. Paul Abramson, John Aldrich, and David Rohde, *Change and Continuity in the 1996 Elections* (Washington, D.C.: CQ Press, 1998), 239.

25. Warren Miller and J. Merrill Shanks, *The New American Voter* (Cambridge, Mass.: Harvard University Press, 1996), 120.

26. Carey McWilliams, "Parties as Civic Associations," in *Party Renewal in America*, Gerald M. Pomper, ed. (New York: Praeger, 1981), 51–68.

27. Paul Allen Beck, "A Socialization Theory of Partisan Realignment," in *Controversies in American Voting Behavior*, Richard A. Neimi and Herbert F. Weisberg, eds. (Washington, D.C.: CQ Press, 1984), 396–411.

28. Frank J. Sorauf, "Political Parties and Political Action Committees: Two Life Cycles," in *Arizona Law Review* 22 (1980): 445–464.

29. Four percent of all voters did not answer the question or considered themselves apolitical. Angus Campbell, Philip E. Converse, Warren E. Miller, and Donald E. Stokes, *The American Vote* (New York: John Wiley and Sons, 1960), 124.

30. Virginia Sapiro, Steven J. Rosenstone, and the National Election Studies, *National Election Studies, 1998 Pilot Study* (Ann Arbor, Mich.: University of Michigan, Center for Political Studies, 1999).

31. Herrnson, *Congressional Elections*, 166–169.

32. Herrnson, *Congressional Elections*, 79–102.

33. Anthony Gierzynski, *Legislative Party Campaign Committees in the American States* (Lexington: University of Kentucky Press, 1992), 50–68, 72–90.

34. John F. Bibby, *Parties, Politics, and Elections in America* (Chicago: Nelson Hall, 1987).

35. Alberto Alesina and Howard Rosenthal, *Partisan Politics, Divided Government, and the Economy* (New York: Cambridge University Press, 1995).

36. Morris Fiorina and Paul Peterson, *The New American Democracy* (Boston: Allyn and Bacon, 1998), 331.

37. Ladd, ed., *America at the Polls 1998*, 24.

38. See, for example, Steven J. Rosenstone, Roy L. Behr, and Edward H. Lazarus, *Third Parties in America: Citizen Response to Major Party Failure* (Princeton, N.J.: Princeton University Press, 1984).

39. See, for example, Paul S. Herrnson, "Two-Party Dominance and Minor-Party Forays in American Politics," in *Multiparty Politics in America*, Paul S. Herrnson and John C. Green, eds. (Lanham, Md.: Rowman and Littlefield, 1997), 39–40.

40. *CQ Weekly Report,* September 21, 1991, 2682.

41. Herrnson, *Congressional Elections*, 134–135, 142–143.

42. While term limits do increase turnover, not everyone is convinced that their net effect would be good. They throw out good representatives with the bad, reduce the incentives for legislators to respond to their constituents, and ensure that legislators will have less experience in the state than many interest groups and bureaucrats.

43. Ron Faucheux, CQ's Special Congressional Forecast Conference, *Election '98: What It Means to You*, Washington, D.C., November 5, 1998.

44. See "1998 Race: California District 46," on the website of the Center for Responsive Politics, at http://www.opensecrets.org/hom/index.asp.

45. Herrnson, *Congressional Elections*, 168.

46. Herrnson, *Congressional Elections*, 218.

47. Burdette Loomis, "The Kansas Third District," presentation at *Money, Media, and Madness: Inside the 1998 Elections Conference*, Washington, D.C., December 4, 1998.

48. Barry Weingast, "Political Institutions," in Robert Goodin and Hans-Dieter Klingemann, ed., *A New Handbook of Political Science* (New York: Oxford University Press, 1996).

49. Shaun Bowler and Todd Donovan, *Demanding Choices: Opinion, Voting, and Direct Democracy* (Ann Arbor, Mich.: University of Michigan Press, 1998), 4.

50. Beyle, in "The State Elections of '96," 200.

51. Clyde Wilcox, *The Latest American Revolution? The 1994 Elections and Their Implications for Governance* (New York: St. Martin's, 1995), 22.

52. Calculated from Norman J. Ornstein, Thomas E. Mann, and Michael Malbin, *Vital Statistics on Congress, 1997–1998* (Washington, D.C.: Congressional Quarterly, 1998), 61–62; and *Congressional Quarterly Weekly Report*, November 7, 1998, 3027.

53. Herrnson, *Congressional Elections*, 70, 216.

PART I
Senate Races

1

So Close and Yet So Far

Two Unpopular Incumbents Meet with Different Fates in California and New York in 1998

SEN. BARBARA BOXER (D) VS. MATT FONG (R) AND
SEN. AL D'AMATO (R) VS. REP. CHARLES SCHUMER (D)

Michael A. Bailey

P eople do not often mistake Barbara Boxer for Al D'Amato. One is a feisty feminist from California; the other, a combative conservative from New York. However, politically at least, they faced similar challenges in 1998.

Both were incumbents with reputations as outspoken partisans. Both had high negatives, especially among moderates. Both were running in states known for big, expensive, and acrimonious Senate races. And both faced strong challenges from experienced opposition.

Despite these similarities, their fates were different. Boxer cruised to victory while D'Amato lost decisively. Clearly, national factors played a role in their divergent fates. But their fates were also determined by choices that the candidates made—choices about issues, about how to advertise, and about how to respond to scandal. A comparison of these choices, and their consequences, can help explain what matters in today's Senate campaigns.

Different Strokes for Different Coasts

No one doubted that Boxer and D'Amato would face tough campaigns. California's previous Senate race, in 1994, featured Dianne Feinstein and Michael Huffington spending almost $35 million trading accusations about who had more egregiously flaunted immigration laws. D'Amato's previous race had been against Attorney General Robert Abrams in 1992. The price tag on the race reached almost $17 million, although it was most notable for flying fur. Abrams called D'Amato a "fascist" (and only reluctantly apol-

---

Originally published in *Campaigns & Elections* magazine, June 1999.

Barbara Boxer   Al D'Amato

ogized) while D'Amato fired back that Abrams was a "sleazebag" who took money from questionable sources.

Brash and controversial, Boxer and D'Amato had many admirers, but both also had many detractors. Boxer's favorables were running just ahead of her unfavorables in the late summer and dipped below her unfavorables at the end of September. D'Amato's favorables were hardly better, languishing in the thirties in the summer before the campaign.

On one point, their 1998 reelection strategies were similar. Both committed early to raising enough money get their message out. Boxer used, among other things, a list of over a hundred thousand contributors to tap individuals for roughly $12 million. Perhaps her single biggest financial asset, though, was one that many thought would bring her down: the first family. The president and first lady's fundraising efforts on her behalf brought in almost $5 million in the two years before the election.

D'Amato was no less assiduous. He used his chairmanship of the Senate Banking Committee to stay in close contact with finance and insurance interests, interests that contributed almost $5 million to his campaign. All told, he raised $17 million between 1997 and 1998 and more than $27 million in total since 1993.

The two senators differed, not only on substance, but also on strategy. Boxer concentrated on popular liberal issues such as gun control, health care, education, and abortion, while covering her back on conservative issues such as crime. On crime, Boxer supported expanding use of the death penalty for federal crimes, eliminating early parole for violent offenders, and increasing penalties for most offenses. On business, Boxer favored targeted tax cuts and exportation of encryption technology, important issues for many Silicon Valley companies.

D'Amato opted for a riskier approach. He not only conceded the issue of personality, but he also went against New York opinion on high profile issues by opposing both abortion and gun control.

Instead, D'Amato forged a two-part strategy: build general support with a reputation for unrelenting pursuit of New York interests and pull in potential swing groups with work on targeted issues. For the first goal, he continued his famous "Senator Pothole" routine, tirelessly serving constituents and seeking out money for New York. To solidify this reputation, he aired a series of "case work" ads on the radio in which New Yorkers described help they had received from D'Amato.

For the second part of the strategy, D'Amato forayed into traditionally Democratic territory. Most visibly, he sought out support from Jewish voters. In his previous two victories, he had won about 40 percent of the Jewish vote, and he hoped to replicate those totals in 1998. He emphasized his strong pro-Israel record and his unceasing work on behalf of holocaust survivors seeking restitution from Swiss banks.

D'Amato also appealed to women, by fighting for more funds for breast cancer research and pushing legislation requiring insurance companies to pay for breast reconstruction surgery for cancer victims. He was particularly interesting in cultivating women voters after his role in pursuing the Whitewater hearings came off as a personal attack on Hillary Clinton.

He also sought to appeal to moderates, by cultivating leaders of traditionally Democratic communities. He actively sought and received the endorsements of former U.S. Rep. Floyd Flake, a prominent African American minister from Queens, and Human Rights Campaign, a gay and lesbian organization. There was little expectation that these endorsements would move many black or gay votes, but the hope was that they would communicate an image of moderation and tolerance.

Lucky Breaks and Gathering Steam

As the incumbents sought to strengthen their positions, challengers began to eye their seats. The good news for potential challengers was that there was a real opportunity to win. The bad news was that this opportunity attracted others, setting up potentially bruising primary fights.

In California, Republican State Treasurer Matt Fong faced a tough contest against car alarm magnate Darrell Issa. Issa had two things going for

The Horses, Handlers, Wagers, and Payoffs

	New York Senate Race, 1998	
	Charles Schumer (D)	*Al D'Amato (R)*
Manager	Josh Isay	John Lerner
Media	Morris & Carrick	Jamestown Associates, Arthur Finkelstein
Pollster	Garin Hart Yang	Jamestown Associates
Expenditures	$16,825,671	$27,422,342
Vote percentage	49 percent (2,450,065 votes)	41 percent (2,058,988 votes)

	California Senate Race, 1998	
	Barbara Boxer (D)	*Matt Fong (R)*
Manager	Rose Kapolczynski	Ron Rogers
Media	Greer, Margolis, Mitchell, Burns	Russo Marsh & Associates
Pollster	The Mellman Group	Moore Information
Expenditures	$15,613,865	$10,818,417
Vote percentage	53 percent (4,410,056 votes)	43 percent (3,575,078 votes)

him. One was money. Lots of it. He was worth $250 million and made it clear he was willing "to spend what it takes" to win. (In the end, he spent $12 million). Second, he had a strong base among conservatives energized by his clear positions on abortion, taxes, and the environment.

Although Issa led for most of the campaign, he wound up losing, largely because of three late developments. First, voters turned against free spending political novices, reacting especially negatively to Al Checchi's efforts to compensate for his inexperience with loads of money in the Democratic gubernatorial primary. Second, a spate of bad stories caught up with Issa. Former business associates accused Issa of arson and theft, while it also came to light that Issa had been indicted for car theft as a young man. These were bad stories for anyone, but especially harmful for an arch-conservative car alarm salesman. Third, Issa let up at the end. Instead of turning up his already high volume of paid media, he kept it flat, allowing Fong to match him commercial for commercial in the final days.

Even with the late push that these developments provided, Fong was only able to squeak to a two-point victory, a victory that may have been Pyrrhic as well as slight. It left Fong's campaign broke. On June 30 he reported $215,000 on hand and more than $700,000 in debt. Boxer, meanwhile, reported almost $4 million on hand and no debt.

In New York, Democratic U.S. Rep. Charles Schumer also came from behind, but he did so more impressively. He faced former vice presidential candidate Geraldine Ferraro and New York City Public Advocate Mark Green. Early on, Ferraro ran well ahead in the polls.

To overcome this lead, Schumer's strategy was three-fold. First, raise lots of money. Second, use it to pound home a record of achievement on gun control, education, HMO reform, and Social Security. Third, stay positive.

Not everyone agreed with this last tactic. Many thought that Schumer would have to attack Ferraro in order to peel voters away from her. The Schumer campaign, however, was horrified by the possibility of a repeat of the Democratic primary of 1992, in which the candidates shredded each other and left a nearly lifeless Abrams for D'Amato to devour.

Ferraro's complacency made it unnecessary for Schumer to attack her. She sat on her lead in the polls, letting her fundraising lag and allowing to persist the perception that she had accomplished little.

If there was any doubt that Schumer was on the right track, it was dispelled for media advisor Hank Morris one day in early August when he toured pool clubs in the Bronx with Schumer. "When people heard his record, they came around," said Morris. By the September 15 primary, Schumer was far ahead and rolled to a surprisingly easy 51–26–19 victory.

Playing to Strengths

Having won their primaries, both challengers were well positioned for strong campaigns. Both played to their parties' strengths, while moderating on other issues.

Fong portrayed himself as a moderate Republican alternative to Boxer. He combined traditionally conservative—and generally popular—stances on taxes, crime, and national security with moderate positions on social issues.

Fong's moderate platform on social issues was supposed to be an asset, but it seemed long on caution and short on appeal. On abortion, he refused to call himself either pro-choice or pro-life. His position was that he respected the right of a woman to get an abortion in the first trimester, but not beyond. On guns, he said the government should maintain existing restrictions on handguns, but should go no further. On gay issues, Fong said that he did not support homosexual behavior but was against discrimination.

Fong also hoped to use his Chinese ancestry and his moderation to cut into the Democratic lead among minority voters. Most promising was the possibility of gaining support from Asian Americans. Exit polling after California's blanket primary found that, even though 81 percent of Asian

Americans of Chinese heritage in San Francisco voted for Gray Davis for governor, 74 percent voted for Fong over Boxer.

In New York, Schumer also played to the strengths of his party, while trying to blur its weak points. On traditionally Democratic issues he was solid. He had become nationally prominent through his work on gun control and had also been active on behalf of abortion rights, social security, and education. But Schumer was also careful to protect himself against charges of being too liberal. In the early nineties, he moved away from opposition to the death penalty, and in the early stage of the campaign he talked openly about limiting the government's role in fixing social problems. He also stayed close enough to Wall Street interests, not only to ensure a healthy donor base, but also to preempt any "anti-business" labeling.

The Quiet Approach

Boxer's campaign made an important strategic decision before they even knew who their opponent would be. They decided to stay off the air during the primary. Dan Lungren, who was running essentially uncontested for the Republican nomination for Governor, chose to go on the air during this time. Many urged Boxer to do the same, to take the initiative and forestall an embarrassing low vote share in the primary. However, Boxer's campaign advisors thought that ads would get lost in the din created by the expensive contested races and would have no effect on voters in the fall. They held firm and stayed off the air.

California's primary was almost four months before the general election, and for the first three months after it both candidates were quiet. For Fong, especially, this was mostly a financial decision, as he had little money. Despite the silence, however, he remained strong in the polls.

When Fong went on the air with commercials, they were cautious and positive. He and his family spoke of tougher crime laws, lower taxes, and school vouchers. They did not explicitly attack Boxer.

Many were surprised by his decision not to attack. One of Fong's main advantages was Boxer's unpopularity. Fong's ads did little to push it along. "It's tough to make something a referendum on somebody when you don't go negative," said Jennifer Duffy, an analyst at Cook and Company.

Boxer also started positive. Her early spots in mid-September touted her record and goals on education and health care. By showing old home movies of Boxer as a young mother and current shots of her as a concerned grandmother, they sought to reassure Californians that Boxer shares their values and agenda.

Shortly thereafter, Boxer's campaign hit its stride. It wanted to make the campaign a choice, not a referendum; that is, it wanted to shift the focus

Thirty-Second TV Spot

"Favorite—Right"

Barbara Boxer for Senate

Produced by: Greer, Margolis, Mitchell, Burns & Associates

ANNOUNCER: This is a Saturday Night Special. It's the favorite gun of street criminals. This is an assault weapon. It's the favorite gun of drug dealers. This is Matt Fong. He's the gun lobby's favorite candidate for the Senate because he's against new bans on Saturday Night Specials and assault weapons. And this is Senator Barbara Boxer. She's pushing for tough bans on Saturday Night Specials and assault weapons. That's why she's the favorite Senate candidate of California's police. Barbara Boxer. The right direction for California.

from Boxer herself and define the race as a choice between the two candidates. Boxer's media consultant Jim Margolis did this by focusing on what he calls "voting decision issues," or issues that swing voters base their decisions on, and issues where Boxer had an advantage.

Three issues were crucial to Boxer's strategy: guns, abortion, and the environment. On each, Boxer portrayed Fong as an extremist and herself as sensible. To ensure that the message would sink in, each was backed with at least 800 gross rating points of air time before being changed.

The first ad was on guns. In ominous tones, it denounced Fong's opposition to further restrictions on guns and then, to lighter music, praised Boxer's work on gun control (see TV spot, above). Another ad was on abortion. It started with an image of Newt Gingrich and an account of how "extremists in Congress have tried over 100 times to restrict a woman's right to choose." Slowly the image revealed Gingrich to be standing behind a Fong for Senate podium. The announcer then lit into Fong's equivocations on abortion and highlighted Boxer's commitment to choice. A third ad was on the environment. "The key here was to focus on health and safety, not tree hugging," said Margolis. In the ad, Fong's statements opposing regulations protecting water and food safety were superimposed over images of children drinking and eating.

Fong's response to Boxer's blitz was weak. He repeatedly asserted that the ads distorted his record, but he never got much traction with this approach. For example, in response to Boxer's gun ad, Fong told the *San Francisco Chronicle* editorial board that he thought low-income people should be able to buy cheap handguns. This undercut his earlier accusation that Boxer, in claiming that he opposed banning Saturday Night Specials, had distorted his record.

Fong's presence on TV was limited, as well. In part this was due to factors beyond the control of his campaign. The national Republican party decided that Republicans could get a better return on money spent in less expensive states such as Nevada, Kentucky, and South Carolina. After all, in the Senate, a vote is a vote, no matter where it comes from.

But Fong's limited TV time was also a consequence of his campaign's huge overhead costs. It spent only 35 percent of its total budget of $10 million on ads, far less than the 60 percent of $15 million spent by Boxer.

When Fong finally went negative the Friday before the election, it was too little, too late. He ran ads featuring his mother, March Fong Eu, a former secretary of state—and a Democrat—calling Boxer "too liberal" and attacking Boxer for distorting Fong's record. "She should be ashamed," said Eu.

Fong was further hurt when word broke a week before the election that he had given $50,000 in left-over campaign money from a past race for state treasurer to a conservative organization working to ban same-sex marriage. Boxer seized on this as validation of her portrayal of Fong, saying that the contribution "shows that he is out of the mainstream."

Fong's response was to pledge support for more money for AIDS research and protection for gay workers. This action was unlikely to swing gays into his camp, while it only further demoralized conservatives wounded by Fong's "pro-nothing" position on abortion. Moderate voters, to whom the pledge was almost certainly pitched, were probably most impressed by an image of vacillation.

Meanwhile, Boxer was bringing together her messages in a single final ad. It used credible third parties to argue that "Fong is wrong" on a variety of issues, referring to statements by police on guns, nurses on HMOs, and the Sierra Club on the environment. Boxer's campaign had planned two tracks of ads, one with their own messages and another responding to Fong's attacks. Without strong attacks from Fong, however, they stuck to their own ads for the duration.

The Aggressive Approach

There was nothing California casual about New York's race. Instead, it was a slugfest from the opening bell.

Twelve hours after Schumer won the Democratic nomination, D'Amato was on the air attacking him. The ads were straight out of the D'Amato playbook: turn the focus on the challenger and make D'Amato look good by comparison.

This was no surprise to the Schumer people. In fact the attacks were so predictable that they had preemptively taped responses the day of the primary, allowing them to go on the air immediately after D'Amato's attacks.

Their early goal was simple: "We knew we would be outspent early, so we just wanted to make sure we would stay alive," said Schumer media advisor Hank Morris. Because D'Amato had a financial advantage, a key element of Schumer's early response was to use ten-second ads to maintain a presence without matching D'Amato's spending. These ads were condensed from thirty-second ads. The ads parried D'Amato's attacks, arguing, for example, that although D'Amato was attacking Schumer on crime, it was D'Amato who had voted against the crime bill that put 100,000 police on the streets.

The tag line on the ads was their most controversial element. It was, "D'Amato: too many lies for too long." Some thought it was too provocative and risked a backlash, but the campaign had found that part of D'Amato's appeal was his bulldog style. By being so provocative early, Schumer made it clear he would not be out-bulldogged.

When it was clear Schumer was not going to wither under D'Amato's Tasmanian Devil style of campaigning, D'Amato floundered. "He was trying to run a formulaic campaign when the formula no longer applied," said Duffy. Beating up Schumer for being liberal was not moving voters. Meanwhile, some Republicans wondered whether the liberal-bashing tactics of D'Amato's longtime general consultant Arthur Finkelstein were right for the race.

D'Amato's best issue turned out to be Schumer's missed votes. At first, it was seen as a typical but minor campaign issue. As Schumer missed more and more votes, however, it became an easier and easier target. D'Amato upped the ante by keying in on missed votes relating to a Holocaust commemoration and a commission to review Holocaust claims.

However, the effectiveness of the missed vote issue was mixed. It appeared to move some voters away from Schumer, but it also alienated many in the media and fed D'Amato's cagey reputation. Many thought that focusing on Schumer's missed votes was a red herring, inconsistent with the widespread belief that Schumer was one of the hardest workers in Congress.

The issue blew up on D'Amato late in the campaign. A week before the election, D'Amato released an ad blasting Schumer for missing more votes in the last twelve months than D'Amato had missed in the last twelve years. The next day it came out that D'Amato had missed almost a thousand votes when he first ran for Senate in 1980 as a member of the Nassau County Board of Supervisors.

This was a case where ignorance was bliss for Schumer's team. Had they known about D'Amato's missed votes earlier, they would have responded early and put the issue to rest. Instead, D'Amato pounded away on it and then, when D'Amato's record came out, he looked like the hypocrite Schumer had been selling him as all along.

Other breaks went Schumer's way. Probably the biggest example was D'Amato's "putzhead" comment. In a private meeting with Jewish leaders two weeks before the election, D'Amato referred to Schumer as a "putzhead" (and referred to Rep. Nadler [D, N.Y.] as "Waddler"). When challenged about this comment, he denied it, stammering, "I just have no knowledge of ever doing it. I just don't. All right? I think it's ridiculous. I think he's probably pretty desperate, and that's why when you ask me do you—I have no knowledge of it. I would never, I have never engaged in that, I wouldn't engage in it. It's wrong. I haven't done it. What, I'm going to do it now? It is ridiculous."

Schumer jumped on the opportunity. In the immediate aftermath, Schumer called the comment a "cheap slur" while Nadler said it "shows a pattern of contempt for people generally, or, perhaps, for Jews in particular."

The incident resonated with voters because D'Amato's comment and denial reinforced an image some already had of him as being mean-spirited and untrustworthy. In this sense, Schumer could not have scripted a better scene in his story of "too many lies for too long."

Even the daily news broke against D'Amato. In late October, an abortion doctor was murdered in Buffalo. This drew attention to the abortion issue and made pro-choice claims about threats to choice extremely vivid. The National Abortion Rights Action League released a biting commercial late in campaign that linked anti-abortion violence to D'Amato's opposition to laws designed to protect clinics.

As the campaign closed, D'Amato went after Schumer's ethics, based on a 1980 investigation of whether Schumer illegally used state workers in his congressional campaign. Of course, the media hated this, as they thought

Thirty-Second TV Spot

"Decades"

Charles Schumer for Senate

Produced by: Morris, Carrick & Guma

ANNOUNCER: D'Amato raises property taxes six times. D'Amato requires government workers to kick back salaries. D'Amato takes hundreds of thousands in speaking fees from special interests. D'Amato rebuked by Senate Ethics Committee. D'Amato conducts partisan hearings on Hillary Clinton. D'Amato votes with Gingrich to cut Medicare. D'Amato votes to cut Head Start, student loans, and against school standards. D'Amato opposes campaign finance reform.

D'Amato: too wrong for too long.

D'Amato—no stranger to being investigated—was being disingenuous. The tone of coverage again was consistent with Schumer's theme of "too many lies for too long."

Schumer, meanwhile, went after D'Amato on all fronts in an ad called "Decades" (see TV spot, above). As newspaper clippings roll by, the announcer lists Schumer's version of D'Amato's career, including votes for property tax increases, a kickback scandal, speaking fees from special interests, a rebuke by the Senate ethics committee, the investigation of Hillary Clinton on Whitewater, votes to cut Medicare, Head Start, and student loans, and opposition to campaign finance reform. It was an exhausting list condensed into thirty seconds.

Democratic Sweep

On election night, Boxer and Schumer swept to victory, both winning by margins that were higher than even their most loyal supporters expected.

So what happened? First, it was clearly a good night for the Democrats across the country. Voters in 1998 cared more about Democratic issues and were turned off by Republican efforts to impeach and remove the president.

Early in the campaign, the conventional wisdom had been that Clinton's scandal would keep demoralized Democrats at home. This was thought to be an especially large problem for Boxer, whose daughter is married to Hillary Clinton's brother and who faced criticism for her restraint about the president's behavior. Many thought that someone who had made her name criticizing Clarence Thomas and Bob Packwood should not pull her punches for partisan, or even family, reasons.

If the scandal had any effect, it was to demoralize Republicans. While turnout was down in both states relative to the last mid-term election, it fell slightly more in traditionally Republican areas. Turnout in New York City fell 10 percent, while it fell 13 percent in all upstate counties and as much as 18 percent in firmly Republican areas such as Oneida County. D'Amato's campaign did little to push Republican turnout, relying instead on the Finkelstein formula of allocating almost all money to TV over get out the vote efforts.

In California, the pattern was similar but less pronounced. Overall turnout was down 3 percent but dropped more in conservative bastions such as Orange County (down 5½ percent), Kern County (down 6 percent) and Madera County (down 7 percent).

It is unlikely that the lower turnout alone explains the results, however. If every single voter who voted in 1994 but did not vote in 1998 had turned out and voted for the Republicans—an admittedly extreme scenario—Matt Fong would still have lost, 52 percent to 45 percent. Al D'Amato would have won, but just barely, 51 percent to 48 percent.

Another factor was that the Democrats kept their base. In California, Boxer conceded nothing on Asian or minority voters. She touted endorsements from prominent Asian American politicians such as Governor Locke (D, Wash.) and Senator Inouye (D, Hawaii) and linked Fong to anti-immigrant Governor Pete Wilson as much as possible.

Among Asians, Fong was able to run 15 points ahead of Republican gubernatorial candidate Dan Lungren, but he still only received 44 percent of the total Asian vote, not much of a boost considering Asians constituted less than 5 percent of the California electorate. Among other minority groups, Fong made no headway, running the same as Lungren and garnering only 13 percent of the African American vote and 23 percent of the Hispanic vote (which was 10 percent behind the 33 percent of the Hispanic vote received by Republican Herschensohn in his race against Boxer in 1992). Fong's only clear success among minorities was in fundraising, as Asian Americans contributed over $1 million to his campaign.

D'Amato, too, had little success penetrating the Democratic base. Despite his tenacious efforts on behalf of the Jewish community, it was difficult for him to differentiate himself from Schumer on Jewish issues. Schumer himself is Jewish, has a solid record on Jewish issues, and is closer to the generally liberal views of many Jewish voters. On election day, D'Amato ran well behind Schumer among Jewish voters, with only 23 percent, far less than the 39 percent he had garnered in 1992. D'Amato also made no inroads among minority or union voters; in fact, his share of the Hispanic vote fell to 17 percent, from 30 percent in 1992.

What really drove the campaign, however, was the ability of the Democrats to drive up their opponent's negatives while presenting policies that appealed to important swing voters. Driving up D'Amato's negatives was made easy for two reasons. First, D'Amato had an eighteen-year history of scandals and support for unpopular policies. Second, and surprising to many, his campaign made many mistakes. "People may have overestimated Al D'Amato," argues Fred Yang. Instead of being a giant killer who always manages to win, D'Amato was able to gain little traction against Schumer's persistent and mistake-free campaign.

Driving up Fong's negatives was tougher, as his caution seldom presented obvious targets. But Boxer's ads found issues people cared about and presented them in stark, easy to understand terms. And they worked. Before them, Fong's favorable to unfavorable ratings among all voters were 55 to 17. By mid-October they had fallen to 47 to 36. Even more remarkable, the ratings among independents went from 55/8 to 28/43. Rarely is the link between ads and results so clear.

Lessons

So what can we take away from these cases? First, for unpopular incumbents, personality is not destiny. Being unpopular does not mean certain defeat. The key for an unpopular incumbent is to keep the campaign from becoming a referendum on his or her performance. Instead, it should be framed as a choice between two rivals. To frame the election in this manner, they must find issues on which to attack their opponents, while offering as few targets as possible.

Boxer found big shiny hooks in Fong's record on abortion, guns, and the environment. D'Amato, on the other hand, could not penetrate Schumer's record. When he tried, on missed votes and ethics, his attacks ricocheted back. Meanwhile, D'Amato—and fate—conspired to give Schumer even more ammunition in the form of inane comments and violence against abortion doctors.

Second, overly cautious and complacent challengers lose. By assuming that Boxer's negatives would bring her down without any help from him, Fong let Boxer redefine the race. Exit polls showed that 43 percent of Fong's supporters were voting against Boxer. That was probably his best issue, and he did not push it as hard as he could have. Schumer, on the other hand, was anything but complacent, working hard to remind New Yorkers why they might have been sick of Al D'Amato.

Third, issues matter. The winners had the advantage of being on the right side of issues that voters—especially swing voters—cared about in 1998. Boxer and Schumer not only attacked their opponents but also presented voters with preferred alternatives, especially on guns, abortion, and education. The losing campaigns had no issue-based connection with swing voters. Their efforts to extend their coalitions to voters who did not share their positions on core issues were largely fruitless.

These two races show that even a vulnerable incumbent is tough to beat; it takes an aggressive challenger campaign that can make the case that it's worth the voters' while to bring in someone new.

2

They Did It Their Way

Campaign Finance Principles and Realities Clash in Wisconsin in 1998

SEN. RUSSELL FEINGOLD (D) VS. REP. MARK NEUMANN (R)

Clyde Wilcox

In many ways, the 1998 Senate race in Wisconsin was a story familiar to students of American politics. It pitted a liberal Democratic freshman senator against a Republican social conservative from the U.S. House. Both candidates raised substantial sums of money, both were aided by outside interests and party committees that spent money on their behalf, and the campaign generated considerable attention. The candidates clashed on abortion and social security. Ultimately the incumbent prevailed in a close vote.

Yet Russ Feingold's victory was anything but ordinary. The freshman senator's most visible public policy priority had been campaign finance reform, as incorporated in the McCain-Feingold bill, which would have limited campaign spending in U.S. Senate and House elections and eliminated party soft money. Running for a second term in 1998 in a swing state, Feingold decided to gamble his political career on his reform principles. He asked the Democratic party to forgo soft money spending on his behalf, agreed to limit his spending to one dollar per voter, and in the final week of the campaign asked contributors to stop sending him money.

The GOP challenger, Mark Neumann, a second-term U.S. House representative from Wisconsin's 1st District, also agreed to the spending cap of one dollar per voter, or $3.8 million. He and Feingold both agreed to limit the amounts that the candidates could give to their own campaigns and the amounts that they could raise from PACs and individuals outside the state. Neumann insisted that he was entitled to spend an additional $700,000 to

Originally published in *Campaigns & Elections* magazine, September 1999.

45

Russell Feingold   Mark Neumann

compensate for Feingold's spending in 1993–96, while Feingold argued that Neumann had spent even larger sums in his various House races.

Feingold's victory shows that candidates can take principled stands on campaign finance and win. But it also shows the complexity of campaign finance issues, for Feingold's campaign did indeed benefit from independent and issue advocacy spending by interest groups, the type of spending that he has criticized and tried to eliminate. On the other side, Neumann's campaign was exceptionally well run, and he came from some 30 points behind to lose by less than 2 percent of the vote.

The Candidates

Feingold, a former Rhodes Scholar with a Harvard Law School degree, began his political career by winning a seat in the Wisconsin state Senate in 1982. In 1992, the thirty-nine-year-old lawyer made his big move and ran for the U.S. Senate seat then held by Republican Bob Kasten, a three-term incumbent. In the Democratic primary, he stood aside as the two leading candidates hurled mud at each other and ignored him. Feingold won the primary and went on to run a campaign that focused mostly on his image as a maverick opposed to Washington politics-as-usual. The campaign is most remembered for its humorous and effective ads. One ad featured an endorsement from Elvis; another showed the candidate at home, opening a closet door and saying, "Look, no skeletons." On election day, Feingold won with 53 percent of the vote.

As senator, Feingold had visited each of the state's seventy-two counties each year, and polls showed that he was well liked but that his support, and his image, was soft. Neumann's pollster, Gene Ulm of Public Opinion Strategies, noted that, "When we asked voters to name accomplishments by Feingold, few could name even one. Those who could usually named campaign finance, which is not the kind of issue that gets voters out of bed and to the polls." Feingold's Senate record was one of fiscal conservatism but social liberalism, and his vote to sustain Clinton's veto of the "partial birth" abortion bill led to a recall effort, which was led in part by Neumann, and which fell short by only 50,000 signatures. Feingold's signature issue from a national perspective was the McCain-Feingold campaign finance reform bill, which had been blocked by a filibuster led by GOP Sen. Mitch McConnell, a staunch opponent of campaign finance regulations and the chair of the National Republican Senatorial Committee.

A former math teacher, Mark Neumann had struck it rich in the home building business. He sold his business in 1992 but did not stay idle long. That year, angry over the rising national debt and high taxes, he decided to challenge incumbent U.S. Rep. Les Aspin (D), the powerful chair of the House Armed Services Committee. With support from Christian conservatives and a $700,000 campaign war chest, Neumann made it a race but ultimately lost, 58–41 percent. On the same day, Bill Clinton had carried the district with 41 percent of the vote, leading George Bush, who received 35 percent, and Ross Perot, who received 23 percent.

When Aspin resigned his House seat to become Clinton's secretary of defense in 1993, Neumann again ran for the seat. This time in a special election, he faced Democratic state legislator Peter Barca, who had heavy support from organized labor. Barca won, but Neumann held his margin to a tiny 1 percentage point.

Encouraged by his strong showing in the 1993 special election, Neumann took on Barca in the regular election in 1994, a banner year for aggressive young conservatives. This time, Neumann prevailed. He won by the razor-thin margin of 1,100 votes, out of a total 170,000 cast.

In 1996, Neumann was opposed for reelection by Kenosha Council President Lydia Spottswood (D), who attacked the incumbent as a "rigid" extremist, even calling him a "creep." In another nail-biter, Neumann defeated his wealthy, labor-backed Democratic challenger by 4,200 votes out of 232,000 cast. That day, Democrat Clinton had beaten Republican Bob Dole in the 1st District by 29,000 votes. As a member of the House, Neumann established a solidly conservative record, especially on social issues such as abortion. He would likely have faced another strong challenge, in what had become a very competitive district, had he run again for reelection in 1998. Instead, he chose to run for the Senate.

Neumann had matured as a candidate during his various campaigns, but his stiff campaign style, his strong opposition to most abortions, and his tendency to argue with voters at campaign events made him an unlikely candidate to mount a serious campaign for the U.S. Senate. In March, the Milwaukee *Journal* wondered if he stood a chance of raising enough money to meet the $3.8 million spending cap.

Since neither candidate faced a primary election, both were able to develop a campaign plan early. Neumann was known to only 60 percent of Wisconsin voters, almost all of whom were from the southern part of the state. His campaign needed to introduce him to voters statewide as an appealing, issue-oriented leader while at the same time softening his personal image, which was often viewed as being cold and unresponsive. In addition to image development and rehabilitation, Neumann hoped to focus his campaign's message on issues like Social Security, tax cuts, and abortion, drawing distinctions between himself and his opponent. Of course, this type of multifaceted campaign would require lots of media buys and a significant war chest. Neumann spent most of his money in the 1998 general election on television, and he received substantial assistance from issue ads run by the Republican party.

Feingold wanted to focus voter perceptions on the promises he had made in the 1992 campaign, and to emphasize his position on campaign finance reform. Feingold was also determined to run essentially positive ads, a tactic that led media advisor Steve Eichenbaum to complain, "You brought me to a gun fight with a butter knife." He decided to save his advertising money until later in the campaign and to devote a substantial amount of his resources to building what he called "the best field organization in the state."

In many ways, the two candidates were very similar. Both were young, ideological, and independent. Feingold was a great worry to Democrats planning for a Senate impeachment trial of Bill Clinton, and Neumann had been kicked off a committee by an angry Newt Gingrich. Both men were hands-on campaigners who insisted on their own vision over the advice of professionals. Ideology, however, was where the campaign gave Wisconsin voters a clear choice. The liberal Americans for Democratic Action gave Feingold a score of 97 for his 1997 votes— and gave Neumann a low score of 10 for his. The contrast was even greater on social issues. In May, the Christian Coalition rated the Wisconsin delegation on its issues, giving Neumann a perfect score of 100 and Feingold a score of 0.

Meet Mr. Neumann

By the end of June, each candidate had raised a little under $2.5 million. Feingold allocated a significant portion of his allowable spending to building a grassroots organization and developing a voter mobilization and turnout effort. Because he believed that voters in Wisconsin wanted a short campaign, he decided to withhold his advertising until after Labor Day. The delay in the start of the incumbent's paid media effort gave the challenger an unexpected opportunity to introduce himself to the state without interference from his opponent. Neumann's ads ran for four weeks before Feingold's spots went up.

Neumann's early biographical ads, which started in mid-August, stressed his working-class roots, his career as a school teacher, and his success at building a business. The Republican party followed those ads with an effective spot that showed school children answering in unison questions such as "Who is the only school teacher running for the U.S. Senate?" and "Who supports smaller class sizes?"

Neumann then ran some negative but quite amusing ads that charged Feingold with supporting odd programs, such as one that proposed to study methane from cow flatulence. The spot showed a mock scientist with a glass jar chasing a cow, apparently without much of an idea of how cows actually produce flatulence. The ad worked in more than one way—it presented a looser and more humorous Neumann, and it encouraged voters to see Neumann as the heir of William Proxmire, a former Wisconsin senator famous for handing out "Golden Fleece" awards that spotlighted wasteful government spending.

The Cook Political Report estimated that the Republican National Senatorial Committee (RNSC) provided money to the state party to buy 2,000 gross rating points of television advertising before Feingold aired anything. This meant that the average Wisconsin voter saw some twenty pro-Neumann ads before Feingold took to the air.

Throughout most of 1998, polls had shown Feingold with substantial, but widely varying, leads—ranging from 42 points, in a survey conducted for Wisconsin Public Radio in February, to 14 points, in a survey conducted by GOP firm Public Opinion Strategies in March, to 24 points, in a survey taken by Wisconsin Survey Research as late as mid-August. By mid-September, both candidates' polls showed that Neumann had pulled even with Feingold, which caught both campaigns by surprise. For the Democrats, this caused a panic and widespread talk that Feingold was not responding forcefully enough. A two-minute "promises kept" ad that aired on every station twice in early September was generally criticized by party activists and by Republicans as wasteful and soft.

Neumann campaign director R. J. Johnson admits that the speed of their ascent caught the campaign by surprise. "We had planned for an underdog campaign, where we might catch Feingold in late October. Instead, we found ourselves even much earlier and had to rethink our entire strategy.

This also changed the media dynamics of the race—by late September the media were focusing on our fundraising and portraying Feingold as the underdog."

Both candidates ended up raising enough money to meet their voluntary cap, but neither violated the limit and both ended up with money in the bank. It is remarkable that in such a tight race both campaigns chose to conserve their money rather than violate their agreed-to limits.

The campaigns ran neck and neck for nearly six weeks, with Feingold opening a narrow lead as the election approached. For a time Neumann defined the issues, even challenging Feingold on Social Security—making the incumbent fight hard to win traditional Democratic voters—and putting Feingold on the defensive on partial-birth abortion. In the final weeks the Feingold campaign pushed hard on the issue of campaign finance reform and recaptured the momentum. Feingold won with 50.6 percent of the vote—a 35,000 vote margin—in an election marked by exceptionally high turnout.

Why Feingold Won

In all close elections there are many competing explanations for the outcome, and Feingold's victory is no exception. Most believe that the campaign finance issue helped Feingold turn the election. Others suggest that Neumann's decision to promote his pro-life position cost him the victory, although there is some disagreement over precisely how this issue cut in the final analysis. All observers note that the record turnout in Dane county, sparked in part by the campaign of Tammy Baldwin for the U.S. House, provided the votes that propelled Feingold to victory. Finally, analysts from both parties suggest that the GOP obsession with impeaching the president succeeded in awakening the Democratic base, changing the composition of the electorate and helping all Democratic candidates, including Feingold.

Follow the Money

Although most surveys show that few voters care passionately about campaign finance reform, they also show that the voters dislike the current system and would prefer effective reform. Indeed, one survey funded by the Joyce Foundation shows that a substantial majority of donors would favor a ban on soft money.

Feingold's campaign highlighted the senator's stand against soft money with an effective ad that showed Feingold climbing a steep hill in northwest Wisconsin against the bright fall foliage. As he climbed, he talked about the problems with soft money, and about why he would not take it. He claimed that party officials wanted him to take the money, but that he insisted on taking the "high road." The ad ended with a panorama of Wisconsin dairy country ablaze in color. Feingold personally credits this ad with turning the election.

Eichenbaum suggests that the ad was especially effective because of its fortuitous timing. Soon after the ad aired, the Democratic Senatorial Campaign Committee (DSCC) aired, over Feingold's objections, a negative ad criticizing Neumann as too extreme for Wisconsin. Feingold sharply criticized the ad and demanded that it be removed from the air. The ad was pulled, and Feingold got a tidal wave of positive free media. Neumann, who had benefited from substantial party spending—much of it paid for with unregulated soft money—fought back with an ad charging that Feingold was taking party money and urging voters to inspect the tag line of pro-Feingold ads.

The timing of Neumann's response was unfortunate, for by this time the Democratic party had exhausted its coordinated ads and had pulled the issue advocacy spot, so voters looked in vain for evidence of Neumann's charge. Tracking polls showed that the issue began to really cut at that point and moved voters in the final weeks.

Allen Raymond of the RNSC agrees that this was the turning point of the campaign, but he complained that Feingold got the full benefit of a strong media buy and then the benefit of the free media that came with his repudiation of the ad. Moreover, he argues that Feingold benefited from substantial issue advocacy and independent expenditures by Democratic groups in the state.

Feingold did indeed benefit from interest group activity. The League of Conservation Voters targeted Neumann as part of the Dirty Dozen, a set of members who the league identifies as having the worst environmental records in Congress, and spent more than $400,000 to defeat him. The league had a full-time manager in the state and a field organizer in Madison. It ran nearly 200 spots in the Milwaukee media market alone, and another 200 in other locations in the state. The league maximized the impact of their ads with an "earned media" campaign that featured a press conference before each ad aired, at which they presented the media with the script and evidence to support the charges. The league's most memorable tool, however, was "Wally the 7 Foot Walleye," a foam fish costume that attracted considerable attention at events. The league made more than 20,000 calls to members of the African American community criticizing Neumann's stand on lead paint. NARAL, a pro-choice group that strongly supports abortion rights, sponsored a grassroots voter identification, made some 60,000 calls in Madison and Milwaukee, and sent two direct mail pieces to pro-choice voters. The Sierra Club made early radio buys, labor groups did some organizing, and other groups helped in various ways.

Neumann also benefited from interest group activity, including spending by anti-tax groups, voter guides from the Christian Coalition, some voter contact by the NRA, and some surprisingly limited organizing by pro-life groups. The Republican party spent at least a million dollars in issue ads for Neumann, perhaps more. Some Republicans grumbled that Mitch McConnell might have been allocating money to defeat his campaign-finance nemesis, although the final margin seems to have justified the allocation.

Focus on Abortion

Neumann cared deeply about abortion, especially "partial birth" abortion, and had indicated that he opposed abortion even in cases of incest and rape. Some Republican advisors urged him to steer clear of the issue, but he insisted on using it in the campaign. He discussed "partial birth" abortion during his stump speeches and raised the issue in debates. In October his campaign ran a strong ad criticizing Feingold for helping to sustain Clinton's veto of the "partial birth" bill. The ad included a somewhat graphic description of the procedure and then listed the members of the Wisconsin delegation who had voted to overturn the veto—every member except Russ Feingold.

Feingold responded quickly with an effective ad of his own. It began with Feingold on stage left and out of focus, introducing himself and claiming that someone was distorting his record on abortion. It then moved center stage and came into focus, as he told voters that he opposed nearly all late term abortions except those necessary to save the life of the mother. He then noted that his opponent wanted to make most abortions illegal, something that most citizens, he claimed, did not want. The ad concluded with Feingold saying he wanted abortions to be "rare, safe, and legal."

There is considerable disagreement on how this issue cut in the election, although some on both sides point to this exchange as an important turning point. The Republican candidate in the second district, Josephine Musser, announced soon after that she could not vote for Neumann because of his extreme abortion views. Neumann campaign manager R. J. Johnson admitted that the issue probably hurt them in the Madison area.

Yet Johnson also argued that Neumann's stance on the issue attracted many volunteers, who were thrilled to see a candidate actually campaign on abortion. The abortion issue helped the campaign raise some of the $2 million it raised through direct-mail and telemarketing fundraising. Exit polls show that among the 20 percent of voters who indicated that abortion was the most important issue, Neumann won in a landslide, but private polls also showed that the issue helped sway toward Feingold some undecided voters, for whom abortion was one of several critical issues.

"Buy Tammy Baldwin Dinner"

Neumann's campaign, which had developed a turnout model with projected vote margins in various counties, exceeded its projected vote total by

150,000 and ran ahead of expectations in many areas. But Dane County, home of the University of Wisconsin—Madison, delivered a resounding 65,000 vote margin for Feingold, who won the entire state by only 35,000 votes. Turnout in Dane County was 55 percent, easily a record for a non-presidential year, and an increase of 26,337 votes over 1994. In twenty-eight polling places, election officials ran out of ballots, and several wards near campus ran out of same-day voter registration cards.

Most agree that this remarkable turnout was driven principally by the campaign of Tammy Baldwin, who built a strong voter mobilization effort that used an army of student volunteers. When GOP candidate Jo Musser announced that she could not support Neumann, she only added to his woes. Neumann's campaign had projected that he would lose the county by 28,000 votes, and the actual vote margin buried him.

Wisconsin Governor Tommy Thompson, whose expected reelection landslide against a weak opponent was held to 60 percent of the vote because of the large Democratic mobilization in Madison, said after the election, "I think Russ Feingold should buy Tammy Baldwin a dinner every week for the next fifty-two weeks for what she did for him. If I was Russ, I certainly would call up Tammy Baldwin and say, 'Thank you so very much.'" (See chapter 6 for analysis of Baldwin's campaign.)

Feingold himself credits Baldwin for helping in Dane County, but he notes that his campaign devoted significant resources to building its own field organization. The campaign hired a field worker in each district and went door-to-door for months, identifying voters. The coordinated Democratic campaign built on Baldwin's network and Feingold's team, as well as on the organizations of gubernatorial candidate Ed Garvey and Attorney General candidate James Doyle—both Madison natives.

The Sleeping Giant Wakes

Another factor—one of the most important, according to Neumann campaign manager R. J. Johnson—was the national reawakening of the Democratic base in the final two to three weeks of the campaign. Much as the 1994 election had energized the GOP core constituency, national trends in 1998 similarly galvanized white liberals and African Americans, and these groups began showing up in Neumann's polls as likely voters in increasing numbers near the end of the campaign. Congressional Republicans' seemingly unending preoccupation with impeaching the president, Johnson argued, demoralized the Republican base and angered core Democrats. Although the GOP did not air any of its "get Clinton" ads in Wisconsin, they were picked up by the national news media and broadcast for voters to see.

Neumann pollster Gene Ulm agrees. His analysis of the tracking polls found that no one issue was driving voters, but rather that the likely composition of the electorate began to change in the final weeks. The newly energized Democrats contributed a percentage point or two to Feingold's total, he argued, pushing him to victory. Feingold personally agreed that the nationwide Democratic trend in the last two weeks greatly helped the campaign.

They Did It Their Way

Ultimately, both candidates ran races that reflected their personal visions, and after the election voters had positive views overall of both men. Feingold emerged from the race the winner despite having limited spending and refused to accept soft money spending. Clearly he will command credibility when he argues for campaign finance reform in the future.

Neumann lost a close race but won new political respect. He significantly altered his image in the state and ran a campaign that Chris Matthews called the best in the country in 1998. He fought hard on the Social Security issue, and although polls showed that 58 percent of voters who cared about that issue most voted for Feingold, this was actually much better than most Republican Senate candidates managed. In California, Democrat Barbara Boxer won some 73 percent of voters who listed Social Security as the most important issue; in New York, Democrat Charles Schumer won 70 percent. Neumann won narrowly among voters sixty-five years and older, but the electorate was much younger in 1998 than it had been in 1994, and Feingold won handily among the youngest voters.

Republicans charge that the campaign has generated a myth—that Feingold was significantly outspent, and that he did not benefit from soft money. It is hard to sort out the impact of the interest group campaigns, of the Democratic soft money ad, and of the free and "earned" media that both campaigns generated. The League of Conservation Voters has a history of success when it targets its "Dirty Dozen," and its ads were quite effective. The Democratic soft money ad was hard hitting, but it was pulled from most stations after a day, and it ran in Milwaukee only three days. The Republican party soft money buys were considerably larger and more significant than the soft money spent on Feingold's behalf by groups and the Democratic party—it was these ads that drew Neumann even early in the campaign.

Yet the difficulty in tracking campaign expenditures, in estimating the effects of the DSCC media buy, in estimating the amount spent by interest groups, in tracking soft money in voter mobilization efforts—all point to the limitations of voluntary agreements between pairs of candidates. Feingold himself sees little future to voluntary agreements and argues that these difficulties make even clearer the case for systematic campaign finance reform.

3
Cornhusker Upset

Underdog Defeats Nebraska's Popular Governor in 1996 Senate Race

CHUCK HAGEL (R) VS. GOV. BEN NELSON (D) IN AN
OPEN SEAT RACE

Doug McAuliffe

On a frigid Christmas morning in Nebraska in 1962, Chuck Hagel's family awoke to a tragedy. Their father had died suddenly. As they consoled each other in the living room, their local doctor joined them. Young Chuck, the eldest of four boys, stepped forward, embracing his mother. "Let me know what I need to do Doc, it's my responsibility now."

Later that afternoon, as Doc Rundquist sat down to Christmas dinner with his family, he turned to his wife and said, "That young boy, Chuck Hagel, he's going to be quite a man."

In politics, there are moments when candidates must step up, be accountable, and display that intuitive ability to perform when pressure is greatest. Rarely have I worked for a candidate who so successfully challenged adversity with determination, courage, and a sense of destiny as did Chuck Hagel in his uphill 1996 U.S. Senate race.

I first met Chuck in the offices of the National Republican Senatorial Committee. He told me he was going to be the next U.S. Senator from Nebraska. He said he knew it would not be easy—a bit of an understatement—but expected ultimate victory.

Work Cut Out

In the late spring of 1995, it was clear that Republican Chuck Hagel had his work cut out for him. The good news was that Sen. Jim Exon, the three-

---

Originally published in *Campaigns & Elections* magazine, February 1997.

Chuck Hagel   Ben Nelson

term Democratic incumbent, had announced his retirement. Popular Democratic Gov. Ben Nelson (who had just been reelected with a solid 73 percent of the vote) said that he did not want to go Washington. Bill Hopprier, who had lost the 1990 gubernatorial primary to Nelson by forty-two votes and was a former chief of staff to both Exon and Senator Bob Kerrey (D-Neb.), expressed interest but said that he would decide later.

Despite what looked like a wide open general election, Hagel faced an immediate and formidable task—winning a Republican primary against popular Attorney General Don Stenberg, the darling of the Nebraska Right-to-Life movement and other conservative groups. Stenberg is aggressive, articulate, and known for his take-no-prisoners partisan jabs at Democrats and his willingness to champion right-of-center causes.

Hagel's pollster, Glen Bolger of Public Opinion Strategies, conducted our first survey in September 1995, which showed the obvious: Stenberg led Hagel 54–8 percent. However, Bolger's analysis uncovered the seeds of a possible primary victory. Only 19 percent of the GOP electorate was committed to Stenberg, and the poll's open-ended questions suggested that Stenberg's lead was vulnerable—his support was driven by the fact that he was the only primary candidate voters knew.

The poll also suggested that Hagel's personal story would motivate voters. Hagel was a war hero who had volunteered for combat duty in Vietnam, where he was wounded twice (he still carries shrapnel in his chest) and decorated for bravery. Hagel's work for Ronald Reagan was also a plus, as was his record as a self-made businessman.

As in any campaign, it was critical not to dismiss the obvious: Nothing beats a great story. And Hagel had a great story.

Call it hubris, but we concluded that our candidate's persona provided us with the opportunity to convey to voters what we came to refer to as the stature gap: Hagel's presence and real life experiences versus those of his opponents.

As the bone-chilling Nebraska winter gave way to the humid breezes of the prairie summer, Hagel embarked on a tour of the state's ninety-three counties. Campaign Manager Lou Ann Linehan, a seasoned nuts-and-bolts political operative, concluded that the only way for Hagel to win was to build a superior campaign organization.

Working mom Linehan understood the psyche of Nebraska voters. They do not just elect politicians, they choose leaders and invest in personalities—warts and all. From Bob Kerrey to Jim Exon, Nebraskans have elected politicians with a sense of independence and prairie populism dating back to William Jennings Bryan.

Throughout the summer and fall, Hagel criss-crossed the state and focused on the necessities of early campaigning: raising money, organizing counties and local communities, securing endorsements, and cultivating the local media.

In late September, the campaign was hit with a reality check. Despite a pledge to serve his full gubernatorial term, Ben Nelson reversed his decision not to run for the Senate. A public poll by Political Media Research and KETV showed Nelson with a daunting 47 point lead over Hagel (65–18 percent).

As the new year turned, Hagel distributed Nebraska-shaped marble paper weights with a prophetic quote from Goethe—"What you do, or dream you can do, begin it. Boldness has a genius, power and magic in it." In January, Stenberg released a poll showing him with a 38 point lead over Hagel (50–12 percent) in the GOP race. In our poll, Stenberg's lead was also large, but his support was soft.

Media Message

After nine months and 40,000 miles, the Hagel ground game was in place. Our team now turned to devising media strategy.

In defining the message, we assessed each candidate's strengths and weaknesses. As in any media-driven campaign, our key strategic goal was to define Hagel—his story and his agenda. Our second strategic objective was to minimize Stenberg's perceived ideological advantage.

As we traveled during the summer, Hagel and I discussed growing up in rural Nebraska. After listening to him vividly describe the many towns he had lived in (his father ran lumber and coal companies in various rural towns), I thought, "Why not make all of rural Nebraska Chuck's roots?" Hagel agreed.

The introduction TV spot titled "Nebraska Roots" weaved together vignettes of Chuck in various towns talking about growing up in rural areas and his Nebraskan values. We described his courage in Vietnam, his work for Ronald Reagan, and his success in building a business and creating jobs. The spot concluded with Chuck on a rural road talking about smaller government, cutting spending, lower taxes, and a call for more personal responsibility. Our subsequent ads defined Hagel as a "Nebraska Conservative" and included significant issue messages.

Bolger's mid-March poll showed that Hagel's campaign was working. Since early February we had aired 3,000 GRPs (Gross Rating Points) of television time with staggering results. Hagel now led Stenberg 41–31 percent, a 55 point shift. Bolger's analysis found three big improvements: Hagel's favorable image had jumped from 10 to 54 percent, he was now perceived as more conservative than Stenberg, and his committed vote outpaced Stenberg's.

Stenberg was boxed in. We anticipated that he would now run to the right on social issues and question Hagel's conservative pedigree. We took the offensive and added to our next series of TV spots several conservative litmus-test issues such as Hagel's support for conservative judges and protecting the second amendment right to keep and bear arms.

At the same time, Lou Ann Linehan's team of coalition supporters went to work lobbying Right-to-Life groups, the Christian Coalition, pro-gun organizations, and other conservative activists.

Initially, Stenberg's media strategy defined his conservative accomplishments as Attorney General and featured the tag line, "A Nebraskan we know and trust." The tag was aimed directly at Hagel's twenty-year absence from the state.

After one week of positive television, Stenberg then launched a full scale assault on Hagel, portraying him as a carpetbagger, a Washington lobbyist, and a less than committed conservative.

Adding to Stenberg's attack were pro-Nelson forces. The Nebraska Democratic Party and the Democratic Senatorial Campaign Committee (which Nebraskan Bob Kerrey chaired) invested hundreds of thousands of dollars in an independent expenditure campaign attacking Hagel for the twenty years he lived in Virginia.

At the height of the negative assaults, our polls confirmed that the race was tightening. However, our media response, featuring average citizens on camera assailing both opponents' attacks as deceitful, distorted, and desperate, helped halt the slide. Hagel successfully raised questions about the desperation of two career politicians (Stenberg and Nelson) personally attacking him instead of talking about important issues like lower taxes and smaller government.

Meanwhile, the campaign's ground game was in full force, dropping tens of thousands of personalized letters to pro-life activists, targeting primary voters, and making more than 100,000 phone appeals.

On primary day, May 14, Hagel defeated Stenberg in a landslide, 62–38 percent. The campaign organizations built by Hagel and Linehan won eighty-five of ninety-three counties.

Stenberg made a classy and crucial step to help Hagel. On election night he drove from Lincoln to Omaha to endorse Hagel on the late evening news. Twenty-four years of GOP infighting were over. We were now ready to take on the "unbeatable" Ben Nelson.

Broken Promises

Despite Hagel's convincing primary victory, most Washington pundits and the PAC community had written this race into the Democrat column.

Unfazed and confident, Hagel made a number of policy speeches throughout the lazy hot summer months while Linehan focused on folding Stenberg's supporters and "Nelson Republicans" into a united GOP organization.

In early July, Hagel appeared before the Lincoln Rotary Club and offered a sweeping tax cut proposal to be paid for with spending cuts. The Nelson camp, flush with over-confidence, assailed Hagel's plan and attacked its credibility.

A May poll conducted by the NRSC showed Hagel trailing Nelson 49–36 percent. The disparity was of little meaning. The important figure was Nelson's number—less than 50 percent.

We surmised that Nelson was now the "functional incumbent" in the race. This was extremely significant. Despite the fact that the governor remained very popular, his vote share in the ballot test was dropping, and we could now see his soft underbelly.

In 1990, Nelson had defeated an incumbent Republican governor by promising to solve the "tax mess" and "provide property tax relief. " During his 1994 reelection landslide, Nelson had signed a pledge to serve his full term as governor.

In Bolger's first general election survey, we asked a series of questions that confirmed suspicions. Voters overwhelmingly felt that Nelson had not fulfilled his commitment to lower taxes and that under his administration property taxes were higher. Voters strongly believed (72 percent) that

Nelson should keep his word to serve his full gubernatorial term and to lower taxes.

We devised a two-pronged strategy. Our first objective was to reintroduce Hagel's story and define his core message: smaller government, lower taxes, and stronger values. Our second task was to link Nelson's broken promise on tax relief with his broken pledge to serve his full term.

Our fear was that Nelson's team would move to control the campaign by attacking Hagel in early September, thus putting us on the defensive and forcing us to play catch-up. When they did not, we breathed a sigh of relief.

As we filmed Hagel's initial TV spots in mid-August, a public poll was released by Mason Dixon showing Hagel trailing Nelson 55–34 percent. Despite this unpleasant news, Hagel intuitively understood his mission: contrast his message of smaller government and lower taxes with Nelson's record of expanding government and increasing taxes.

In late August, we went back on television with our initial general election spot focusing on Hagel's story and message. Our next three spots were designed to highlight the adverse effects of high taxes. Utilizing portraits of Nebraskans and Hagel talking on camera, we established the predicate that higher taxes were hurting people, while implicitly positioning Nelson as the villain.

After four weeks of television, the next Public Opinion Strategies survey showed that Hagel now trailed Nelson by nine points (47–38 percent). Ten days later, Nelson's lead was down to 47–44 percent.

Linehan's organizational operation was again in high gear. Metro Omaha Right-to-Life withdrew its endorsement of Nelson (known as a pro-lifer) after his appointment of a pro-choice judge. The statewide Right-to-Life group also endorsed Hagel after having previously only endorsed the Democrat. We also made headway among gun owners, who had been traditionally favorable to Nelson.

Internally, the Nelson team saw their lead slip and launched a series of attacks which continued through the rest of the campaign.

Upping the Ante

In early October, Nelson attacked Hagel's call to eliminate the Department of Education and claimed that Hagel would cut student loans. We had anticipated this attack and were on the air immediately with a spot filmed weeks earlier.

Speaking directly to camera, Hagel said Nelson wanted to give more of Nebraska's education dollars to Washington bureaucrats, while he (Hagel) would rather give the money to "states like Nebraska and local school districts to reward teachers, help students, and improve schools."

Nelson's advisors then returned to the attack they had used in the primary, assailing Hagel's twenty-year absence from Nebraska. They upped the ante by running a spot that used strong language to imply Hagel's business success was due to his lobbying background and actions to "rig federal auctions" for cellular telephone licenses. Nelson's attacks lacked full documentation and were criticized by the state's largest newspaper as "deceiving" and "dead wrong."

It was the critical moment of the campaign.

Our internal polls showed the attacks helped Nelson regain the lead, 44–41 percent. Under heavy fire, we made a decision to do two things. First, to use scathing press editorials against Nelson combined with Hagel on camera (also filmed weeks earlier) to counter Nelson's attacks. Second, to focus on Nelson's tax record and his failure to keep his word.

It was critical that we remain on message and avoid a protracted argument over the negative attacks on Chuck. Our message of lower taxes and smaller government, contrasted with Nelson's record of high taxes and broken pledges, was working. It had put Nelson into a box from which there was no exit—unless we gave him one.

With Nelson under fire for his attacks on Hagel, we moved in for the kill and launched two spots that provided documented evidence of Nelson's failure to deliver on promises. At the same time, we sent out hundreds of thousands of direct mail pieces focusing on these same issues.

The Nelson campaign responded with a television spot claiming higher property taxes were not the fault of the governor. He was now making an argument that voters did not believe.

We were now in control of the race.

A week before the election, Hagel moved ahead of Nelson by six points. Our tracking polls over the last week showed Nelson stuck in the 40–42 percent range. Bolger's turnout model projected that the lead could go as high as 15 points!

On November 5, 1996, Chuck Hagel defeated Ben Nelson 56–42 percent. It was a stunning upset by any measure.

4
How to Beat an Incumbent

The Hard-Fought Senate Race in South Dakota in 1996

Sen. Larry Pressler (R) vs. Tim Johnson (D)

Karl Struble

O nly one U.S. Senate challenger defeated an incumbent in 1996. He was also the first to beat a Senate committee chairman in twelve years. And despite running in a state with a Republican majority where Bob Dole beat Bill Clinton, he was the first Democrat to oust a Republican Senator in six years. That is what Tim Johnson and the team he assembled accomplished on November 5.

Looking for the Differences

First, let's start with a few basic truths about elections. All campaigns are about differences. Those differences can be about policy, personality, values, experience, party, gender, race . . . you name it. Voters, however, take these differences and interpret them, attributing them to character traits like smart, honest, effective or "cares about people like me." Ask any voter why they support a candidate. The reasons given are almost never "voted for the ABM treaty" or "reformed welfare"; they are usually a list of character traits. Good campaigns decide what character traits they wish to own and which traits they wish to associate with their opponent. Thinking about an election this way forces a campaign to examine differences between candidates as voters do, rather than dissecting and communicating arcane issue differences only elites understand or care about.

It may be surprising, but virtually every major office incumbent who loses does so because he or she lacks one crucial character trait: "cares about

---

Originally published in *Campaigns & Elections* magazine, June 1997.

people like me." The electorate concludes that the incumbent has lost touch and is not on their side. This alienation from the electorate normally happens for one of three reasons: 1) scandal, 2) issue differences, or 3) incumbent arrogance. In the case of U.S. Senators, this arrogance normally shows up as having "gone Washington," and the abuse of the perks and privileges of office.

Often candidates with serious ethical problems decide not to run again, like Sen. Don Riegle (D, Mich.) or Sen. Alan Cranston (D, Calif.). Gov. Ed DiPrete (R) of Rhode Island, whom we helped defeat in 1990, lost because his administration was embroiled in a kickback scandal that destroyed the electorate's trust. In a case like this, the challenger, our candidate Bruce Sundlun, only had to appear to be a credible alternative to win. Other times, like in the 1991 victory for the New Democratic Party of British Columbia, Canada, it is necessary to remind voters of the incumbent's record of scandals to make sure the electorate acts on the need for change.

The second way incumbents go down is when the opponent is able to sharpen the candidates' differences on issues, demonstrating that the office-holder is not on the voters' side. Tom Daschle's election in 1986 over incumbent Sen. Jim Abdnor (R, S.D.) is an example of the use of issue differences. In this election, we used the farm crisis and farm policy along with Social Security as validators that Jim Abdnor had lost touch with average South Dakotans.

Larry Pressler bit the dust for the third reason. We documented Larry's arrogance and abuse of office. We made his conduct and indulgence in the perks and privileges of his incumbency "the issue" in the race. We made him own this trait, driving a wedge between him and his constituents. Often more than one reason is combined to prove an incumbent is unfit for office. Or one reason works off others, as you will see in the Johnson-Pressler Senate race.

Assets and Liabilities

To learn how to sell your arguments to the public, you must analyze what assets and liabilities you and your opponent have, and what their effect on the race will be. In South Dakota, incumbent Senator Pressler had five significant advantages:

1) Pressler was popular. He possessed a 65 percent favorability rating and had never lost an election in twenty-two years.
2) South Dakota is a Republican state where GOP identifiers outnumber Democrats 46 percent to 36 percent.
3) Pressler was ideologically conservative in a state where conservatives outnumber liberals by better than two to one.

Tim Johnson's "Message Box"

TIM ON TIM
Tim Johnson is different from most politicians. He's on our side. He's taken on the powerful to fight for the needs of average South Dakota families.

- votes to protect Medicare and education
- fights for family farmers and water projects
- plan to hold down pharmaceutical costs
- raise minimum wage
- v-chip/cleaning up the Internet

TIM ON LARRY
Larry Pressler has changed. He's gone too Washington and sold out South Dakota families to promote policies that benefit the rich and powerful.

- votes to cut Medicare, education, farm programs
- votes to give tax breaks to the rich and corporations
- junkets, first-class travel, abuse of office, and campaign finances

LARRY ON LARRY
Larry Pressler is a common sense conservative. He is changing Washington to get government off the backs of South Dakota families and re-establishing traditional family values.

- passed Telecom bill
- helped pass welfare reform
- pro balanced budget amendment

LARRY ON TIM
Tim Johnson is a liberal. He supports the tax and spend policies that are ruining our economy and permissive values that are destroying the American family.

- votes against a balanced budget, welfare reform, and tax cuts
- abortion

4) As a senior senator and committee chairman, Pressler had clout and a commendable record of delivering money and projects to the state.

5) Finally, Pressler had a significant resource advantage. He started with half a million in the bank, out-raised us in every quarter, and out-spent us $4.4 million to $2.9 million.

In most cases, those advantages would be enough for an incumbent to be reelected. However, our candidate was not like most challengers, and we were not without assets of our own. Tim Johnson, as the state's lone Con-

Larry Pressler

Tim Johnson

gressman, had been elected statewide five times. He started with even better personal favorability numbers than Pressler—with 74 percent positive and only 16 percent negative. We had an experienced campaign team of consultants and staff who had worked together for years and knew how to win in South Dakota.

Most importantly, we had a great candidate. Tim Johnson, while not charismatic, was a good Congressman who shared the values of average people and had not forgotten who he represented. He oozed sincerity, was straightforward, a good father and husband—in short, just the kind of friend or neighbor you would like to have, someone you could trust. He was also committed to the race, focused on doing what was needed to win, and disciplined.

As we looked at our assets and liabilities, we saw that our candidate possessed the personal discipline that all challengers need. We had to overcome party, ideology, and money barriers, and we could only do that if we were smarter with our money and more focused with our message.

After months of research on our record and Senator Pressler's, several focus groups, two benchmark surveys, and countless meetings and discussions, we set our strategy and message. More than a year before the election, we constructed a "message box" and then set out to execute it. We chose to exploit the opposition's weakness on junkets, personal use of campaign funds, and abuse of perks as proof that Pressler had "changed" (see "Tim on Larry"). We theorized that it would then be easier to get voters to believe

Pressler would vote with powerful special interests and hurt average South Dakotans if they first perceived he had become too "Washington."

Conversely, we portrayed Johnson as what he is: the "Ward Cleaver" of South Dakota politics: a solid citizen with good family values who stands up for the little guy (see "Tim on Tim"). Unlike many Democratic challengers, we eschewed the "too extreme" argument on Pressler because it was less believable. Instead, we went directly to the question of who is on your side.

We also anticipated what Pressler wanted to say about himself (see "Larry on Larry") and what he wanted voters to believe about Johnson (see "Larry on Tim"). It should never be underestimated how important it is to understand what your opponent's message is going to be when formulating and executing your own strategy.

The great Chinese philosopher and warrior Sun Tzu wrote, in *The Art of War,* that if you do not know yourself and you do not know your opponent you will be imperiled in every single battle; if you know yourself, but do not know your opponent, you will win one battle and lose the next; but if you know yourself and you know your opponent, "you will not be imperiled in a hundred battles."

The simple exercise of filling out the four quadrants of a message box is quite illuminating and forces campaigns to understand themselves and their opponent. It can help enforce discipline on your campaign and gives structure to virtually every campaign activity from press releases to literature to paid media.

Plus, if you understand the opposition strategy, you will often know whether to counter an attack or ignore it because it is off message. This was particularly important in this race because Pressler's resource advantage meant we could not always respond.

In our judgment, we needed to save our resources for the end. They wanted a long war, to exploit their resource advantage. We wanted a short war to make our resources more comparable in the endgame.

They wanted to label Johnson a *liberal* and have ideology and partisanship determine the race. We wanted values and empathy for the public to emerge as the question.

We wanted voters entering the voting booth asking who is most like them, who understands them, who is really on their side.

Finkelstein's M.O.

When you start your campaign is not always up to you. Arthur Finkelstein, Pressler's strategy and message guru, true to his M.O. in other races, launched early. Pressler and Finkelstein attacked earlier than we wanted, earlier than we anticipated, earlier than any candidate in any other race in

The Horses, Handlers, Wagers, and Payoffs

	Tim Johnson (D)	*Larry Pressler*
Media	Struble, Oppel, Donovan	Arthur Finkelstein
Pollster	The Mellman Group	Arthur Finkelstein
Estimated spending	$2.9 million	$4.4 million
Votes	166,511 (51.3 percent)	157,912 (48.7 percent)

America. They attacked in July of 1995, a full sixteen months before the election.

Their attack started with trumped-up charges that we were behind "independent expenditure" ads being run in the state that were criticizing Pressler about cutting nursing home care. They followed that quickly with the first of more than forty separate negative ads calling Tim Johnson a liberal. They attacked Johnson for voting for the biggest tax increase ever, for opposing welfare reform, on school prayer, abortion . . . the list was endless.

Over the next year, Pressler and the National Republican Senatorial Committee ran more than 35,000 rating points of television time. That level is more than three times the number of ads typically run in the average competitive Senate campaign. Astonishingly, over two-thirds of Pressler's ads were negative, and all of them—every single negative ad after the first commercial—concluded with the refrain that Tim Johnson was a liberal. The ads were focused and tough; in fact, perhaps too tough for South Dakota. Focus groups were repulsed by the simplistic nature of Pressler's ads and what they saw as name-calling. Voters had a sense of who Tim Johnson was, they knew he was a Democrat, but instinctively they could not buy that he was a liberal. The word did not fit the person.

We worked the press and newspaper editors to exploit factual errors in Pressler's ads and to condemn his overly negative approach. We started to sell these media opinion leaders the basic elements of our message box that Larry had "changed," and our efforts bore results. More than a year out, editorials characterized our opponent's ads as "cheap shots" and "false." These editorials became the validators for our response ads.

Sporadically, we responded to Pressler's almost continuous attacks—undermining their credibility and seeding the idea that the old Larry Pressler we knew would not have stooped so low and been so dirty. We had no illusions about our strategy. We knew that thousands of negative rating points run against Johnson would have an effect. Our best hope was to keep the race even until Labor Day, when we could mount a continuous two-track positive and negative campaign.

Thirty-Second TV Spot

Tim Johnson for Senate

"Frequent Flyer"

Produced by: Struble, Oppel, Donovan

VIDEO: Travel postcards from around the world with Pressler photo.

ANNOUNCER: Paris, London, Hong Kong . . . Larry Pressler has traveled the world at our expense. When you add up Larry's taxpayer paid junkets, he's spent more than a year overseas . . . free trips to sixty-five foreign countries . . . including the Riviera and Rio. Pressler was named junketeer-of-the-year . . . and one of the Senate's most frequent flyers . . . It's a long way from Humboldt to Hong Kong . . . and it makes you wonder . . . Is Larry Pressler really on our side?

In reality, we started TV ads in June of 1996. *We went positive.* We talked about values and issues that put Johnson squarely on the side of average families. *We targeted women.* We constructed simple, direct, sentimental ads that spoke of pocketbook issues and reinforced our candidate's own family values. We made positive ads on traditional subjects like education, Medicare, farm policy and welfare reform. We also produced value-laden ads with special appeal to women on subjects like teenage pregnancy, domestic abuse, and gambling on the Internet. Often we used female voice-overs. We pictured Johnson listening, not just talking. Our scripts consciously employed conciliatory language and touted constructive solutions that studies show appeal to female voters. We did this not to dupe voters but rather to communicate accurately who our candidate really was and to attract our natural constituencies.

A TV spot titled "Solid" was typical of this style. While the ad could be viewed as a laundry list of positives, in reality it was a vehicle for saying that Tim Johnson is not like most Washington politicians, he is like you. Coincidentally, this ad ran more than any other one we produced. "Solid" saw almost 2,000 rating points during September and early October. It was the positive counter-position from which we opened attacks on Pressler's character. It also served as a reminder that this race was not about ideology.

Consciously, we saved our bullets for the end. The campaign spent thousands of hours researching Pressler's record and his foreign travel and use of perks and campaign funds. We spent months educating various members of the press on Pressler's transgressions. We documented every vote he missed to earn a speaking fee. We matched his votes with special interest checks. We identified almost half a million dollars in unexplained personal expenses reimbursed by his campaign. We found thousands of dollars spent on first-class airfare, luxury hotel suites, limos, opera tickets, and a copy of the social registry. We could even prove that Pressler spent more time in foreign countries than he did in South Dakota one year, and that he had cumulatively spent more than a year overseas at taxpayer expense since he was in the Senate. It was quite a compelling case.

The press ate it up. Our campaign systematically doled out the information piece by piece to reporters in D.C. and South Dakota. The result was a series of damaging articles that accurately depicted a senator who had let his position go to his head and who used his office for personal benefit. We used the headlines generated as validators for our ads. They added credibility, making our commercials seem fair and believable.

The most provocative of these ads was a script called "Frequent Flyer" (see TV spot, facing page). It combined headlines of Pressler's junkets with postcards from exotic destinations and footage of a tropical beach. It was designed to cut through the clutter using these cartoonish images coupled with a sound track that flipped from jazz to calypso music to a Chinese gong at the end. The ad confronted voters with the reality that Larry Pressler had changed and questioned whether he was really on their side.

Within days of our earned and paid media assaults, tracking polls conducted by our pollster, the Mellman Group, showed a meteoric rise in Pressler's negatives on abuse of office and a deterioration of empathy traits like "cares about people like me." Consequently, we opened up a 5 to 10 percent lead in early October.

In fairness, it must be pointed out that Pressler also succeeded in driving up a perception that Johnson was "too liberal." Over the course of the campaign, we endured a steady but less substantial erosion on this trait. Fortunately, it affected the view of Republicans more than Independents or Democrats. Nevertheless, the race closed up at the end with Pressler's partisan and ideological advantages holding back a Johnson blowout.

The race was the longest and most expensive in South Dakota history. It was by far the most negative the state has ever seen. Ultimately, we overcame our liabilities in ideology, party, and money because our message was more believable and more compelling.

The opposition made a fundamental mistake: It is not enough to simply maintain someone is a liberal. Pressler, or rather adviser Finkelstein, did not connect the dots and make the anti-liberal argument relevant to voters. Besides, the pejorative use of the label "liberal" was offensive to many South Dakotans and did not fit the style and substance of Tim Johnson.

We chose to run on a message voters could understand and buy. Tim was like them and Larry had "gone Washington." After all, it is very easy for the public to believe twenty-two years in Washington would change anyone.

We spent our resources smarter, had a simple, believable, meaningful message and we executed it better. The victory was sweet, the margin slim, and the result was the only U.S. Senate challenger to win in 1996.

5

The Senator from Central Casting

How Fred Thompson Turned Tennessee Politics Upside Down in 1994

FRED THOMPSON (R) VS. JIM COOPER (D) IN AN
OPEN SEAT RACE

David Beiler

The status quo of Tennessee politics, dominated by Democrats for so long, exploded in 1994, as Republicans captured the top three slots by convincing margins. Democrats had held every statewide office for the past eight years; in 1994, they barely won one—a seat on the Public Service Commission. Jim Sasser, the man expected to become Democratic Leader of the next U.S. Senate, was beaten by 14 points—by a political unknown.

Much of the sudden and dramatic shift in GOP fortunes in the land of Andrew Jackson could be traced to the electorate's enthusiastic reaction to Senate candidate Fred Thompson, a straight talking attorney and actor who had succeeded in defining Tennessee's political agenda. Thompson's star quality—already evident in films such as *Hunt for Red October* and *In the Line of Fire*—soon took center stage in Washington, where he was chosen to deliver the GOP response to President Clinton's mid-term address to the nation in December.

The Prince and the GOPer

Not so long ago, the drawling Thompson was anything but the center of adulation. As late as August—when a treasureless salesman held him to little more than three-fifths of the vote in the Republican primary—Thompson looked like a longshot in the race to complete the last two years of Al Gore's Senate term. Opponent Jim Cooper had the strongest credentials of any non-incumbent candidate in the country. A Rhodes Scholar son of a former

---

Originally published in *Campaigns & Elections* magazine, May 1995.

Fred Thompson

Jim Cooper

governor, he had already put in a dozen years in Congress at the age of forty; his much-touted health care bill was a major impediment to the far more sweeping program proposed by President Clinton. Cooper was a legitimate national figure, and his campaign coffers reflected it, even though he had decided not to accept PAC money.

By contrast, Thompson's political career appeared stillborn. Ever since his high-profile role as the young minority counsel in the Senate Watergate hearings of a generation ago, Thompson had been considered a potential candidate for statewide office. As the years and opportunities passed, the once-rising political star began to look like a political Kahoutek—all hype and no happening. After playing himself in a 1985 Sissy Spacek film about a crusade against corrupt state government, Thompson launched a side career in the movies as a character actor, a move that seemed to categorize him as little more than the question to a thousand-dollar jeopardy answer: "After uncovering the secret Nixon tapes, he later played a presidential chief of staff in the movies."

Now that he was finally in the field, campaigning for the Gore seat, Thompson was being roundly criticized for what appeared to be a laconic start. He still bristles about it today:

It seems like the experts are always fighting the last war and really don't have the ability to project—here in Tennessee especially. The way they saw it, Cooper had a million dollars going in, was the fair-haired boy of the health care industry, and was an effective campaigner. The fact of the matter was the only race he'd ever had was that first race for Congress twelve years ago.

True enough, but that first race had left a deep impression. Running in a newly created, marginal district that sprawled 300 miles across the state, Cooper faced Cissy Baker, whose father (Howard Baker) and grandfather (Everett Dirksen) had both served as Republican Leaders in the U.S. Senate. Baker spent a record $1.2 million, but Cooper crushed her by a two to one margin. One indicator of the effectiveness of the Baker campaign was its bumpersticker, whose black letters on a yellow background proclaimed one word: "Cissy." It was not often found on the back of the rural district's many pickups.

Laid Low

A self-proclaimed "New Democrat" whose path to the nomination had been cleared by the Nashville establishment, Cooper had gone a long way toward alienating his party's liberal support base. He recently had voted against shifting the tax burden toward the wealthy, had voted for NAFTA, and had been fingered by the White House as the most dangerous opponent of the president's elaborate and ambitious health care designs.

All that made Cooper a particular persona non grata with Tennessee's labor unions, who burned a copy of his health care plan at a March 10 rally in Chattanooga. "You don't reckon he's putting that bill in because it's good for the people, do you?" bellowed Marty Berger of the Garment Workers. "You don't think he wants to grow up to be a Senator, do you?"

The idea that the Congressman was a tool of special interests gradually took hold, despite his refusal of PAC money. A March 21 Cooper fundraiser in the insurance capital of Hartford, Connecticut, drew a hundred protestors chanting "shame!" and led to unflattering headlines back home, such as the Nashville *Banner*'s "Insurance Execs Fill Up Cooper's Collection Plate."

For his part, Thompson generally laid low on the issues that threatened an intraparty revolt against the presumed Democratic nominee. He took no position on the controversial GATT trade treaty that would soon be coming before Congress and offered no specific alternatives to the Cooper health care plan, which he claimed was too expensive and restrictive. Instead, he harped on Cooper's insurance industry funding, reportedly lobbied GOP senators in Washington to avoid compromise on health care, and carefully laid plans for an image-driven campaign that would draw on the widespread disaffection with Congress among middle class voters.

Remarkably, it would be the only non-incumbent Senate campaign in the country whose advertising would virtually ignore the opposition—even that favorite GOP punching bag, Bill Clinton.

"It was something I had in mind from the very beginning," Thompson recalls, explaining why he passed up a concurrent chance to run for a full six-year Senate term, challenging liberal establishment figure Jim Sasser.

"One of the reasons the open seat appealed to me was that I thought I could talk about what I wanted to do instead of complaining about the other guy. It worked out that way . . . [and] was responsible for a major part of our success."

Unique Strategy

Success looked a long way off when Thompson formally opened his campaign on April 18. Cooper was leading him by a three to two margin in most surveys and had outraised him three to one. The Democrat's $2.5 million war chest was the largest of any open seat Senate campaign in the entire country. Although the March *Campaigns & Elections* had tabbed Thompson the "upset pick of the year," this was a rare assessment. "Fred's frittered away his chance," a Republican activist reported from Nashville.

The filing deadline was a month away, and Thompson faced only nominal primary opposition from Memphis salesman John Baker. The early low profile was "more or less the plan we laid out in September [1993]" reports Thompson manager Bill Lacy. "We knew little attention was going to be paid to our race during the primary season, with a big, well-financed field shaping up in the Republican primary for the other seat. So we concentrated on raising money for the big media push that would start the day after the primary, in mid-August."

A native of Cookeville, in populist/Democratic middle Tennessee, Lacy was a veteran GOP operative from the highest levels, having managed Bob Dole's 1988 bid for the presidency. Coming on board the campaign at its inception the previous fall, he had helped put together a crack team of professionals that included pollster Linda DiVall and media maven Alex Castellanos, a veteran of Jesse Helms's 1990 comeback and the Bush reelection effort. But it was clear this candidate would need little instruction in how to communicate to the voters, particularly the key swing "3-M" cohort: Moderate, Middle-class, and Mad.

"The people around me had the confidence to sublimate their own ideas and professionalism," Thompson fondly recalls. "They let me go with what I felt I had to do."

Thompson's instincts told him to avoid negative attacks in his advertising until fired upon, concentrating instead on articulating a reform agenda and conveying empathy for the disillusioned working class. It was a unique strategy among the nation's major races, and it initially appeared to be going nowhere.

The Thompson campaign ran only one TV spot during the primary season: an interesting thirty-second bio that recounted his various adventures as a prosecutor, Watergate investigator, crusader against corruption in the Governor's Office, and actor. Riding high in the polls and awash in cash, Cooper avoided joint appearances over the summer, citing the contested GOP primary.

The pair finally clashed for the first time at a convocation of the state bar association in June, with Cooper acting like an incumbent and Thompson relishing the role of challenger. Known in Washington as a policy wonk, Cooper studiously ticked off the details of his background and health care plan. To preempt being stuck with the "Washington Insider" label, he tried to position Thompson under the mantel of campaign heavy. "We've seen very little in the way of negative campaigning," he cautioned ominously. "That may be about to change."

Tennesseans deplore incivility in their politicians, and Thompson was not about to rise to the bait with his advertising, despite his underdog status. But for the more studious voters who were noting these face-to-face showdowns, he was more than willing to demonstrate his opponent's alleged unworthiness. Cooper was guilty of "the old congressional two-step," Thompson charged, pushing a health care plan favorable to the insurance industry while raking in contributions from it. Furthermore, he had "ignored the need for congressional reform while voting to increase his own salary."

Red Pickup and Plaid Shirts

The day after the August 4 primary, Thompson leased a red pickup from a Knoxville car dealer, emblazoned the doors with his campaign logo, and set off on a trek that would carry him to every one of Tennessee's ninety-five counties that he had not already hit in his quest for office. Wearing jeans and plaid shirts, the one-time bicycle assembler pressed the flesh at county fairs and country stores and in small hamlets far off the beaten campaign trail.

The shift in tactics caused no great commotion until the Cooper campaign ridiculed it as "a Hollywood actor driving around in a rented stage prop." As the news media took note of the amusing controversy, Thompson and the truck became overnight celebrities.

It was a sequence of events reminiscent of the very first media campaign, the presidential contest of 1840. A Democratic newspaper berating Whig

Around the Track
Tracing the Tennessee Senate Race by the Numbers

Candidate	Survey 1 (late July)	Survey 2 (mid-September)	Survey 3 (mid-October)	Returns
Thompson (R)	33/49 percent	39/62 percent	46/85 percent	61.1 percent
Cooper (D)	45/88	41/84	40/89	38.9
Undecided	22	20	14	

The first percentage in each column refers to support; the second refers to name identification.
SOURCE: All surveys by Mason-Dixon/PMR for *The (Nashville) Tennessean:* 1) taken July 24–26 of 838 likely voters (margin of error +/– 3.5 percent); 2) taken September 15–19 of 814 likely voters (margin of error +/– 3.5 percent); 3) taken October 8–10 of 804 likely voters (margin of error +/– 3.6 percent).

nominee William Henry Harrison as an antiquated back-bencher sneered, "set him up on the porch of a log cabin with a barrel of hard cider, and he will sit contentedly for the rest of his days." Heretofore known as the party of privilege, the Whigs adopted the log cabin and cider barrel as campaign symbols and swept Democrat incumbent Martin Van Buren out of office in a "tidal wave of apple juice."

The new-found Thompson imagery had a similar effect. Following up on the avalanche of populist publicity, the part-time actor wrote and recorded a series of "talking head" spots that used farm scenes as a backdrop. Dressed in his now-trademark uniform of denim and flannel, a folksy-but-firm Thompson harkens reform from the heartland:

> They have no idea, do they, the career politicians. How the laws and taxes they put on us affect us. So let's stop Congress from exempting themselves from the laws they make for the rest of us. Let's take away their million-dollar pensions and pay raises. Same laws that apply to us ought to apply to them. Who knows? Maybe they wouldn't make so many laws if they actually had to live under a few of them.

Usually closing with footage of the red pickup hurtling through the countryside along a rail fence, the farm ads put Thompson's numbers on the move. By mid-September he had pulled even in the polls, and Cooper had begun to panic, charging in a radio debate that Thompson was concealing "his secret life . . . as a foreign agent" from the voters. Slowly the race was being defined as John Wayne meets Miles Silverberg.

The Horses, Handlers, Wagers, and Payoffs

	Fred Thompson (R)	Jim Cooper (D)
Manager	Bill Lacy	John Cooper
Media	National Media	Strother/Duffy/Strother[1]
Pollster	American Viewpoint	Hickman-Brown Research
Expenditures	$3,792,835	$3,976,246
Votes	878,426 (61.1 percent)	559,356 (38.9 percent)
Amount spent per vote	$4.32	$7.11

1. Succeeded the Campaign Group.

Bronk vs. Wonk

In an attempt to turn the tide, the lisping Democratic lawmaker did his best to appear tough in an ad that called on him to recount the attempted burglary of his home by a man with a pitchfork. The episode was plainly overblown, with Cooper describing his home-alone wife's alarm and declaring the arrested criminal "got off." In fact, the incident took place in Washington; the burglar avoided serving time there only because he was subsequently given a much longer sentence in another jurisdiction. As his numbers continued to wane, Cooper put Al Gore's old media firm, the Campaign Group, on the bench and called in Strother Duffy—specialists in southern populism.

Castellanos became concerned that the Democrats would soon use their larger media budget to drive home the charge that Thompson's common-man image was another movie role, that he was really an elite lobbyist for special interests. He urged the reluctant candidate to discredit his opponent first, loading into attack ads ammunition that he had already fired in debates. Thompson finally relented, allowing the production of a single negative spot ("Stripes"). But he dictated that it be held in reserve and used only in response to Cooper's first negative advertising.

Like duelists from Andy Jackson's time, warily keeping each other in their sights long after the count of ten, the candidates showed remarkable restraint, neither wanting to take the first ungentlemanly plunge into the quagmire of negative advertising. With only a month left on the campaign schedule, this had so far been the only competitive Senate race in the country that had avoided muddying up the voters' living rooms.

Finally, a Mason-Dixon poll published October 14 in *The (Nashville) Tennessean* reported that Thompson had pulled six points ahead. Steaming over what he regarded an artful subterfuge, an exasperated Cooper found his vox populi, dubbing his homespun opponent a "Gucci-wearing, Lincoln-driving, Perrier-drinking, Grey Poupon–spreading millionaire Washington special interest lobbyist." The mud-caked message soon hit the airwaves in a spot that featured Thompson's Washington home.

The gloves were off, and "Stripes" was finally unleashed. It opens with Cooper piously explaining he does not take PAC money because "I don't want to be beholden to special interests." It then recreates a clip from an ABC News broadcast that identifies Cooper as the biggest recipient of insurance industry largesse in the entire U.S. House. After citing the Democrat's several votes for tax hikes and congressional pay raises, the thirty-second devastation concludes with priceless footage of Cooper chasing after a jogging Clinton on the Mall, looking like Sweet Pea trying to tag along in Popeye's wake. "Jim Cooper," a voice disdainfully offers. "He's running with the wrong crowd."

NRA Push

In the final ten days, with Thompson's advertising shifting to inspiring spots that recalled the campaign's grassroots images and message, Tennessee registered as the epicenter of a national Republican earthquake. The see-saw governor's race turned into an eight-point GOP win, while Sasser's precarious lead over surgeon Bill Frist slid into a landslide loss.

A major force that energized Republican turnout across the board was a massive outpouring of gun owners, mobilized by the National Rifle Association, which has, according to public opinion studies, a following of over 450,000 members and "perceived" members in Tennessee. Their efforts were aimed at the grassroots and helped move countless nominal Democrats into the Thompson and Frist columns.

At center stage, Farmer Fred was burying Gentleman Jim by more than 22 points, rolling up the biggest non-presidential year vote total in Tennessee history. A month later he was being cast by all major TV networks as the national spokesman of the Republican Party. Before he was even sworn in to his first elective office, Thompson was asked on a top-rated public affairs program if he would be running for president in 1996.

What makes this latest figure on our political landscape so compelling a force?

It is a stirring television image. Draped in the homespun raiment of the backwater, the Man of the People looks out of place in the political arena— where the other gladiators all evince the image of formal, authoritative conformity. An entertainer by trade, he speaks engagingly, amusingly, in the vernacular—but straight-on; no phony, studied double-talk here. And he is seething with the discontent of the ignored masses:

You wouldn't be doing the [people] any good voting for this bill. You'd only be making rich men out of the land-grabbers and speculators who've been trying to get it passed. Now, just who are these scalawags? Well, one of them could be the President himself . . . [but] I'm sure he has only the good of the country at heart. No, it's just a few thievin' varmints hangin' on, givin' dinners and fancy parties, reachin' for whatever they can get their hands on. But they're a no-account lot about as natural as flies around a molasses barrel. The real scalawags in this here capital of the brave and free is us—you and me . . . It's nobody's fault but our own if a bill like this gets passed.

No, that is not a Fred Thompson commercial from 1994, though it might as well be. It is a Walt Disney production from 1954, a scene from the first TV mini-series, "Davy Crockett: King of the Wild Frontier." Actor Fess Parker's drawling Crockett is railing away on the floor of Congress, scolding the members for caving to fat cat special interests.

The Crockett saga became an instant international sensation: its theme song camped out in the Billboard Chart's number one slot for seven weeks; raccoons became an endangered species as millions of kids clamored for Davy-style coonskin caps. Re-run every other year for a decade, "Davy Crockett" profoundly influenced baby boomers in their formative years. Writing fifteen years later in *The Strawberry Statement,* student radical James Simon Kunen declared that the series had led him to question the powers-that-be. Of Walt Disney, Kunen wrote: "The old fascist never knew he was creating a generation of revolutionaries."

Forty years ago, Fred Thompson was a working-class adolescent in Crockett's bucolic hometown of Lawrenceburg, Tennessee (pop. 10,000). One can scarcely imagine the impact Parker/Crockett must have had on him, but it seems evident today in the way he speaks to the unblinking eye that carries his message to millions:

Let's limit the terms of career politicians and open the system to average citizens. Let's stop their automatic pay raises and make them live under the laws they make for the rest of us. To restore our confidence in our government again, Congress needs a major shakeup. I'm Fred Thompson. If you'll help me, I'll lead that fight.

If Tennessee voters are any indicator, the idealistic-turned-surly boomers have found their voice in this reincarnation of their childhood hero. Those wishing to stay in power had better listen.

PART II

House Races

6

Professionalism, Progressivism, and People Power

Baldwin's Victory Blends All Three in Wisconsin's 2nd District in 1998

TAMMY BALDWIN (D) VS. JO MUSSER (R) IN AN
OPEN SEAT RACE

David T. Canon and Paul S. Herrnson

Tammy Baldwin's victory in Wisconsin's 2nd Congressional District signifies two important firsts in politics. Baldwin is the first woman elected to Congress from Wisconsin in the state's history. She is also the first openly gay candidate elected to Congress in the nation. Baldwin's success in breaking down the barriers that have kept members of traditionally underrepresented groups from serving in Congress brings added significance to her victory over Republican Josephine Musser.

Wisconsin's 2nd District is evenly divided between the rural counties of the south-central part of the state and Madison and its suburbs. The rural areas, which contain 36 percent of the district's residents, are largely agricultural and fairly conservative. Madison, the state's capital and home to the flagship campus of the University of Wisconsin, comprises about a third of the district. Sometimes referred to as "The People's Republic of Madison," it is one of the few remaining bastions of 1960s liberalism. The rapidly growing Madison suburbs are the battleground where swing voters have determined recent congressional elections. Their support enabled Republican former U.S. Representative Scott Klug, a television news broadcaster, to defeat sixteen-term Democratic incumbent Robert Kastenmeier in 1990.

Klug's announcement in February 1997 that he would not run for a fifth term attracted a great deal of attention. It was the first time that the seat had been open in forty years, and national and state leaders of both parties considered the seat one of their best prospects. Wisconsin State Democratic Chairwoman Terri Spring summarized her party's perspective on the 2nd

---

Originally published in *Campaigns & Elections* magazine, May 1999.

Tammy Baldwin Jo Musser

and neighboring 1st District as follows: "They're Democratic seats, and we want them back. The interest [in Washington] is intense."

Republican leaders maintained that the politics of the district had moderated during Klug's tenure and that the coattails provided by popular GOP Gov. Tommy Thompson would work to their candidate's advantage. However, Spring was right about the partisan makeup of the district. The 2nd District has not delivered a majority of votes for a Republican presidential candidate since 1960, and Bill Clinton carried the district by 18-point and 22-point margins in 1992 and 1996, respectively. National political handicappers first reported that the district leaned Democratic and later rated it a tossup after the primary.

A Flurry of Activity

The open seat stimulated a flurry of activity in both the Democratic and Republican parties. Three of the biggest Democratic names in the district, state Sen. Joe Wineke, county executive Rick Phelps, and state Representative Baldwin, started their campaigns soon after Klug's announcement. A fourth Democrat, house spouse Patrick O'Brien, was a late entrant, spending only $300 on the race.

In contrast, the Republican contestants were notable for their lack of experience in elective politics. Led by former state Insurance Commissioner Jo Musser, they included Sauk County beer distributor Donald Carrig,

The Horses, Handlers, Wagers, and Payoffs

	Tammy Baldwin (D)	*Jo Musser (R)*
Manager	Paul Devlin	Ruth DeWitt
Media	Will Robinson	David Welch Associates
Pollster	Diane Feldman	Linda DiVall
Expenditures	$1,067,404	$871,544
Votes	53 percent	47 percent

former congressional aide Nicholas Fuhrman, University of Wisconsin history professor John Sharpless, DeForest chiropractor Meredith Bakke, and minister and former firefighter Ron Greer. Some party activists privately complained that they lacked a big-name candidate. This general malaise among Republicans prompted a tongue-lashing from Klug, who told them to "quit the whining and get to work."

Baldwin had begun to lay the foundation for a U.S. House campaign early in 1996, when she attended a candidate training session sponsored by the Women's Campaign Fund and took a trip to Washington to discuss her political future with representatives of several women's organizations, including EMILY's List and the National Organization for Women.

All three of the major Democratic contenders assembled impressive campaign teams and brought in Washington-based firms to produce their media. Collectively they had raised $551,983 by the end of 1997. In comparison, Republicans had raised only $92,099.

The pattern of lavish spending continued through the primary. Phelps, who had secured Kastenmeier's endorsement, spent more than $607,000 in the primary, and Wineke spent $346,000. Baldwin topped both of them, spending $642,000 in the nomination bid. Carrig and Musser led the Republicans in fundraising during the primary. Carrig spent more than anybody, $712,000, including $457,000 that came from his own pocket. Musser was also generous with her checkbook, contributing almost $290,000 of the $414,000 she spent in her primary campaign. Bakke spent $247,000, Greer spent $187,125, Fuhrman spent $144,000, and Sharpless spent $73,000.

Money became an important issue. Wisconsin is known for its squeaky-clean politics. Democratic Senator Russell Feingold put campaign finance on the media's agenda by championing campaign finance reform, limiting his own spending, and seeking to limit spending by the outside groups that supported him.

Phelps and Wineke raised the campaign finance issue by proposing to cap spending at $250,000 for each candidate and to limit funds accepted

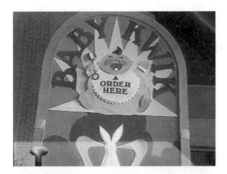

Thirty-Second TV Spot

"Baby Kwik"

Tammy Baldwin for Congress

*Produced by: MacWilliams
Cosgrove Smith Robinson*

ANNOUNCER: Having a baby shouldn't be like getting fast food.

TALKING HEAD: Welcome to Baby Kwik, your baby is ready, please drive through.

ANNOUNCER: But insurance companies and some HMOs tried to make it that way, forcing women out of the hospital less than a day after giving birth.

TAMMY BALDWIN: That's why I fought to require insurance companies to give new mothers at least two days in the hospital after having a baby. Because families need time to get off to a healthy start.

ANNOUNCER: Tammy Baldwin for Congress.

TALKING HEAD: Do you want fries with that too?

from sources outside the district to no more than 40 percent of total spending. Baldwin refused, recognizing that her status as the only woman and gay candidate in the primary would provide her with an advantage in raising money through national donor networks.

In addition to campaign finance, the candidates in both primaries debated education, taxes, and health care, though there were few significant differences among the candidates in either primary. Notably, in the GOP primary all of the candidates but Greer attempted to portray themselves as the rightful heir to Klug, despite the fact that he chose not to endorse anyone.

Baldwin and Musser both emphasized their gender, but Baldwin made it more central to her campaign. While positioning herself as a policy-oriented candidate, she repeatedly pointed out that Wisconsin had never sent a woman to Congress and ran television ads saying that "Tammy Baldwin will take on the issues that most congressmen won't." Her ads focused on issues that topped women's concerns, including equal pay for equal work, protecting Social Security, quality education, combating nursing home abuse, and health care reform. One ad highlighted her opposition to drive-through maternity stays (see "Baby Kwik" TV spot, facing page). Others emphasized her support for family and medical leave and affordable health care coverage (she favored a single-payer universal health care system). Some of these ads were broadcast during television programs that attracted largely female audiences.

Baldwin also mobilized young voters. One of her ads, which ran in both the primary and general election campaigns, focused on "Generation Xers" and was broadcast on MTV and during "Ally McBeal" and other shows with large student audiences. It featured a college-aged woman in a dorm room who tells the audience, "There is a way to make a difference right here and right now. There is one candidate who cares about our issues: Tammy Baldwin." The woman goes on to tout Baldwin's candidacy. She then urges young people to vote, describing Wisconsin's same-day registration system (which allows people to register at the polls), and urging them to telephone Baldwin's campaign headquarters if they do not know where to vote or want more information. The ad, which closed with the woman asserting that "making a difference is easier than you think," also contained a reference to Baldwin's web site.

According to Paul Devlin, Baldwin's campaign manager, every time the ad ran, all ten phone lines in the headquarters would light up. The person handling the phones would yell out "Bucky," which was their unofficial name for the ad (after the University of Wisconsin mascot "Bucky Badger"), so that others in the office would pick up a line.

Despite her focus on gender, students, family concerns, and traditionally Democratic issues, Baldwin's homosexuality seemed destined to become a factor in the campaign. Although none of her Democratic opponents focused on it, initially the press did. Her campaign manager had to battle with the local press for about a month before they would discuss her candidacy without describing her as "Tammy Baldwin, the first lesbian member of the state assembly."

The only Republican who made an issue of Baldwin's sexual orientation was Greer, whose alleged gay-bashing had cost him his job at the Madison fire department. He aggressively attacked Baldwin and the gay community. His attacks, highly publicized attempts to reclaim his job, and his race—he

Thirty-Second TV Spot

"Mud"

Jo Musser for Congress

Produced by: David Welch Associates

ANNOUNCER: We'll be right back after this commercial message.

VOICEOVER: Uh oh, it's another Tammy Baldwin ad. Baldwin believes with enough mud-slinging, we won't see Jo Musser's true record. The truth? As insurance commissioner, Jo Musser protected us from losing our policies. She fined the insurance companies for taking advantage of seniors. And Jo Musser collected millions in claims from companies refusing to pay. If Tammy Baldwin had a record like Jo Musser, she wouldn't have to hide her record in mud.

ANNOUNCER: And when we come back, Tammy Baldwin goes negative again.

is an African American—brought him a wave of statewide and even national press coverage. A fundraising letter in which he labeled Baldwin "a left-wing lesbian" brought him national support in conservative circles but also had some unintended effects.

These tactics helped mobilize Madison's politically active gay community and drew the attention of homosexuals nationwide, many of whom responded by contributing to Baldwin's campaign. Furthermore, all of the other Republican candidates publicly criticized Greer's attacks, and the eventual nominee, Musser, was a supporter of gay rights who refused to raise it as a campaign issue.

On September 8, Baldwin won 37 percent of the Democratic primary vote, followed by Phelps, who captured 35 percent. Musser's victory was even narrower. She won with 21 percent of the GOP vote, only 395 votes more than Greer, who garnered 20 percent. Carrig, the top spender in the GOP field, finished fourth with 17 percent of the vote.

Not So Fortunate

Baldwin was able to unify Democrats immediately after her primary. Musser was not so fortunate. She needed to build bridges to the four out of five Republican primary voters who had not supported her, but Greer did not make this an easy task. He first asked for a recount, and later he threatened to wage a write-in general election campaign. Contending with these possibilities delayed Musser from focusing on the general election. Carrig was also lukewarm about Musser's campaign, because of comments she had made about him during the primary.

Although both campaigns had assembled professional teams, replete with experienced managers, media consultants, and pollsters, Musser's organization was plagued by internal dissension. It went through five different campaign managers, and Republican insiders report that it had no clear lines of authority and a chaotic decision-making process. By contrast, Baldwin's campaign had a well-organized decision-making process.

Baldwin also enjoyed a financial advantage. She raised more than $1.5 million, setting a record for Wisconsin U.S. House races. According to the Center for Responsive Politics, 54 percent of her funds came from out of state. The efforts of EMILY's List, the Gay and Lesbian Victory Fund, and other liberal organizations helped her collect more than $213,000 from ideological PACs and liberals. She also benefited from the direct mail sent by the Sierra Club and Citizen Action. Various Democratic committees transferred nearly $1.2 million to help finance a coordinated campaign that helped Baldwin, Feingold, and other Wisconsin Democratic candidates mobilize their base.

Musser raised $875,000, drawing heavily on the health insurance industry and other business interests. Only 11 percent of her funds came from outside Wisconsin. Americans for Term Limits also spent $200,000 attacking Baldwin for refusing to sign a pledge to serve no more than three terms. The Republican Party spent nearly $500,000 on issue advocacy ads attacking Baldwin on tax increases. The GOP also transferred more than $2 million to help finance voter mobilization activities intended to help Musser, Neumann, and other Republican candidates.

Distinguished Herself

Baldwin's message emphasized that she was a different kind of candidate who had vision. She distinguished herself from other politicians by stressing her youth, gender, and commitment to bipartisan solutions to national problems. She articulated her vision by framing Social Security, protection for the elderly, and workplace fairness issues around the experiences of her ninety-two-year-old grandmother and two-year-old cousin.

Baldwin also used an innovative web site. In addition to the usual information about the candidate's issue positions, press releases, and text from her television and direct mail ads, Baldwin's site provided information designed to make it easier for individuals to vote. Students who typed in their dormitory or off-campus address, for example, would learn the location of their polling place. The site even provided a picture of the building in which the polling place was located.

Baldwin's web site played a significant role in encouraging student voter turnout, especially in the primary, which took place only two weeks after students had arrived in Madison for the start of the fall semester. It received 45,000 "hits," and a mirror site set up by a student received an additional 10,000 "hits."

Musser's late start enabled Baldwin to define Musser negatively on health care, the issue that could have been her greatest asset. By running ads that detailed Musser's contributions from insurance PACs and state support for insurers over consumers during Musser's tenure as commissioner, Baldwin painted her GOP rival as a tool of the insurance industry.

Musser, who was on the defensive for most of the campaign, responded by running ads attacking Baldwin on taxes and crime. The hardest-hitting ad of the campaign, which featured a convict endorsing Baldwin, was produced by Klug (who was brought in during the closing weeks to shore up the Musser campaign), but it proved to be too little, too late.

Baldwin also enjoyed a tremendous advantage in the field. Her campaign attracted the support of approximately 3,000 volunteers, including 1,700 from the University of Wisconsin. Volunteers participated in literature drops, mailings, and phone banks. They also registered and mobilized voters and participated in the Democratic party's coordinated campaign. Musser recruited about 375 volunteers and did not use them as effectively.

Turnout Was Heavy

Baldwin emerged with a 7.2 percent victory margin in an election that produced a 49 percent turnout—13 percent higher than the national average. Turnout was highest in Madison, which gave two-thirds of its vote to Baldwin, and lowest in the rural areas, which were predictably more supportive of Musser. Turnout was so heavy that about twenty-five precincts ran out of ballots. Some voters waited in line for two and a half hours after the polls closed to get a chance to vote. Campaign workers from the Feingold and Baldwin campaigns bought pizza for hungry voters who had not had a chance to eat dinner before coming to the polls.

The differences between the two candidates and their campaigns go a long way toward explaining the outcome. Baldwin's political experience, well-oiled campaign organization, popular thematic message, and strong field organization worked to her advantage. Musser's lack of campaign experience, organizational disarray, unfocused communications, and failure to inspire a large army of volunteers harmed her efforts. The recipe of professionalism and people power was a winning combination in Wisconsin's 2nd District.

This race also has important implications for campaigns across the nation—about both the positive and negative aspects of today's campaigns. In many regards, the 2nd District race was worthy of its historical stature. Baldwin and Musser held twenty-eight joint appearances and debates in the fifty-six-day general election campaign. Media coverage of the campaign was extensive and the candidates clearly articulated their policy views. Baldwin's campaign energized the electorate in a manner rarely seen in modern politics. Her grassroots field effort was modeled on the old precinct networks of an earlier era, and it worked.

The Bottom Line

Paradoxically, the campaign also epitomizes everything that is wrong with today's political campaigns: massive amounts of money (about $4.5 million spent by the candidates in the primary and general election; the total for the election including outside groups approaches $6 million), requiring both candidates to spend substantial time dialing for dollars rather than talking to voters, floods of soft money spent by outside groups on negative ads, poll-driven messages that shied away from tough issues such as entitlement reform, and hard-hitting ads that turned off many voters.

Ultimately, this campaign demonstrates that modern elections cannot ignore grassroots organization and get-out-the-vote efforts. In an era in which campaigns are increasingly waged on the airwaves, it is refreshing to note that an old-fashioned focus on people power can make a difference.

While it is impossible to return to the William Proxmire era of politics, the lesson of the most recent battles may be that the pendulum had swung too far in the direction of television-based campaigns, and that it is time to put more resources into field organization and getting people to the polls.

Jo Musser made precisely this point in assessing why she lost: "We forgot about the fundamentals. We have to get away from the formula-based media campaigns and back to the grassroots."

A national trend, perhaps?

7

Winning in Unfriendly Territory

A Republican Victory in New Mexico's 3rd District in 1998

BILL REDMOND (R), ERIC SERNA (D), AND CAROL MILLER (GREEN PARTY) IN A SPECIAL ELECTION

Chris Wilson and Mike Burita

In 1996, Bill Redmond was the Republican nominee for Congress, running against popular Democratic incumbent Bill Richardson. Richardson had represented New Mexico's heavily Democratic 3rd District since its creation in 1982 and had won reelection with impressive margins ever since. The 1996 race was no different; Richardson easily defeated Redmond 67–30 percent.

When Richardson resigned his seat to become U.S. Ambassador to the United Nations later that winter, most pundits wrote the special election off as an easy Democrat victory. Even highly regarded political analyst Charles Cook wrote in March that it was "safe to assume Democrats will hold on to the currently vacant seat of U.N. Ambassador Bill Richardson in New Mexico." An April 28th *Roll Call* article was titled: "Democrat Still Favored to Hold New Mexico Seat."

These generalizations were almost universally accepted as the conventional wisdom not only in Washington but also by most observers in New Mexico. Apparently, the state's political elite saw the garnering of the Democratic nomination as tantamount to election.

Eric Serna, a State Corporation Commissioner who started lobbying party insiders for the Democratic nomination before Richardson's appointment became official, secured the nod on the first ballot. Bill Redmond won the Republican nomination to face Serna in the upcoming special election on the second ballot. Although he had lost heavily to Richardson only a few months earlier, Redmond was committed to running an aggressive cam-

---

Originally published in *Campaigns & Elections* magazine, July 1997.

paign. He put together a professional campaign team and fully recognized the unique strategic scenario which relied upon (a) the turnout dynamics of a special election and (b) the presence of a formidable third-party candidate, Carol Miller of the Green Party.

Flawed Candidate

From the beginning, opposition research revealed what many in New Mexico already knew: Democrat Serna was a flawed candidate with a history of ethical problems. Most recently, Serna had used the phone in his state office to place calls to party officials who would be selecting the Democratic congressional nominee. In addition, Serna had raised campaign contributions from industries he regulated as a corporation commissioner; he was accused of pressing staffers, and those with business before the commission, to buy jewelry from him; and he had used a state airplane to fly to horse races.

Our campaign tested all of the above, and more, in the benchmark survey we did for Redmond. The poll took on a special significance, as it had to tell us not only what our message should be but also who (demographically, ideologically, geographically) would be voting in the special election. To accomplish all of this we designed an extremely tight screening process that eliminated any respondent who either was not registered, was not a self-described "definite" or "probable" voter, did not say that they voted in all or most local elections, or did not know that the election would be in the month of May.

The poll's findings were encouraging. Redmond only trailed Serna by 9 points (38–29 percent) and Green Party candidate Miller garnered a promising 7 percent. Almost one in four (23 percent) voters were undecided.

Most significantly, two findings showed that the race was winnable for Republican Redmond. First, a plurality of voters said restoring "honesty and integrity to government" was most important to them in deciding their vote. Second, when voters learned more about the two major candidates, Serna's numbers dropped while Redmond's held steady.

Based on these results, the campaign team crafted a message that couched the race in these simple terms: Eric Serna is a corrupt politician; Bill Redmond will return honesty and integrity to government.

Recent conventional wisdom has held that character does not matter—with Bill Clinton's success as exhibit A. But New Mexico voters disagreed. By repeatedly reminding the electorate of Serna's lack of ethical discretion, we were able to drive his negatives to above 40 percent.

While Redmond traveled across the district, meeting voters and sharing

Thirty-Second TV Spot

"Scandal"

Bill Redmond for Congress

Produced by: Pearson Communications

ANNOUNCER: With Washington engulfed in money scandals, New Mexicans have a choice: Send another corrupt politician to add to the scandals or send an honest man to Washington. Bill Redmond's life has been spent making things better, saving marriages, counseling young people, and fighting for better education for our kids.

REDMOND: I'm Bill Redmond. I'll fight to end the money scandals and bring honesty back to government. I'll work full time for you and your family, and I respectfully ask for your vote on May 13th.

ANNOUNCER: Send an honest man to congress. Elect Bill Redmond.

his positive conservative message, the on-site campaign team (which, for most of the period, consisted only of a campaign manager) put together an impressive ground organization.

The campaign then took the fight directly to the district's Republican voter base. Strategy, mail, and media were handled by former RNC regional political director Dave Pearson. Pearson put together an impressive mail and phone program that touched each Republican voter several times. For instance, the 60,000 targeted GOP households received 460,000 mail pieces urging them to: first, vote by absentee ballot; second, vote early; and third, turn out on election day.

Phone calls were important as well. The absentee ballot piece was followed up by an automated call from Governor Johnson urging fellow Republicans to fill out and return the absentee ballot. The early-vote mail piece was followed up by an automated call from Republican Party of New Mexico chairman John Dendahl asking GOPers to vote early. The week before the election, Republican voters received an automated call from their U.S. senator, the popular Pete Domenici, exhorting them to get out and vote. Finally, Republicans received a similar automated call from Redmond

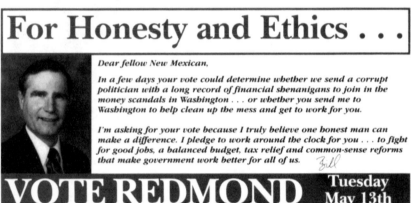

Redmond campaign mailers, above and on the facing page, challenging Serna's ethics.

the weekend before the election. A live volunteer calling effort reached another 10,000 favorable GOP households.

Democrats were targeted with mail sent from the state GOP. Democratic households in the upper Rio Grande valley (where Democratic candidates traditionally get 57 percent of their vote) received two mailers the Thursday and Friday before the election. Both pieces focused on Serna's ethical issues.

Three's Company

The Redmond campaign's next step was a mail piece that sent the Democratic party establishment into a tailspin. It had on one side a reproduction of a local newspaper article that chronicled Serna's "troubling ethical history" and on the other side an article praising Green Party nominee Carol Miller.

Republican Party of New Mexico
2901 Juan Tabo NE, Suite 116
Albuquerque,NM 87112

NONPROFIT ORG.
U.S. POSTAGE
PAID
MAILED FROM
ZIP CODE 24506
PERMIT NO. 28

As your Corporation Commissioner, Eric Serna, used your tax dollars to *commute* to the horse races in government planes like this . . .

As your Congressman, Eric Serna will undoubtedly think bigger!

Eric Serna took the taxpayers for a ride when he and his cronies jetted off to Ruidoso in the taxpayers' airplane to take in a horse race. And when an Albuquerque legislator demanded that Mr. Serna and his friends pay back the taxpayers for taking the brand new $1,000,000 Gulfstream Commander on the racing junket . . . Mr. Serna refused! United Press International reported that Mr. Serna ". . . went along to check out the new airplane . . ." (UPI 8/10/83) **Check out the new airplane indeed!** The fact is Mr. Serna has a long history of financial shenanigans . . . from pressuring his employees and others into buying his jewelry, to taking money from companies he regulates, and campaigning in cars "donated" from people with business before his commission and even openly campaigning from his taxpayer supported office.

If he goes to Washington, who will stop him?

This piece was crucial. By showing that the Redmond campaign was taking Miller seriously, it energized Miller supporters. Serna supporters were demoralized and his base was fractured.

By legitimizing Miller as a liberal alternative, we helped her peel away crucial Democratic voters from Serna (she actually carried Santa Fe County, a Democratic stronghold, on election day).

Redmond's ads, also produced by Pearson, drove home the same message throughout the district. By introducing a softer, conservative message through testimonials, the campaign was able to eliminate the much-discussed gender gap. In fact, our final brushfire poll showed Redmond leading among women by a larger margin than among men! Several ads were used to deftly drive home the same message that Serna was corrupt and that Redmond would restore honesty and integrity.

The Redmond campaign refused to surrender either the women's vote or the senior vote. By identifying Redmond as a warm, caring person, we were able to blunt Serna's textbook Democratic attacks of extremism that hurt so many Republican candidates in 1996. This GOP campaign fought back when attacked and went right after Serna's record.

Tight Screens

The NRCC and the campaign commissioned a final Fabrizio, McLaughlin poll two weeks out. Again, we used a tight sample screening process in our polling to identify likely voters in what would be a low-turnout special election. The wisdom of the campaign's strategy was confirmed: the survey showed Redmond had moved into the lead. Although the undecideds were heavily Democratic, non-linear psychographic patterns showed that if voters, of all parties, continued to break in similar patterns, then Redmond would win by between two and four points.

The importance of the sample screening delineation used in the polling cannot be overemphasized. It was validated when the NRCC, for legal purposes, used another polling firm to handle tracking in the final ten days. They chose a less stringent screening process than the one we used and, as a result, mistakenly showed Serna winning throughout.

Finally, the Redmond campaign, through an extensive paid phone program designed by John Grotta, identified potential Democratic swing voters. Grotta developed a GOTV (get out the vote) script identifying district Democrats on several issues and then used those issues to push them toward Redmond. This effort identified one in three Democrats as supporting Redmond. Those voters were then moved into the GOP universe and targeted with the Republican GOTV effort. The remaining two-thirds were called with an issue-specific script coupled with the campaign's message of corruption versus integrity.

Big GOP Turnout Skew

Election day was not the normally frivolous experience it often is. Ballot security was a must and was directed by the NRCC and the state party to perfection. Poll watchers were sent throughout the district to ensure a fair election.

As the numbers began to flow in on election night, the campaign's strategy proved its worth. In what was called by the Santa Fe *New Mexican* "one of the biggest upsets in New Mexico political history," Bill Redmond defeated Eric Serna by 3,000 votes (43–40 percent) to capture this "safe

Democratic" seat. Green Party candidate Miller garnered an impre
not altogether surprising, 17,079 ballots for 17 percent of the tota

The final tally would show Serna and the Democratic party outspending
Redmond and the Republican party by a significant margin.

Although the GOP strategy was sound and the campaign was expertly
run on the ground, not enough can be said for the personal effort of the
candidate. Redmond's passion convinced skeptics that he could win. His
ideas had an immeasurable impact on voters. His enthusiasm roused a
number of Democratic and Hispanic voters that might have stayed with
Serna had a lesser candidate been the GOP nominee. Redmond's animated
campaigning and passionate conservatism energized and mobilized the
Republican base to turn out in record numbers (54 percent compared to 23
percent Democratic turnout).

8

Beating B-1 Bob

Underdog Ends Conservative's Congressional Career in California's 46th District in 1996

REP. BOB DORNAN (R) VS. LORETTA SANCHEZ (D)

Bill Wachob and Andrew Kennedy

In some respects, the contest for California's 46th Congressional District was an aberration on the 1996 electoral map. A study in political contrasts, the race matched Democratic challenger and political newcomer Loretta Sanchez with eight-term incumbent Robert Dornan—a Republican firebrand noted for his searing political rhetoric.

The campaign to beat congressman Dornan can best be summarized by the following words: *hard work*—nobody worked harder than Loretta Sanchez; *persistence*—even in the face of many naysayers, Loretta Sanchez pushed on; *change*—Orange County is changing, Sanchez knew it, Dornan did not; *risk*—the willingness to risk a different approach and use cable television; and *repetition*—as in repetitive, message-driven television and mail.

Divisive Style

Tenacious, confident, and eternally optimistic are the best words to describe Loretta Sanchez. In early January, with the primary three months away, Loretta termed herself "the candidate to beat Bob Dornan." She tackled her campaign responsibilities with extraordinary enthusiasm. But she was different—at one point even taking bags of mail to the post office so they would be sure to drop on time, after she had put labels on the mail herself. A prolific fundraiser, Sanchez made a priority of campaign activities that gave her candidacy its distinctive grassroots appeal. Precinct walking, candidate meet-and-greets, and civic forum appearances—she excelled at

Originally published in *Campaigns & Elections* magazine, February 1997.

Loretta Sanchez   Bob Dornan

them all. Her campaign odyssey through the 46th District seemed a home-coming for the thirty-six-year-old Democrat, whose family roots in Orange County stretch over half a century.

Having served in the House of Representatives off and on for nearly two decades, Dornan had seen his ties to the district grow tenuous in recent years. His divisive and confrontational style, his arch-conservative ideology, and his Cold War rhetoric no longer resonated with Orange County voters, whose real-life experiences were far removed from the apparitions domi-nating Dornan's political prism. Moreover, his quixotic quest for the GOP presidential nomination left him scrambling for money in the final months of his reelection campaign. Appearing to take the support of his con-stituents for granted, Dornan's last-minute appeals for another term proved unconvincing.

Changing Demographics

A blue collar community, full of older homes and younger families, the 46th District in the 1990s is a cultural melting pot that has undergone significant change. Its image as a mostly white, middle-class bedrock of Nixonian conservatism is a distant memory. Of its 570,963 residents, 50 percent are Hispanic, 35 percent Caucasian, 12 percent Asian, and 2 percent African American.

,o, Dornan defeated Democratic challenger Michael Farber
,7 percent, with Libertarian Richard Newhouse receiving 6
,an outspent his rival $2.3 million to $302,000. In 1992,
led Bill Clinton in the district 40 percent to 37 percent; Ross
Perot ɔ៶៶. a sizable 23 points. Historically known as a bastion of Republi-
canism, the 46th District has become increasingly Democratic in recent
years. Orange County's changing demographics worked in favor of Loretta
Sanchez's candidacy. In the spring of 1996, voter registration favored the
Democratic Party by 46 percent to 40 percent. The appeal of a Latina busi-
nesswoman whose platform addressed the needs of working families struck
a resonant cord with voters.

Her election, though by a razor-thin margin, nevertheless proved a significant milestone in Orange County politics: the region's only district with
a Democratic plurality had sent its first woman and Hispanic representative
to Congress.

Repetition, Repetition

Our firm, the Campaign Group, Inc., was hired in January 1996 to provide general consulting and electronic media for the Sanchez campaign.
M&R Strategic Services was hired at the same time to produce direct mail
for the campaign. In August, John Shallman was recruited to oversee the
day-to-day campaign. Shallman, a respected veteran of Los Angeles politics,
uniquely understood the components necessary to defeat an incumbent
member of Congress. It was Shallman who set realistic fundraising goals
and put together the tactics necessary for victory. He did a superb job jug-
gling all of the balls to fund television, mail, and voter outreach efforts.

Another key decision was the hiring of Lake Research to do polling.
Celinda Lake and Peter Feld provided invaluable insight into targeting and
issue groupings that were key to defeating an incumbent such as Bob Dornan.

The value of this team was its ability to work together and to use its past
experiences to model a unique campaign that looked beyond conventional
wisdom.

All good campaigns need a mantra to live by. Tip O'Neill's was "All politics is local." James Carville's was "It's the economy, stupid!" The Sanchez
campaign mantra was "Repetition, Repetition, Repetition!" Keep the message local and simple and say it to as many voters as possible and as many
times as possible. When you think you have said it enough, say it again.

Our goal in the March 1996 primary election, and again in the fall general election, was to achieve a critical mass of message frequency in the
most cost efficient way. With this in mind we decided to use persuasion

mail as a main communications medium. After a thorough cost analysis, v. also chose to use a medium that Dornan and past Orange County campaigns failed to use—cable television spots.

The decision to adopt this strategy was by no means easy to come by. The campaign team was divided, with the Orange County advisors arguing against the use of cable television as too inefficient and expensive. If the cable television strategy failed, they argued, the campaign would be broke. It was a high-risk play.

However, we needed to move poll numbers—quickly. If we did not, we would not have the resources necessary to wage the fall campaign. If it worked, Sanchez would have enough resources to compete effectively with Dornan in the crucial final weeks. We knew from earlier polling that the incumbent was weak, with his reelect rating hovering around 30 percent.

The cable television strategy was put into place. Buying on as many as three cable systems and at least six networks per system, including ESPN, USA, LIFETIME, and CNN, our goal was to get as much message frequency as possible over a three week period. Two early spots, one thirty seconds and one sixty seconds, featured Sanchez as a homegrown leader of Orange County, fighting for secure jobs and safe neighborhoods, good schools for our children, and college loans for the middle class.

In three weeks, the poll numbers moved. Sanchez went from 25 percent of the vote to 43 percent—putting her in a virtual dead heat with Dornan. This rapid movement also worked to convince the Washington, D.C., political action committee community that Dornan was in fact in serious danger.

With Dornan in an obvious panic and searching for a life boat, we began airing two additional spots, both thirty seconds. One ad contrasted the candidates on the issues of education, seniors, crime, and choice. The second spot was a hard-hitting negative, defining Dornan as an out of touch elected official more concerned with his own stature than the needs of the district. These spots continued through the final three weeks of the campaign.

Turning on the Spigot

The Sanchez direct mail program was enhanced by a unique feature of this district: extremely low voter turnout. In 1992, approximately 110,000 people showed up to vote in the 46th District—which is about half of a normal turnout in other districts in California. Through targeting that included the elimination of Republicans in traditionally conservative precincts, we lowered our mail universe to a highly manageable 40,000–50,000 voters. Keeping costs low by adhering to a simple message and easily identified targets enabled us to get more frequency. By combining print jobs, we were

ι low cost program that included ten mail pieces to the
εrse and an additional five pieces to smaller segments of the

the mail program was to reach swing or persuadable voters
as γ.   ο communicate with low-frequency voters who viewed
Sanchez's campaign favorably for GOTV (get out the vote) purposes. The
early mail pieces were designed to take full advantage of suspicions about
Dornan's record in Congress, while ensuring that they also would define
our candidate as the right alternative.

The attack mail pieces focused largely on Dornan's record as an out-of-
touch member of Congress who took fifty-four foreign junkets, drew a
huge salary, and had a million-dollar pension waiting for him—while he
was voting against Medicare, Medicaid, and increases in the minimum
wage. They also took him to task for wasting taxpayer money by giving use-
less floor speeches in the U.S. House to enhance his own national exposure
before C-SPAN audiences while voting to cut funding for police.

About two weeks before election day, Dornan turned on the spigot of
negative advertising against Sanchez. By this time, our polling numbers had
shown us drawing even and our goal was to neutralize Dornan's ability to
question Sanchez's record. As planned, the tone of our direct mail shifted.
We counterattacked by drawing attention to his uniquely nasty nature. One
mail piece used Sanchez's mom as the messenger, pointing out Dornan's
broken promise to talk about issues rather than launch personal attacks.
The same mailer directly rebutted each of Dornan's arguments about
Sanchez with evidence of his hypocrisy. Another piece titled "Distortion"
highlighted a press advisory written by Project Vote Smart that lambasted
Dornan for distorting their information on Sanchez's positions.

We also mailed pieces from credible third parties that were designed to
increase Sanchez's credibility as a candidate. These mailers, in the aggre-
gate, reduced the credibility of the GOP attack against Sanchez. Dornan also
damaged his own effectiveness by cramming too much text and hyperbole
into each mail piece.

In the final days we shifted the tone of the mail campaign again, revert-
ing to positive messages to ensure that the last impression of Sanchez
would be favorable. A piece titled "Babies" showed two children sitting on
an American flag with the subtitle: "Vote for Us." It focused on Sanchez's
interest in helping working families and ensuring that education funding
would be protected.

Direct mail, combined with six weeks of message-driven cable television
spots, suffocated Dornan's response and effectively put out his bombastic
flame. For every piece of mail he sent, we had at least two to counter. In the
final week, ten pro-Sanchez pieces dropped, including, serendipitously, four

created and paid for by independent expenditure campaigns. Dornan had, we estimate, six pieces in the last week with no television.

While the bulk of the Sanchez mail assault focused on persuasion, John Shallman worked with the coordinated campaign and a local Assembly candidate to fashion a considerable get-out-the-vote and absentee mail program targeted to the Hispanic community. In the end, while the mail and cable television campaign brought Sanchez even with Dornan, our election day turnout program sent her over the top. More absentee ballots were ultimately sent in by Democrats than by Republicans, an uncommon trend in southern California. Sanchez outspent Dornan $760,000 to $681,000. On election night, Sanchez was behind by 233 votes. However, after a week of counting late absentees, Sanchez won by over 900 votes.

A tireless challenger, Sanchez won because she had a plan, stuck to it, and deployed the latest in campaign targeting and communications. Her well-known opponent was an out-of-touch incumbent who took the race for granted. He relied on outdated tactics and shrill attacks.

In the end, even "B-1 Bob" was no match for a hard-working candidate with a good grassroots campaign that had both message discipline and tactical sophistication.

9

Incumbency and Base

How a Black Incumbent Won Renomination in a New Majority-White District in Georgia in 1996

REP. CYNTHIA MCKINNEY (D) DEFEATS
SEVERAL OPPONENTS IN PRIMARY

John Rowley

It is 5:20 A.M., July 2, on the streets of Atlanta. The early morning stirring of construction workers preparing for the Olympics is ignored by a solitary figure in a phone booth scanning a copy of the *Atlanta Constitution*.

He is reading the editorial page. On the phone listening are Democratic U.S. Rep. Cynthia McKinney and Nashville-based media consultant Bill Fletcher.

As they listen, the staffer struggles with his emotions as he reads that, for the first time ever, after two terms in the Georgia House of Representatives and two terms in Congress, his boss has been endorsed by the morning newspaper.

But, unless this endorsement is quickly integrated into McKinney's advertising, few people will ever know it happened.

Because of the pending Fourth of July holiday, there is a narrow window of opportunity to cut through the Independence Day clutter and maximize this important endorsement.

Tracking polls show that McKinney is teetering just above 50 percent. A slip below this mark will force an uncertain runoff election played out through the media muddle of the summer Olympics in Atlanta (one of the most expensive markets for broadcast television due to the games).

Including the endorsement in the campaign's TV and radio commercials could provide the push needed to win the primary outright. But there is a hitch. Any new media needs to air immediately to have a significant

Originally published in *Campaigns & Elections* magazine, September 1996.

impact. By 5:45 A.M., Fletcher's recommendation that the campaign integrate the endorsement into all communications is accepted.

We put into motion the creative, management, and technical chore of producing new radio and TV spots touting the endorsement.

As we began the process we did not know that the afternoon newspaper in Atlanta was preparing to endorse Comer Yates, McKinney's principal challenger in the primary. We did not know even after it happened whether Yates's team would air the endorsements on television or radio.

By the end of the day on Tuesday, a new flight of radio commercials had been written and produced in Nashville. They were transferred to an Atlanta production house via state-of-the-art 3D2 equipment from a studio on Music Row and were airing in Atlanta during afternoon drive time. A new TV spot was delivered the next morning.

Twelve hours after the endorsement hit, the campaign's paid ads had been totally changed to highlight it, and the momentum needed to push McKinney toward a primary victory—without the need for a runoff—had been set into motion.

Yates received the endorsement of the afternoon newspaper the same day McKinney was endorsed by the morning newspaper. Unlike McKinney's campaign, his campaign did not incorporate the endorsement into their paid advertising.

Most voters never knew that Yates received the endorsement.

The maximization of this newspaper endorsement is not the only story of the McKinney campaign—but it is a prime example of how old-fashioned coalition politics blend with modern campaign techniques to produce a dramatic victory.

In Trouble

In 1992, Cynthia McKinney became Georgia's first African American congresswoman in the newly drawn 11th District, which had a 64 percent black electorate. In 1995, the Supreme Court declared her district unconstitutional, ruling political boundaries could not be drawn based primarily upon racial makeup. Many observers thought that would end McKinney's congressional career, figuring she would not survive in a two-thirds white district.

In the July 9 Democratic primary, McKinney faced three white male challengers in the new district, where only 33 percent of the voters were black. Her campaign played out against the backdrop of Georgia's racially charged political environment. The conventional wisdom, especially in Washington and downtown Atlanta, was that McKinney was in trouble.

Cynthia McKinney

In one of McKinney's late radio spots, voters are asked to "ride a train called 'History.'" On primary day, voters in Georgia's new 4th Congressional District did just that.

Shafting Attacks

To attract the broad coalition of moderate and liberal men, labor groups, small business owners, women, African Americans, senior citizens, members of the gay and lesbian community, and environmentalists, McKinney needed a compelling and unifying positive message.

The campaign went up early on cable television and Atlanta radio with a message focused on McKinney's support of the minimum wage and anti-crime measures, as well as her opposition to Medicare cuts and tax breaks for the rich.

The spots also included the story of McKinney's fight for poor Georgia landowners who had been abused by a huge mining conglomerate and her work to get better housing for a 108-year-old woman.

These stories reinforced her image as a solid Democrat voting for mainstream issues and illustrated her record of constituent services and advocacy.

Several weeks earlier, the creator of the theme from the popular 1970s TV and movies series "Shaft," pop icon and music legend Isaac Hayes, literally walked into McKinney's campaign office and volunteered the end of the next day, production for television spots, radio spots for a television program, audio for phone bank messages, all Hayes, were in the can.

After one week of positive television on cable, a thirty-second TV spot featuring Hayes was added to the media mix. The ad was designed to soften the blow of anticipated attacks. Hayes's message: "Don't be fooled by the negative campaign and all this mud throwing. Cynthia McKinney is a fighter for justice, for people and for the future—and America needs her compassion and experience in Congress."

The McKinney campaign ignored the attacks of her primary opponents and let "Black Moses" do the talking.

Fifteen-Minute Special

As the campaign prepared for late attacks and intense local and national media coverage, consultant Fletcher recommended the production of a long-form video to deliver Cynthia McKinney's messages and career history.

Creating a positive diversion, the fifteen-minute program was aired more than a dozen times on cable TV during the last week of the campaign. Air times were advertised heavily by literature drops and in local newspapers.

"The Pride of Georgia" television special gave highly motivated voters who were seeking more information about Cynthia McKinney a personal introduction to their congresswoman.

Isaac Hayes opened and closed the program, appealing to Georgians to "join me as we prove that the old prejudices are dying away." McKinney was featured in long sound bites from an open meeting with senior citizens, and her themes were documented and magnified by passionate testimonials from supporters in the old 11th District and the new 4th District.

The program also gave the free media something to write about and helped defuse the barrage of late attacks from the opposition.

Targeted Buying

Comer Yates was well-funded and placed a larger broadcast TV buy than McKinney. To counter Yates's buy, McKinney used a combination of ten-second and thirty-second spots to boost the number of gross rating points and to reduce the overall cost per point.

Louisville-based Media Plus Communications, working through our firm, Fletcher and Rowley Consulting, Inc., helped develop the media buy for McKinney, which was designed to reach the most likely voters. McKinney's buy was heavy on network news programming and daytime programming and was especially focused on senior citizens who remained undecided until late in the race.

Tracking polls indicated that Yates and another McKinney opponent, state senator Ron Slotin, were gaining ground with 19 percent and 7 percent, respectively. The polls suggested that Yates or Slotin would have to attack McKinney to have a chance of forcing a runoff election. The day Yates's first piece of attack mail landed, McKinney's campaign began airing radio spots that counterattacked Yates with revelations about his work as a lawyer for huge corporations and that attacked Slotin for missing votes in the Georgia Senate. A few days later, it dropped a piece of mail that mirrored the radio counterattacks, while also stressing all of McKinney's positive messages.

The counterattacks quashed Slotin and Yates's growth potential. The combination of a compelling positive message and a series of attacks hamstrung the opposition's communications to a net gain of virtually zero.

As the media focused on the attacks and counterattacks flying between the camps, McKinney personally oversaw a week-long get-out-the-vote effort that utilized targeted phoning, neighborhood rallies, and door-to-door activity. In addition to the efforts of the campaign, there were also extensive member-to-member communications between a wide array of groups that endorsed McKinney, including labor, environmental, women, and other advocacy organizations who wanted to "ride the history train."

A key element of the McKinney election-day turnout strategy was 42,000 phone calls that featured a prerecorded introduction by the candidate and then a message from Isaac Hayes. It was highly successful: turnout among African Americans in this district was 15–20 percent higher than it was statewide on the same day. Said telephone contact consultant Tony Parker, of the Parker Group: "It was one of the most focused campaigns I've seen in a long time. It proved that the systematic targeting of a well-planned message roll-out works."

The result: McKinney wiped out the field with 67 percent of the vote. Yates was limited to 24 percent and Slotin finished with 6 percent.

In the *New York Times* the day after the election, one Georgia political analyst called the margin "amazing."

AP reporter David Pace reported that an analysis of the election did not reveal significant turnout differences between black and white voters within the district. His analysis did reveal that McKinney had received at least 36 percent of the vote in several predominantly white areas.

Cynthia McKinney's nomination in Georgia's 4th District offers an example for a racially polarized America.

Sensing the historic proportions of her victory, McKinney concluded her victory speech by saying:

Today—the people of Georgia have taken a step toward justice by rejecting the patterns of the past.

Today—I have been lifted upon the shoulders of the people of Georgia—black and white.

And from this position I have a clear view of the horizon.

And through the smoke of burning churches—I see a better place.

Through the haze of extremism—I see where we're going friends and neighbors—and it may not be the Promised Land—but it is a place where America keeps her promises.

I see an America of opportunity for our young people, dignity for our workers, and security for our seniors.

Those are your values.

Those are my values.

We are all on the train called History—and we are ringing the bell called Freedom. Let freedom ring.

10

Coming On Strong Down the Stretch

Republican Leaves Democrats in the Dust in Kentucky's 2nd District in 1994

RON LEWIS (R) VS. JOE PRATHER (D) IN AN
OPEN SEAT RACE

Al Cross

In May 1994, baptist minister and Christian bookstore owner Ron Lewis became the newest member of Congress because Republican leaders gave him the right message, the right strategy, and the right tactics for the special election, while Democrats had the wrong candidate, the wrong tactics, and the wrong president for Kentucky's 2nd District.

The man Lewis beat by 10 percentage points, Joe Prather, had solid, traditional credentials: nineteen years in the state legislature, the last eleven as chief elected officer of the Senate; extensive statewide campaign experience on his own and for others, most recently for Governor Brereton Jones. As Jones's chairman, Prather assembled the organization and chose many of the county Democratic chairmen who made the nomination. Even before the seat was vacated by the death of William Natcher, Prather had such support that Owensboro mayor David Adkisson, a younger and more telegenic candidate and a protégé of U.S. Senate Majority Whip Wendell Ford, backed off.

Prather had the social-conservative credentials that a Democrat needed to succeed Natcher. A Roman Catholic, he is an opponent of abortion, as was Natcher, and led efforts to rescind Kentucky's ratification of the Equal Rights Amendment. But his record and personality were those of a traditional politician, and that was a drawback in the minds of some Democrats, including state party chairman Grady Stumbo. Stumbo tried to persuade Jones to call the special election for May 10, the earliest possible date under

Originally published in *Campaigns & Elections* magazine, July 1994.

state law. Jones scheduled it for May 24, primary election day money. That reduced one of the Democrats' great advantages.

"The problem we obviously had was lack of time," said Republican U.S. Senator Mitch McConnell, the state's chief Republican strategist.

Thoroughly Electable

Republicans had long thought they could capture the 2nd District seat when Natcher left the scene, but when he took ill and died after the filing deadline, most despaired. Neither candidate in the GOP primary was well known, and even if a stronger candidate won the special election in the spring, he or she could not run in the fall for the full term.

That did not deter McConnell, who met with Lewis at the Bob Evans Restaurant near the senator's home in Louisville on Saturday, April 9, the day after Lewis beat primary foe Bruce Bartly for the special-election nomination. "I really didn't have much of a feel for him before then," McConnell said. "I became convinced that this was a thoroughly electable candidate."

Because the election was in five weeks, "I said to Lewis that this race had to be a referendum on something," McConnell recalled. "There was not enough time or money to develop the details of who Ron Lewis is or who Joe Prather is. The key was, what will it be a referendum on? I said, 'I think the only thing that people already know about is the president of the United States, and we don't know what shape he's in within the 2nd District.'"

Lewis had little money for polling. On April 11, McConnell called Representative Bill Paxon of New York, chairman of the National Republican Congressional Committee (NRCC), and alerted him to Lewis's potential. The NRCC commissioned a poll, and the poll results showed that the strategy of making the election a referendum on Clinton strategy promised to work even better than McConnell had expected. The poll, by the Wirthlin Group, showed that only 30 percent of likely voters would vote to reelect Clinton, while 55 percent said it was time for someone new.

When the results arrived on April 28, "I was pleasantly surprised," said state Republican chairman Terry Carmack.

Kentucky political observers already knew that Clinton's liberal social agenda (gays in the military being the chief example) had hurt him in the state as it had in the rest of the South, and that he had a special problem in Kentucky—his health-reform plan's huge increases in taxes on tobacco, a mainstay of the state economy.

Perhaps as important were the results to a question about party preference in the special election. In a district that is 68 percent Democratic in voter registration but that voted for George Bush in 1992, the Democratic edge was only 36 percent to 31 percent.

Ron Lewis

"When I saw that," Carmack said, "I knew people were willing to hear a message."

National Implications

To get the message out, Lewis needed national Republican money, but GOP leaders had another special election to worry about first in Oklahoma's 6th District.

"Paxon said a lot of their enthusiasm would depend on what happened in Oklahoma," on May 10, McConnell said.

"If they won in Oklahoma, it was a shot at maybe going all out because of the potential national implications."

Meanwhile, Kentucky Republicans took steps to shore up Lewis and build their case. John McCarthy, the state party's political director, was dispatched to Lewis headquarters to control spending. "McCarthy's job was to see that no checks were written unless McConnell and I approved them," Carmack said.

Meanwhile, Lewis continued to raise money, reaching $45,000 by May 4, "further evidence that this was a very credible guy that we had somehow missed because he had not been in our circles," McConnell said. He and Republican Representatives Jim Bunning and Hal Rogers helped persuade

Paxon and Barbour just before the Oklahoma election to make effort in Kentucky.

"After Mitch and Jim and Hal gave us such high remarks about Ron we decided to roll the dice before Oklahoma," Paxon said. Carmack said the deal was sealed when, at Barbour's suggestion, he agreed to follow the lead of the Oklahoma chairman and run the campaign. McConnell said Barbour "felt very strongly that we needed to have somebody on the ground who we had confidence in."

Carmack, a McConnell protégé, went to some lengths to conceal his departure from party headquarters.

"A key part of this was keeping quiet," McConnell said. "We said to everybody, 'We can't alert the other side early.' It was important they think as long as possible that this was a chip shot."

At Prather headquarters a few miles away, there was a quiet confidence but an occasional, vague sense of foreboding. Prather had heard about the GOP poll, and knew it had tested the effect of his votes for taxes as a legislator, as well as Clinton's unpopularity, which he knew from his own polling. "We looked at that and said that if somebody came in here with $200,000 we could be in trouble," Prather advisor Larry Hayes said.

But Prather kept trying to emulate Natcher, not only by refusing to take PAC and out-of-state money, but rejecting aid from the Democratic Congressional Campaign Committee as well. That left him without any advisors who had worked in a truly contested federal campaign, except Washington-based media consultant Peter Fenn.

That may have led to a key miscalculation. Hayes said after the election that the Prather campaign figured Lewis would get about $50,000 in national Republican purchases, plus direct money from party committees and leadership PACs. The actual figure turned out to be about $180,000, of Lewis's total spending of $225,000. Prather, who had pledged to use his personal money to stay even, ended up being outspent by about $40,000.

"What we didn't count on," Hayes said, "was that they would double up."

Unaware of the impending Republican deluge, Prather failed to sandbag his levees. He delayed the beginning of his TV campaign until Friday, May 13, the same day Lewis took to the air. "To run media longer, we would have required a sizable amount of contributions on my part," Prather said, "and I just chose not to do that."

It was, again in hindsight, another mistake. "We knew that every day he wasn't on the air was time he couldn't get back," Carmack said.

"We wanted to get on no worse than simultaneously," McConnell said, "and have a chance of defining the race."

They did.

the start of the TV battle, Prather was stuck with a
ad, while Lewis pummeled him with a tough and
he and Clinton were both professional politicians
ment deals ("Whitewater," the screen said) and raised
crease in history"). The images were memorable: a
photo of Prather morphing" into one of Clinton and then back into
Prather, and back-to-back photos on a spindle that finally spun so fast they
appeared to be one image.

Prather and Fenn replied with an ad saying that Washington special
interests were trying to buy the seat of the saintly Natcher, but the spot was
almost entirely defensive, told voters little about Prather, and did not refute
the referendum-on-Clinton theme. After a week of morphing and spinning,
the Republicans switched to a spot in which Lewis made an effective case
for himself, saying that Clinton did not want him in Congress because he
would not "rubber-stamp his plan for socialized medicine." Prather, whose
manner and voice are somewhat ponderous, never spoke in an ad. The
closing line in Lewis's ads, "He's one of us," alluded to Prather's political
history.

A late surge of Washington money—mainly from House Republicans'
campaign committees, jumping on the bandwagon after their victory in
Oklahoma—allowed Republicans to buy twice as much TV time as they had
planned and spend much more on phone banks and radio, a medium that
Prather largely ignored. Meanwhile, term-limits and anti-tax groups targeted Prather in radio spots placed by the same buyer who was working for
Lewis; the National Rifle Association mailed an appeal to its 15,000 members in the district and followed up with a get-out-the-vote phone call; and
the Christian Coalition distributed up to 90,000 copies of a "voter guide"
that said Prather supported "registration of firearms." (Gun control, which
Natcher always opposed, is a big issue in the district, and Prather favored
the Brady Bill and the registration of assault weapons.)

The impact of Lewis's ads, and the lack of TV punch for Prather, was
clear the Saturday afternoon before the election, as Lewis walked a precinct
in Louisville's outer suburbs and introduced himself to Mose Rushing, who
was watering his lawn.

"Yeah, I saw you on TV," Rushing told him. "You make a nice speech."
He said likewise to a reporter who hung around to talk after Lewis moved
on. "He's the one who said Clinton wouldn't want him," Rushing said. "I
liked his forcefulness." Rushing does not fit the stereotype of a Ron Lewis
voter. He is an African American who works at a chemical plant and voted
for Bill Clinton in 1992. "I like Clinton," he said, "but you've got to have

somebody who's strong to push him, you know, make him stay on the ball."

Rushing could not name Lewis's opponent. Told Prather's name and asked if he recalled anything about him, Rushing said, "No, I don't think I've seen him."

PART III

State and Local Races

11

The Body Politic Registers a Pro⸱

Jesse Ventura's Stunning Victory for Governor of Minnesota in 1998

JESSE VENTURA (REFORM PARTY), NORM COLEMAN (R), AND SKIP HUMPHREY (D) IN AN OPEN SEAT RACE

David Beiler

D ean Barkley sensed that something was out of order. Then a fairly well-known candidate for the U.S. Senate, he was marching in a July 4 parade when he noticed that his aide-de-camp was attracting the crowd's attention.

"Next time, you'll be the candidate," he told Jesse Ventura. A former pro wrestler who now earned his Harleys as a radio shock jock and action flick bit player, Ventura chuckled at Barkley's outrageous thought.

He would be the first of many—including most of Minnesota's political establishment—to laugh at Ventura the candidate. But they are not laughing anymore. Ventura is their new governor.

That Ventura would be so easily dismissed by some of the best political minds in the country is the real man-bites-dog story here, though it was largely overlooked by the national media horde that trampled the tundra of the Gopher State in November. True, Ventura's Reform Party held no state or federal offices; true, he was being outspent 15–1 by his Democratic and Republican rivals right up until five weeks before the election. But the dynamics of American voter behavior have been changing for years, in ways yet unfathomed by many big-league strategists.

"It could happen anywhere," warns pollster Fred Steeper, who worked the race for Ventura's GOP opponent. State Democratic executive director Kathy Czar agrees: "If you're up against a third-party candidate with name recognition and media skills, you'd better take them seriously, even if they're short of money."

Originally published in *Campaigns & Elections* magazine, February 1999.

The Horses, Handlers, Wagers, and Payoffs

	Jesse Ventura (Ref)	Norm Coleman (R)	Skip Humphrey (D)
Manager	Doug Friedline	Chris Georgacas	Amy Finken
Strategist	Dean Barkley	Luntz Research	Eric Johnson
Media	North Woods Adv.	Larry McCarthy	Squier Knapp Ochs
Pollster	None	Market Strategies	Fairbank, Maslin
Budget	$625,000 (est.)	$2,750,000 (est.)	$2,100,000 (est.)
Votes	768,000 (37 percent)	713,410 (34 percent)	581,497 (28 percent)

The warp-speed rise of Ventura offers more than just a wake-up call; it can provide a crash course in the cartography of a new electoral order.

Heavy to Hero

A notorious bad guy in the repertory theater known as the World Wrestling Federation, Ventura continued to nurture his notoriety after retiring from the canvas in 1986. Stints in such movies as "Predator" and as a ringside commentator for TBS eventually gave way to a steady gig as a radio talk show host in his hometown of Minneapolis. Ventura's public tough-guy image notwithstanding, environmental issues propelled him to his first political involvement.

Concerned that stormwater runoff was being dumped into wetlands near his neighborhood, Ventura complained to the City Council of Brooklyn Park, home to 60,000 suburbanites. Dissatisfied with the official response, the riled 250-pound grappler successfully ran for town mayor in 1990, quintupling voter turnout in the process.

The job was, in essence, to chair a part-time legislative body. At its meetings, Ventura chewed tobacco. He occasionally skipped them altogether as he made movies and personal appearances around the country. But his forceful leadership made its mark, and he left office after one term with his popularity intact.

Meanwhile, Barkley had been paving the way for an outsider's takeover of state government.

Inspired by Ross Perot's example, Barkley launched an independent run for Congress in 1992. The lawyer/marketer spent only $64,000, but he received endorsements from the two major Twin Cities newspapers and ultimately won an impressive 16 percent of the four-way general election vote.

Setting his sights higher in 1994, Barkley ran for the U.S. Senate and won official status for the Independence Party with his 5 percent showing. After the IP affiliated with the Reform Party in 1996, Barkley launched a second Senate run and improved to 7 percent.

Jesse Ventura

Campaigning for the Senate often landed Barkley a guest slot on Ventura's radio show, where the host was fond of comparing the major parties to Los Angeles street gangs, dubbing them the ReBLOODicans and DemoCRYPTS. Ventura chaired Barkley's 1996 campaign but resisted Reformers' suggestions that he run for governor.

The fledgling party had been gaining ground on other fronts, however: Reformer Steve Minn won a nonpartisan seat on the Minneapolis City Council in 1993; two years later, radio talk jock Barbara Carlson—the earthy ex-wife of former Gov. Arne Carlson (R)—ran a strong race for mayor of Minneapolis as the Reform endorsee.

By the fall of 1997, Ventura had grudgingly agreed to be a gubernatorial candidate, and Barkley—now operating a car wash business—had drafted a campaign plan with designated manager Doug Friedline, proprietor of a pull-tab gambling operation housed in a Minneapolis bar.

Barkley's scenario anticipated that the Democrats and Republicans would nominate pro-life candidates, leaving Ventura the only pro-choice alternative in a pro-choice state. That did not happen, but everything else in his plan did play out as expected: Get Ventura into the debates and excel there; raise half a million dollars for a last-minute media blitz; hit the 1992 Perot mark of 24 percent in mid-October polling; energize the youth vote.

But months would pass before the campaign got off the ground. A New Year's fundraiser went poorly, and the candidate seemed to be dragging his feet. On January 17 of election year, the staff delivered Ventura an ultimatum: Kick in $10,000 of seed money or make an official announcement. Otherwise, they would toss in the towel.

Ventura soon announced, but the treasury remained bare for months.

Back in the Real World

Despite its potential for crowd appeal, the Ventura campaign drew scant attention in the early days of 1998. Governor Carlson was stepping down, and the Republicans had a wide-open, three-way race to succeed him. But a trio of historic marquee names had kept tongues wagging about the Democratic primary for more than a year.

It was the battle between "My Three Sons"—chips off three of the most venerated blocks of political timber ever produced by Minnesota's Democratic Farmer-Labor Party. One was Mike Freeman, son of former governor and Kennedy cabinet member Orville Freeman; the two others (former state senator Ted Mondale and Attorney General Hubert H. "Skip" Humphrey III) were sons of former U.S. senators who later became vice presidents and presidential nominees. The pedigreed trio were joined by pro-life state senator Doug Johnson and state auditor Mark Dayton, heir to a department store chain.

Backed by the party's more liberal elements, such as the AFL-CIO and U.S. Sen. Paul Wellstone, Freeman edged Humphrey for the party endorsement in June but trailed him in polls for the September primary. A suburban candidate with a suburban running mate, Mondale sounded moderate New Democrat themes that fell flat with traditional Democratic constituencies. Dayton, who lost a 1982 Senate race, had feminist backing and imaginative, plentiful advertising. Johnson ran a clever campaign, contrasting himself against the "silver-spoon" candidates, though he seemed out-of-tune with the party's social liberalism.

Humphrey, who had made a disappointing run for his father's old Senate seat, won a $6 billion tobacco settlement for the state in May, which many pundits felt would propel him into the governorship. But his flip on the abortion issue (to the choice position) bothered some voters.

The Republican intramural initially had four players. Moderate state senator Roy Terwillegar started early and visited all eighty-seven counties and logged 45,000 miles on the campaign trail. But when a March poll had him at 4 percent, he folded his tent.

That left the GOP field to three pro-life conservatives, the most extreme being Allen Quist, who had won the party's gubernatorial endorsement in 1994 but went on to lose the primary.

Lieutenant Governor Joanne Benson was also running to succeed Carlson—the man who put her there—plainly without his blessings, but backed instead by U.S. Sen. Rod Grams.

The presumed Carlson candidate was St. Paul mayor Norm Coleman, who had switched from the DFL in 1996. A pragmatic conservative, Coleman won support from such luminaries as U.S. Rep. Jim Ramstad, House Minority Leader Steve Sviggum, and national GOP guru Vin Weber.

Around the Track: Following the Race with Media Tracking Polls
(figures are percentages of total vote)

	Late August[1]	Six Weeks Out[2]	Three Weeks Out[3]	Two Weeks Out[4]	Ten Days Out[5]	November 3 Results
Ventura (Ref)	13	10	15	21	23	37
Coleman (R)	29	29	31	34	33	34
Humphrey (D)	43	49	44	35	34	28
Other/Undecided	15	12	10	10	10	—

1. Mason-Dixon/PMR.
2. Market Solutions Group for *Minneapolis Star-Tribune*/KSPM.
3. Mason-Dixon/PMR.
4. Market Solutions Group for *Minneapolis Star-Tribune*/KSPM.
5. Mason-Dixon/PMR.

Coleman was backed by an organization skippered by former party chair Chris Georgacas. He proved to be an appealing candidate and led the caucuses virtually everywhere in the state. The June convention endorsed him on the fourth ballot.

Bodily Charm

The reputation Barkley had established as the state's leading nonpartisan moderate paid big dividends in January.

Former U.S. Rep. Tim Penny, a fiscally conservative Democrat, had recently organized the Minnesota Compact, a good-government group devoted to making campaigns more substantive. Highly regarded by both parties, Penny succeeded in making the compact a key part of the upcoming gubernatorial debates. At Penny's request, Barkley became codirector, boosting Ventura's chances for inclusion in upcoming debates.

Minnesota's primaries are not held until September, and the long nomination season also played into Ventura's hand. He was invited to many debates and forums, throughout the spring and summer, sponsored by local civic groups across the state. Barkley's strategy called for his candidate to accept as many such opportunities as possible. The forums were so numerous and the election so far away, little attention was being paid to these events by the press or the public. But they afforded a raw, novice candidate the opportunity to prep for prime time.

"Jesse's style never changed," explains Barkley, "but those early forums let him get comfortable with the format and learn about the issues . . . before the pressure was really on."

Thirty-Second TV Spot

"Endorsed"

Skip Humphrey for Governor

Produced by: Squier Knapp Ochs Dunn

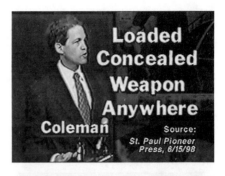

SHERIFF GARY WALLER: You can't tell if someone is carrying a loaded concealed weapon. That's why it's so dangerous. Norm Coleman wants to change state law and let just about anyone carry a loaded concealed weapon anywhere. It's a bad idea. Skip Humphrey has crime fighting experience. He got mandatory prison terms for felons who use guns. As governor he is someone we can trust.

ANNOUNCER: Our police believe in him. So can we. Humphrey for governor. Believe in Minnesota.

Meanwhile, Ventura began building a base among his wrestling fans. They were not hard to find.

As their candidate marched in a seven-block parade down the streets of Minneapolis on St. Patrick's Day, Reformers found eager takers for ten thousand pieces of literature. At a major wrestling event in April, pandemonium broke loose as Ventura made a grand entrance, unannounced, yet well-advanced. A few days later, he energized thousands of protesters on the capitol steps with a blast against the legislature for its vote to return only half of a $4 billion budget surplus to the taxpayers.

A celebrity in Minnesota's popular culture, Ventura started the campaign with widespread name recognition (64 percent), surpassed by only three other candidates: Democrats Humphrey and Mondale and GOP frontrunner Coleman. Comprising mostly young, disaffected, middle-class males, Ventura's initial audience hardly fit a high-turnout profile or a dowager's idea of decorum, but he did not hesitate to round it up and put it in a political harness.

A typical Ventura event found the candidate regaling college students within easy driving distance of his suburban Minneapolis home, quoting philosophers such as Jim Morrison and Jerry Garcia. His schedule was spotty before he was compelled to leave his radio program in July (having finally filed as a candidate), and sparse even thereafter. Though he began to venture beyond the Twin Cities media market in August, he was soon sticking to the homefront again. The results were telling on election day: He lost only one county within a hundred miles of his base but lagged elsewhere.

"That was by design," explains Ventura's free-spirited media man, Bill Hillsman of North Woods Advertising. "We had to make efficient use of the candidate's time, and the Twin Cities media cover 80 percent of the state."

The candidate impishly claims his close-to-home schedule was dictated by his determination to not miss a practice of the high school football team for which he serves as a volunteer coach. But in truth, this populist revolution was a front-porch campaign, driven by Twin Cities journalists looking for colorful copy. The media mountain came to the Minnesota Mohammed, and it was rarely disappointed.

"The press doesn't go out and make their own story," says Barkley. "You've got to give it to them. They'll take it if you can make it meaningful and interesting. And it helps to be colorful and controversial."

Before a student rally at St. Cloud State, Ventura, a community college drop-out, rejected the idea of further state subsidies for tuition. "If you're smart enough to get here," he bellowed, "you're smart enough to figure out how to pay for it." On the flip side, Ventura was fond of decrying the proliferation of laws designed to "save stupid people from themselves," suggesting to do so was interfering with the evolutionary process.

When a debate moderator tried to preface a question by asserting, "To be governor of Minnesota, you have to be an expert in agriculture," Ventura quickly admonished, "No, you don't." His capacity for political sacrilege seemed boundless.

But the refreshing Reformer was not all swagger and shock; he often took substantive positions that resonated with those who felt Minnesota's paternalistic government needed a tug on the reins: Return the surplus, forget subsidies for sports moguls, let people carry a gun so they can protect themselves. And while you are at it, cut the student/teacher ratio.

Faced with a horrendous 4 to 1 gender gap, Ventura named elementary school teacher Mae Schunk his running mate for lieutenant governor. He explained that, if elected, he would leave education policy to the sixty-four-year-old schoolmarm.

"Ventura won all the debates," opines Wy Spano, "because he always gave a straight answer, even if it was 'I don't know the answer.' "

Editor of the newsletter *Politics in Minnesota*, Spano was amazed at how directly Ventura's approach ran contrary to standard professional advice: "Unlike the practiced politicians he was up against, he never stayed on message, deflecting the tough questions. That really set him apart. Voters figured the politicians were just telling them what they wanted to hear, and only Jesse was telling them the truth. . . . They'll vote for someone they disagree with, if he's the only one they can believe."

No More Play Time

Ventura's quest hit a watershed on July 21, when he was finally compelled to formally file his candidacy and was immediately relieved of his radio show. Play time was over.

After six months in the field, the campaign had raised a pitiful $12,000. To qualify for the $326,000 in public matching funds, the campaign would have to raise another $35,000 by the end of August, in contributions of $50 or less.

A Ventura T-shirt—bearing the snarling slogan "Retaliate in '98"—had been introduced at Fourth of July parades and was beginning to sell briskly at $20. Hundreds flew out of the Reform Party booth at the state fair in August, and $62,000 had been collected by the end of the month.

Even though the threshold for the state subsidy had been met, the $326,000 taxpayer subsidy could not be collected until a month after the election, and then only if Ventura topped 5 percent on election day. That level of performance seemed assured, as Jesse was posting between 11 percent and 13 percent in the polls. But bankers are not conditioned to take polls as collateral.

A program soliciting small personal loans from supporters was heralded on Ventura's Internet Web site and produced about $1,500 a day. The candidate spoke at the Reform Party convention in Atlanta but failed to raise much money from the national party cohorts.

On September 15, the Democratic primary had predictably been swept by Humphrey, who piled up 37 percent against 19 percent for Freeman. Enthusiasm was palpably low: Turnout failed to crack 20 percent, the lowest in the fifty years that records had been kept.

The 18 percent third place posted by Johnson proved the biggest surprise. Much of the credit for this obscure pro-lifer's impressive showing went to his quirky TV spots, which engagingly appealed to Minnesota's populist tradition. They had been crafted by Hillsman, the same media iconoclast whose ads had helped win Wellstone a Senate seat in 1990 despite being outspent nearly 5 to 1.

Five days after the DFL primary, Barkley received a letter from Hillsman offering his services to the Ventura campaign.

"Bill was a perfect fit," the Reform strategist admits, "but he had always been close to Democrats. I hadn't thought he'd do it."

"I liked Dean and respected his positions for years," explains Hillsman, "and I had watched Jesse at all those candidate forums over the summer. . . . I was impressed."

Coming aboard with less than six weeks left to the campaign, Hillsman immediately returned the Ventura effort to a fixation on Twin Cities free media. His first act was to stop the candidate from taking a three-hour road trip to Mankato for an interview on a public access cable station.

While the scramble continued to get a loan to cover expenses pending payment of the public subsidy, Hillsman began crafting radio ads designed to attract immediate media attention. Drawing on Ventura's tough-guy image and background as a Navy SEAL in Vietnam, he composed an attitude-laden jingle to the strains of the theme song from "Shaft": "When the other guys were cashing their government checks / He was in the Navy, gettin' dirty and wet / Well, they try to tell you he can't win / But we'll vote our conscience and we'll vote him in."

Right on.

Debunking the Debates

What the major-party candidates had in terms of monetary advantage, they gave away by their lack of inspiration. In an early debate, Coleman had gaffed that "we're going to have to redefine the family farm," suggesting that small operations simply were not viable anymore. He had spent months on the cowpaths ever since, desperately catering to farmers and trying to shed his image as a city kid from Brooklyn. He went even further than Humphrey in advocating farm subsidies and in forgiving property taxes on cropland.

"It was an absurd spectacle of someone trying to be something he wasn't," assays Spano. But it finally began to pay dividends in early October. Two state senators recognized as leaders on farm issues—one a Democrat, one an independent—unexpectedly backed the Republican.

Coleman, looking more like a liberal panderer, failed to tie down the swing-vote suburbs, a constituency he felt was safe against big-spender Humphrey. But there was another wolf at this door, one whose pro-choice position might eventually resonate with suburban Republican women.

The idea that Ventura could siphon off Coleman votes had occurred to Humphrey's strategists. Buying the conventional wisdom that the wrestler's macho, libertarian appeal synched better with Republicans than Democrats, Humphrey refused to debate Coleman unless Ventura was also included.

Fresh from his primary triumph, and shortly after the death of his mother, Humphrey opened up a huge twenty-point lead in mid-September polling and appeared ready to coast to victory with a prevent defense. Trapped in third place and being outspent massively, Ventura looked less like a threat than a way to pull some votes off of Coleman.

Attention was now focused on the three debates sponsored by the League of Women Voters, all due to be carried on statewide television.

At the first such event, in Brainerd on October 1, Coleman again pitched for rural votes, while Humphrey tried to shoot down charges he would raise taxes as governor. While concentrating on Humphrey, Ventura attacked both major party entries for their partisan posturing and lack of leadership, but he drew only condescending smiles from his rivals.

The following day's headline in the *St. Paul Pioneer Press* declared: "Leaders battle, Ventura charms." The entry in Barkley's log reads: "Jesse hits a home run." Media interest in the Reformer began to perk up; money or no money, he was plainly on the move. And at Humphrey's expense.

"The biggest mistake of the campaign was Humphrey's insistence that Ventura be in the debates," declares Coleman pollster Fred Steeper. "Like Perot in '92, Ventura connected instantly with that middle-class swing vote that had been parked with Humphrey, largely from recognition. . . . He became the champion of the little guy against the established powers. . . . Humphrey performed poorly in the debates and couldn't hold them."

Spano agrees, reporting the AFL-CIO phone bank nearly shut down two weeks out, after it was found to be reaching as many voters for Ventura as Humphrey.

By October 10, with his lead cut by a third and Ventura rising into the mid-teens, Humphrey began skipping the lesser, late debates. He was markedly more aggressive in the second televised event on October 11, charging Coleman with running up an astronomical debt in St. Paul. Humphrey's media campaign became so pointed, Coleman filed suit in all eighty-seven counties, charging that Democratic ads had violated the state Fair Campaign Practices Act by lying about his record. Humphrey was such a spendthrift, Coleman charged, "he doesn't know what a budget is."

Rising above the bickering, Ventura continued to endear himself to the public and press with expressions of candor most major party candidates would have considered fatal. Running counter to his macho image—but straight after Humphrey's crumbling support—he endorsed gay rights, declaring "love is bigger than government."

"Ventura could have been stopped by bringing the public's attention to the import of his libertarian, outrageous positions," insists Steeper. "It wouldn't have been difficult. He had left such statements in the public record all year long."

Naked and the Dead

But the big boys were not biting. The idea that a destitute third-party wrestler could actually win was beyond their concept of plausibility. Pundits and major party pols presumed Ventura's vote would follow the classic third-party pattern of falling away in the closing days of the campaign. Both Coleman and Humphrey tried to position themselves as the beneficiary.

"Neither wanted to be the one to stick Jesse with the 'emperor's clothes' routine," offers DFL executive director Kathy Czar. "They didn't want to alienate his voters by bursting his bubble."

The Late Fade Theory of third-party candidates relies on the assumption that such candidates will not have the resources to effectively compete in the final media battle. It also assumes that the "wasted vote" syndrome will kick in, that disaffecteds will grudgingly turn to the major parties—or not turn out at all—once they realize their candidate cannot win.

Neither of these assumptions applied to Ventura.

On October 20, a *Star-Tribune* poll reported that Humphrey's lead had vanished and that the Reform Party standard bearer was up to 21 percent. That helped the Ventura campaign close on a $266,000 loan from the Franklin National Bank the next day.

The draft had been arranged by Minneapolis alderman Steve Minn, chair of the Reform state convention, and it had required the taking out of an insurance policy that guaranteed payment.

The cash infusion came at the precise moment it was needed to launch Hillsman's long-planned TV flights. The first spot used the simple graphic of an American flag, the voiceover decrying the debilitating effects of partisan division as the camera panned over the alternating red and white stripes; it then shifted into a paean to Ventura's unifying influence as the screen zoomed to a star on a true blue field.

The soft allegories were a letdown for the newsies, who expected more fireworks from the Ventura/Hillsman combo. "I could tell the press was disappointed," a sensitized Hillsman recalls, having been inculcated by the Wellstone race in the value of crafting spots for free media attention. "I knew, however, we had something coming down the production line that they would really push."

The press pleaser was a takeoff on Ventura's days as a WWF star, when he had his own toy "action figure" on the market, popular enough to buy

Thirty-Second TV Spot

"Action Figure"

Jesse Ventura for Governor

Produced by: North Woods Advertising

ANNOUNCER: New from the Reform Party.

BOYS: Yeahhh!!

ANNOUNCER: It's the new Jesse Ventura action figure! . . . You can make Jesse battle special interest groups.

BOY (imitating Jesse): I don't want your stupid money!

ANNOUNCER: And party politics!

BOY: We politicians have powers the average man can't comprehend.

ANNOUNCER: You can also make Jesse lower taxes, improve education, and fight for the things Minnesotans . . . really care about!

BOY (imitating Jesse): This bill wastes taxpayer's money! Redraft it!

ANNOUNCER: Don't waste your vote on politics as usual! Vote Reform Party candidate Jesse Ventura for Governor.

him a Porsche with a single month's royalties. Two boys were depicted playing with a new version of the figure—Ventura in a business suit—as he battled "Evil Special Interest Man" (see TV spot, facing page).

"I don't want your stupid money," one kid had Ventura hoot, as the corrupting lobbyist took a well-deserved sock.

True to its billing, "Action Figure" grabbed gobs of free newscast airtime as campaign money began pouring into Ventura's coffers at the rate of $10,000 per day. And the hoopla over it helped douse the only major media crisis suffered by the campaign on October 21.

Asked if he supported legalizing prostitution and drugs, Ventura answered no, but said that legalizing prostitution might bear a second look, as "Nevada doesn't seem to have a problem with it."

"It was the worst timing," shudders Barkley, who at that very moment was getting ready to ink the bank loan. "I was afraid it would blow the deal."

But in the end, the damage was minimal. Humphrey and Coleman both took their first swings at the issue, but they were too absorbed in the task of destroying each other to bother following up. The news media was simply too enamored of the breaking story of Ventura's new-found viability to risk nipping it in the bud. For the first time, reporters began speculating about a third-party win.

"How would you deal with a legislature that includes no members of your party?" reporters asked, to which the brawny candidate responded by rolling up a sleeve and flexing a bicep. The copy and visuals were just too good to ignore.

The identities of Coleman and Humphrey were becoming merged into one gray, dispiriting backdrop against the vibrant color of Ventura's civic carnival. Coleman's platitudinous ad campaign had been pushing the slogan "Norm Coleman: The Only One." Now Humphrey blended in with spots trumpeting "Only Humphrey."

The dissing duo polluted the airwaves with attacks and counterattacks at their October 24 debate, Humphrey charging "Norman" with seeking "straight tax dollars for his cronies," while Coleman derided the Democrat's pledge to push for Medicare benefits in Washington as a promise Humphrey had made and broken a decade before. The beleaguered moderator was reduced to endlessly shouting "Stop!"

As the flak thickened, big guns from the major parties rolled into the state to fire a few partisan rounds, led by First Lady Hillary Clinton, USDA secretary Dan Glickman, and erstwhile GOP ticket-mates Bob Dole and Jack Kemp. To Clinton's calling him a "sideshow," Ventura dryly responded: "If I were her, I'd be more concerned about leaving Bill in the White House."

Now leading among all men and voters under forty-five, Jesse was looking less and less like a freak to be gawked at. But to push to a winning plurality, he had to sober up his image, tighten his gender gap, and maintain a sense of bandwagon momentum that would run over any remaining "wasted-vote" qualms.

Hillsman quickly and effectively met these challenges, one by one. He produced a new version of "Action Figure" that introduced a new "war-wagon" accessory: the RV that Ventura would use to barnstorm the state in a nonstop performance over the campaign's last seventy-two hours (see TV spot, facing page).

To drive home the point that his candidate had a record of public service and had discussed issues more thoroughly than had his opponents, Hills-man produced "The Thinker" spot, playing against Ventura's nickname, "The Body." To assure viewers he had not suddenly begun to take himself too seriously, the statuesque statesman winks at the camera in the closing shot.

Filmed a week before the election (with a bodybuilder double minimiz-ing Ventura's studio time), "Thinker" hit the air on Saturday night and proved to be the crowning blow. News accounts juxtaposed "The Thinker" clips with reports of Ventura rampaging across the countryside, exhorting student masses to storm the polls.

Hi-Tech Nervous System

In addition to the ads and news coverage, the campaign's Web site was a particularly effective mobilization and information tool. Early in the race, Ventura realized that the Internet was "tailor-made" for his kind of low budget, unconventional campaign. "It's reaching a huge amount of people at a very low price," he was quoted as observing.

Phil Madsen, director of the campaign's Web site and an initial organizer of Minnesota's Reform Party, was quoted as saying that the "Internet for us served as the nervous system of the campaign. The Web site was the differ-ence; it was the mobilization."

According to American University researcher Rebecca Strauss, much of Ventura's use of the Internet was as a behind-the-scenes coordinating tool. The campaign's big closing event, a seventy-two-hour final drive through the state, was organized and coordinated entirely by email through its Web site. Madsen sent out an email to his 3,000-member list, called "JesseNet," inviting volunteers to a meeting; more than 250 people showed up to help organize the tour.

Another big factor in Ventura's favor was Minnesota's unusual election law. It gives voters the right to register at the polls on election day. That made Ventura's impact particularly hard to gauge, especially for pollsters who never showed the full force of the Reform surge.

In the end, voter turnout hit 61 percent of the voting-age population (the highest in the country), and 16 percent of the total election-day elec-

Thirty-Second TV Spot

"Drive to Victory"

Jesse Ventura for Governor

Produced by: North Woods Advertising

ANNOUNCER: Presenting the latest accessory for the Jesse Ventura action figure! The Victory RV! A full-size RV that Jesse rides on his seventy-two-hour Drive to Victory! . . . You, too, can join the Drive to Victory. Check our Web site at www.jesseventura.org to find out how!

KID (imitating Jesse): I only answer to the people of Minnesota!

ANNOUNCER: The Jesse Ventura Friday-to-Monday seventy-two-hour Drive to Victory.

JESSE: I can't do it without you!

ANNOUNCER: Join in and meet the man, the action figure, and our next governor!

torate had registered at the polls, a figure unseen since the law's inception in 1974. Analysts estimate more than three of every four new voters opted for Ventura.

The result would stun political analysts across the country. Only a few local pundits predicted a Reform Party win, and of the national predictions, only *Campaigns & Elections'* Internet handicapping service, *The Political Oddsmaker,* came close, calling Ventura an even bet to win. The final vote percentages were Ventura 37, Coleman 34, and Humphrey, the initial frontrunner, 28.

Not surprisingly, the late-night comics had a field day with the Minnesota results (make that a field week), and Minnesotans soon grew testy about their ridiculed voting behavior. Several days after the Ventura earthquake, David Letterman introduced a special segment titled "What the Hell Happened in Minnesota?" a question he intended to pose to a caller chosen at random from the state's phone books. After identifying himself and his "little podunk show on CBS," Letterman pitched his query. He quickly received a click and a dialtone.

"We've circled the wagons," explains Wy Spano. "Everybody defensively insists Jesse will do just fine."

But there is no shortage of political operatives ready to answer Letterman's question.

"Jesse's participation in the debates was probably the most important factor," says Kathy Czar. "He came across as real and established his credibility. After all, he makes his living in radio and has got the sound bite routine down pat."

Steve Minn points to Minnesota's unusually reform-minded election laws: same-day registration, public financing, and a provision by which the first $50 donated to any candidate for state office is rebated by the state. "I don't think it could happen anywhere else," he admits, though he concedes that the threshold for third-candidate credibility may have been lowered.

A widely perceived arrogance of the state's power structure was key to Ventura's appeal, an attitude that was sustained "in the elevator," as Minn puts it: reassuring word of mouth among friends and coworkers that bolstered their own inclinations. The vaunted opinion makers were bypassed and disregarded with revolutionary relish.

"I was fooled because conditions here are so good," explains Spano. "Unemployment is the lowest in the country, home ownership is the highest, test scores are at the top. We have the best-run state in the Union. You naturally assume people who have all that will vote for the status quo."

Although times are good in Minnesota and around the nation for now, more and more voters are coming to the conclusion that a two-dimensional electoral system does not represent their will very well, or even respect their opinions. They see two hypocritical political parties ignoring the public interest while they tear at one another and operate as slaves to a corrupt campaign finance system.

If a Jesse Ventura can win the highest elective office in one of America's most prosperous states in the most prosperous of our national times, political professionals should start asking, then what power structure is, indeed, truly secure?

12

'Bama Bash

Endorsement Backlash Saves a Governor from Primary Defeat in Alabama in 1998

GOV. FOB JAMES (R) VS. WINTON BLOUNT (R)

David Beiler

More than a generation later, the images remain indelible: Governor "Big Jim" Folsom on an election eve TV hookup, flapping his arms and squawking like a chicken until he fell off the stage.

His successor, George Wallace, confronting federal marshals at the schoolhouse door after declaring "segregation forever!"

Alabama's colorful, in-your-face political traditions are legend. Yet, even against this backdrop, Gov. Forrest "Fob" James (R) seemed to have stumbled out of a time warp in hyperspace.

In the eighteen months leading up to the election, James had declared a U.S. Supreme Court decision on school prayer null and void, claiming the Bill of Rights does not apply to the states in such matters; he had implied that he would use the National Guard, if necessary, to keep a replica of the Ten Commandments hanging in a courtroom; he had become the first governor in history to secede from the National Governors' Association; and, in a performance before the state Board of Education mocking the theory of evolution, he had traipsed across a room emulating an ape being transformed into a human being.

In performing these dramatic acts of defiance, James had shown administrative audacity reminiscent of Andrew Jackson and made constitutional arguments that hark back to John C. Calhoun. Presented with a colorful flair and a common touch, the whole production at times evoked images of the 1830s—replete with minstrel show.

The Great Unwashed applaud. The elites are appalled.

Originally published in *Campaigns & Elections* magazine, October/November 1998.

agers, and Payoffs		
ames		Winton Blount
ny Baker, Mike Burton		Sonny Scott
)h Reed		Tom Perdue
itegic Perceptions		BrabenderCox
in McLaughlin & Assoc.,		Wirthlin Worldwide
Market Research Institute		
Budget	$3,000,000 (est.)	$6,000,000 (est.)
Votes	256,702 (56 percent)	203,658 (44 percent)

Sudden Opposition

One of those elites refused to stand for it, mounting a challenge to the governor within his own party—an action that would have been considered heresy in the tightly knit southern GOP of the not-so-distant past. Winton Blount III, multimillionaire son of a postmaster general of the United States, filed for the Republican primary at the last minute. And he was not the only one with a representative waiting at the secretary of state's door on filing deadline day, April 3.

James himself played the waiting game until the final ten minutes, raising speculation he might repeat his performance of sixteen years ago, when he declined to seek a second gubernatorial term. But while conventional speculation had long expected James to climb back into the ring and suspected Blount would follow, the third entry would have been considered the sheerest fantasy only three days before.

Indeed, the candidacy of former governor Guy Hunt (R) was not a legal possibility at the time. Convicted of converting inaugural funds to his personal use and removed from office in 1993, Hunt was not even eligible to vote. Then, in rapid succession over a four-day period, he produced a $210,000 restitution check, was pardoned by the state Parole Board, and filed at the deadline to run for his old job.

Although twice elected to the state's highest office, Hunt has never been taken too seriously by political pundits and operatives. Simultaneously a farmer, Primitive Baptist preacher, and Amway distributor, Hunt had won only 26 percent of the vote when he ran as the GOP nominee against Democrat James in 1978. That was before a bitter split in the Democratic Party boosted him from obscurity to the governorship eight years later. Governor Hunt's luck continued in 1990, when the Democrats challenged him with the liberal head of the state teachers' union.

Thirty-Second TV Spot

Winton Blount for Governor

*Produced by: The Perdue Group/
BrabenderCox*

BLOUNT: Four years ago, Fob James
personally asked for my support. He
said he would be a leader and move
the state forward. I trusted him. Like
many of you, I supported him. For a
long time, I gave him the benefit of
the doubt. But Fob James broke his
word. He hasn't moved our state
forward. Fob James turned his back
on Alabama. Now Alabama needs a
new leader. I want to be that leader.
I want to be your next governor.

ANNOUNCER: On June 2nd, vote
Winton Blount for governor.

Although many Republicans felt Hunt had been driven from office by a
Democratic cabal, the controversial former governor unveiled his surprise
1998 primary campaign with negative ratings more than doubling his positives and slim prospects for raising significant campaign cash. He remained
popular with much of his old fundamentalist base, however, giving rise to
suspicions that his candidacy was orchestrated by anti-James, pro-Blount
forces to split the social conservative vote.

"I can't prove it," admits Ted Bryant, political reporter for the *Birmingham Post-Herald*, "but I believe Blount had to be involved. Hunt and James
pulled from the same direction: the rural, religious right vote."

Blount's base was quite different: suburban, "good government" and business oriented, a constituency that would have easily carried the nomination for him in the not-so-old days when country clubbers controlled the Dixie GOP.

"James alienated much of the business community by refusing to push hard for tort reform," assesses University of Alabama political scientist Pat Cotter, a partner in Southern Opinion Research. "He had tried to put a prominent trial lawyer on the Auburn board and reportedly had substantial financial backing from trial lawyers."

The governor's novel crusades on social issues have also struck many business folk as bad for the state's corporate image. "They're fed up with his goofiness," explains Bryant.

By contrast, Blount's business credentials were sterling. Although the family fortune had been created in construction, Blount made his mark in car dealership and the manufacture of plastics. Taking the helm of the Alabama Business Council in troubled times, he led it to renewed success. Despite his business bent, the fifty-four-year-old entrepreneur was no political novice. His father, "Red" Blount, had been the state's GOP nominee for the U.S. Senate after serving in Nixon's cabinet and had run third in the 1994 GOP gubernatorial primary.

But pedigree is not as helpful as it used to be in the Southern GOP. Republican primaries in Alabama are beginning to look like Democratic primaries of forty years ago: rural, working-class, white populists pitted against "good government," urbanized, upper-class whites. If played right, it can be a hospitable environment for a throwback politician like James.

"He has an almost nonpartisan appeal, built upon an image of standing up for the average man against the odds," reports Cotter. James pollster John McLaughlin concurs, assessing the governor's support as "solid and intense."

But in addition to the James base, the electorate also includes an equally large cohort of intense James detractors. "They've been there for quite a while," recalls reporter Bryant. "Ever since his first term back in the '70s."

Football and Free Weights

The Fob James who first entered the governor's mansion in 1978 seems a far cry from today's populist fire-breather. An old Auburn football star who had made millions pioneering the production of plastic free weights, he was hailed as a standardbearer of the New South. Under his leadership, state government was dedicated to the pursuit of economic development with its back turned squarely against the divisive, old-style politics of race. He appointed the first black member of the state Supreme Court, a man who subsequently became the first black to win a statewide election in Alabama.

"I was fairly impressed with how forward-looking Fob was in that first term," recalls Bryant, citing the creation of a $450 million trust fund from offshore-drilling licenses.

But the late 1970s and early 1980s were tough times nationwide, and James honored a campaign pledge not to run for a second consecutive term. "It probably helped to know he was unlikely to win reelection anyway," speculates Cotter.

That did not stop the barbell baron from trying to return to the governor's mansion in every election held since. A member of the Republican Executive Committee in the mid-1970s, he resigned to make his first gubernatorial run as a Democrat. After comeback attempts were cut short in the Democratic primaries of 1986 and 1990, James tried again as a Republican in 1994, following a brief flirtation with an independent candidacy. This time he was successful, edging acting governor Jim Folsom Jr. (D), the man who succeeded to the mansion after Guy Hunt's exit, by a bare percentage point in a year of a national GOP sweep.

The second edition of Governor James was more populist and accessible. He instituted a weekly call-in radio program, fielding unscreened questions from his listeners. "That's really kept him in touch with the people," says James campaign press secretary Donny Claxton, who gives the show much credit for the governor's large, hard-core following. "He covers everything from potholes to the biggest budget initiatives. It's been a fantastic forum."

A strong streak of social conservatism, which became more apparent in James during his 1994 primary runoff campaign against moderate state senator Ann Bedsole (R), increasingly asserted itself through the second term. By early 1997, James was crusading to keep a replica of the Ten Commandments hanging in Circuit Judge Roy Moore's Etowah County courtroom, where proceedings always begin with a Baptist prayer. When Moore defied a court order directing him to take down the plaques and drop the prayer, James waded in with both barrels: "The only way those Ten Commandments and that prayer will be stripped from that court is by force of arms," he bellowed, instantly establishing himself as a national champion of fundamentalist Christians.

When DeKalb County's system of school prayer was struck down by a federal judge, James insisted on taking his appeal to the U.S. Supreme Court. And after his ape-to-human impression before the Board of Education, the governor bought nine hundred copies of a book debunking Darwinism and distributed them to biology teachers across the state.

Thirty-Second TV Spot

"Teach"

Fob James for Governor

Produced by: Strategic Perceptions, Inc.

JAMES: Last year, Alabama students' scores exceeded the national average in every grade and in every subject for the first time. We increased state funding to public schools to improve academics and eliminate substandard classrooms. We gave authority to teachers to restore discipline and required the state superintendent to take over and correct any school not meeting academic standards. A state that will not tolerate a losing football program no longer has to tolerate a losing academic program.

First Heat

James's born-again political status appeared complete with the announcement that his campaign would be guided by campaign consultant Ralph Reed, former executive director of the Christian Coalition.

Reed's influence seemed evident in the governor's primary campaign, which often focused on social issues, perhaps to woo away fundamentalists who were torn between James and Hunt. In a particularly memorable TV ad, teacher Brenda Bobo gave moving testimony as to the effects of a federal court order that took prayer out of her classroom.

Blount signed on seasoned consultant Tom Perdue to guide his effort, with Perdue partner Sonny Scott running the day-to-day campaign. Ironically, Perdue and Scott had been hired by James the year before to clean up the organization of the governor's office, particularly communications. The duo left after only two months amid rumblings of acrimony. Perdue claims James asked him to script the reelection effort; James has denied it.

"The entire operation was a disgusting mess," says Perdue of his stint in the governor's office. "His staff was in a time warp . . . everybody was doing their own thing . . . there was a lack of interest on anybody's part . . . all due to an egocentric management style."

While still working for James, Perdue was contacted by Blount, who was exploring a race for lieutenant governor. That interest cooled, but then, two days before the filing deadline, the call came.

"He had just received a poll that showed him behind [James] 66–14 percent," declares an incredulous Perdue. "Everybody told him not to run, but he did it anyway."

At first, it appeared the Blount campaign would be a feel-good lark. To boost his name recognition in the first week, the challenger sponsored a car in the Touchstone Energy 300 stock car race at Talladega.

Early spots celebrated his business leadership. The governor was not yet in the gunsights. James's reelection effort was equally self-absorbed in the early going. Cognizant of the fact his spartan, minimalist style of government had not made him popular with public employees, the governor began mending fences.

Speaking to statewide confabs of teachers and state employees in mid-April, James emphasized what he had done for them lately. It was a fairly easy task before the state workers, as he had granted them an 8 percent pay increase the month before. Teachers were a tougher sell, and education became an early focus of the James media campaign.

In a spot titled "Teach" (facing page), first aired May 5, the best was made of a not-very-proud situation. "Last year, Alabama students' scores exceeded the national average in every grade and every subject for the first time," crowed the spot crafted by Fred Davis of Strategic Perceptions, but the figures were a bit misleading. They referred to SAT exams, which in Alabama are taken by a relatively small elite of students who expect to attend competitive, out-of-state colleges. The overwhelming majority of Alabama students take the rival ACT exams, where most of them still fall below the national average.

Other statistics used to extol James's tenure were more legitimate: violent crime, down 17 percent; unemployment, at a twenty-five-year low; welfare rolls, off 40 percent. But many other states are posting similarly impressive figures. The incumbent's simple slogan, "Alabama needs more Fob," rang hollow with a great many voters.

"Fob James has done thousands of good things but hasn't received much credit," insists Davis, blaming the disconnect on poor PR work by James and the old staff that had put Tom Perdue in such a lather.

Despite his image difficulties, James was buoyed by his devoted base of religious conservatives and states rightists. A University of South Alabama poll taken in November 1997 showed that 58 percent of the voters backed defiance of the school prayer court order. And a 42 percent plurality agreed that state governments should not be bound by the rulings of federal judges.

The threat that Hunt might split that base never materialized, as he faded from the start. By Hunt's own admission, he began with no money or organization, and he attracted little along the way. Although the discredited former governor began the race polling in second place, it was clear by tax day that the primary battle was a two-way match between James and Blount.

Hunt and Blount agreed that tort reform was sorely needed and that James was responsible for its lack of progress. By mid-May, Blount was thrashing the incumbent for being backward-looking and bad for business.

James declared that Blount had officially lobbied the legislature for $424 million in tax increases, berated his challenger's refusal to sign a no-tax pledge, and challenged him to release his tax returns.

A controversy erupted on May 20 when the James campaign produced a tape of a telephone interviewer using "push" questions that implied the governor was a right-wing extremist who encouraged lawbreakers and militia groups. The phone assault was commissioned by Blount, charged the governor's men, who simultaneously released a month-old interview transcript in which Blount denounced the practice of push-polling.

Scott admitted responsibility, but Perdue still seethes over the charge: "[Blount] was referring to a slanderous poll that was used against him in '94. Ours wasn't a push poll. We were merely trying to see which issues carried more weight."

The primary balloting on June 2 offered only one mystery: Would James avoid a runoff? In the end, he fell 3 points short of the required 50 percent plus one. Blount scored a surprisingly strong 41 percent, only 7 points behind the incumbent in his own party's primary. Blount carried all the big-city counties, Hunt prevailed only in his home enclave, while James swept everything else.

Hot Water

The four-week GOP runoff campaign was bound to be freewheeling not only because of the bitter animosity between Blount and James but also because of an intriguing tactical technicality: the Democrats were now loose. Lieutenant Governor Don Siegelman (D) had easily won the Demo-

Around the Track: Following the Race with Media Tracking Polls
(figures represent percentages of total vote)

	Early April[1]	Late April[1]	June 2 Primary Results	Three Weeks Out[2]	One Week Out[3]	June 30 Runoff Results
James	35	39	48	42	48	56
Blount	14	30	41	44	43	44
Hunt	18	14	8	—	—	—
Others	14	9	3	—	—	—
Undecided	19	8	—	13	9	—

1. Southern Opinion Research for the *Birmingham News* and the *Huntsville Times*.
2. Political Action Consultants.
3. Mason-Dixon/PMR.

cratic gubernatorial nomination in the first primary, so few high-profile races were to be found on the Democratic side of the second primary. Alabama Democrats have a rule forbidding runoff participation by anyone who voted in the GOP primary. It got them into hot water in 1986 when it inspired the courts to replace their gubernatorial nominee.

But Alabama Republicans have no such rule. Primary-voting Democrats are welcome into their runoff kitchen, should the leftovers at home look too bland.

That fact now made for some interesting strategies. Plenty of conservative populists lived in rural districts that still elected Democrats at the local level. But with the Democratic nominations largely decided, they might be persuaded to cross over into the GOP runoff and vote for their soul mate, James.

An even more intriguing element was some 50,000 African American voters in Jefferson County, thought to be widely influenced by Birmingham's black mayor, Richard Arrington. If Arrington could move some of that constituency into the Republican runoff, he might find himself in the curious role of GOP kingmaker.

Soon after the primary ballots were counted, emissaries of the two Republican contenders began making a rather public display of courting Arrington's favor, though it now appears the move may have been a feint on James's part.

Meanwhile, the prospect of Democratic primary votes seemed to transform the GOP contest into a Democratic intramural of old, replete with name-calling, race-baiting, lurid charges, and backdoor intrigue.

It seemed to really get going when Blount suggested Alabama did not need to have its governor "dancing around a stage like a monkey" (a reference to

James's 1995 performance before the Board of Education). Whereupon the stocky incumbent retorted: "If I dance like a monkey, he must dance like a fat monkey" (an obvious reference to the challenger's rotundity).

In case the point was missed, First Lady Bobbie James immediately called Blount "a big fat sissy," and the governor began referring to his opponent as "win-TON."

It went downhill from there. A three-page list of accusations arrived in news media mailboxes, associating Blount with several episodes of unethical personal and business behavior, including arson and the murder of his first wife. When a panelist asked about the charges during a debate, James dismissed the document as a "smear sheet" and urged: "Let the dead rest."

Indeed, Blount had his own Chappaquiddick, an incident that, ironically, dated from the same year as Ted Kennedy's moral debacle: 1969. Driving a speeding car while intoxicated, Blount had an accident in which his wife was killed.

Only one major media outlet—a Huntsville TV station—reported the twenty-nine-year-old story in any detail. The James campaign actually produced a TV spot that made use of the sensational event, but it stayed in the can.

"I wish the Pollies had a category 'Best Spot That Never Aired,'" laments James media consultant Fred Davis. "That one would win hands down. It was devastating, but the governor wouldn't let us use it."

Davis feels the story was fair game because it dramatized the arrogance of elitism, a theme the James campaign was trying to hang on the patrician Blount.

"He was so drunk he couldn't stand up. . . . The real scandal was the way he got off. His daddy swooshed in from Washington in a helicopter, and that poor woman was buried before the sun went down."

That the governor's camp would even consider such a blow is an indicator of the heat generated by Blount's own campaign.

Blount's campaign, mostly in a blitz of radio ads, accused James of several acts of malfeasance (such as improper funneling of state business) with regard to a variety of enterprises owned by his family: a landfill, docks, a bridge, and an oil company.

"Those charges were almost hilariously absurd," assesses Davis. "They didn't even try to document them. . . . After a while, people didn't believe anything they put up."

James pollster John McLaughlin agrees: "They tried to bury this governor, and they failed."

Perdue claims the charges were well-documented and challenges the James team to "re-read their poll numbers. If those ads hadn't worked, we wouldn't have kept running them."

God and Race

With Hunt out of the contest, James decided to cool the religious rhetoric, having assumed that the fundamentalists were now safely secured. The campaign theme became a mix of touting favorable economic and crime stats and dismissing Blount as a pampered aristocrat led around by "out-of-state consultants."

Somehow, it did not matter that James himself had a New York pollster, a California media man, and Ralph Reed (who, like Perdue, hung his hat in Atlanta).

Reed assented to the subtle shift in tactics, though not before convening a group of conservative religious leaders on June 15 and urging them to "encourage your people to go to the polls [and fulfill] their godly responsibility."

"That last month, it looked as if the governor had gotten it toned down," Davis wistfully remembers. But then, just eight days before the runoff, the U.S. Supreme Court turned away James's appeal in the school prayer case. The stage was set to move the issue to the front burner for the home stretch—on terms not favorable to the incumbent.

The problem was the governor's legal appeal was an obvious grandstand play. Rather than sign on to the Republican attorney general's appeal working its way through proper channels, James had filed directly with the high court with little chance of being heard—using the thirty-page document to deliver a political attack on the court itself.

"Because of this court, a few people claiming freedom from religion can silence others in public places," bellowed the appeal, filed by James's son, Forrest III. It went on to accuse the justices of "disobeying the supreme law by taking for themselves the unconstitutional power to decide religious issues for the whole nation." The provocative diatribe even called on government officials and citizens to defy Court decisions they consider unconstitutional.

"Ninety-nine percent of the people on the [James] team were against the wording of it," reports Davis, who adds that the younger James drafted the document entirely on his own. "That didn't fly with the governor, though. He's a firm believer." (Tom Perdue scoffs at that notion. "Fob James is no more interested in the Ten Commandments or school prayer than the man in the moon. All he's interested in is successful publicity.")

"It was terrible timing," concedes Davis, "but you can't tell when the Supreme Court is going to act on those things. I thought Blount would take advantage of it. He should have."

Having secured the endorsement of Guy Hunt, Blount was still trying to cut into the fundamentalist vote, quoting scripture in his television ads. The chance to stick James with the extremist label just before the balloting was forfeited.

The day after the high court action, Mayor Arrington held a news conference to announce his endorsement of Blount. There was immediate speculation, fueled by Reed, among others, that the mayor might lead as many as 40,000 anti-James blacks into the GOP primary.

"The very next day I got a flier in my mailbox," says an amazed Ted Bryant. "It had pictures of Blount, Arrington, and Frank Watkins [Arrington's unpopular political guru] in a '70s afro."

The missive accused Blount of making a deal with Arrington that would give the controversial mayor assurances of substantial state financial support for Birmingham and veto power over certain appointments in a Blount administration. Nearly 300,000 were mailed to white, conservative, mostly rural Republican voters. Black Birmingham minister Joe Dickson took credit for this ostensibly independent initiative, but it was financed with $120,000 from John Teague, a former state senator, now a lobbyist, who is reportedly friendly with James.

In the week that remained before the election, copies of a get-out-the-vote budget allegedly to be used to finance the Arrington forces and paid for with $92,000 from Blount were circulated to Alabama news rooms. And just before the balloting, a second flier on the Arrington endorsement— more pointed than the first—appeared in thousands of mailboxes in conservative areas. It bore a copy of the Arrington organization's sample ballot, which carried a notation by Blount's name: "With Blount vs. Siegelman, we will control either way." On the reverse, pictures of Arrington and Blount loomed above the bold caption, "Who will rule Alabama?"

James released a letter that he had received from Watkins outlining concessions that were expected in return for an Arrington endorsement, and his campaign made the most of Blount's alleged sellout to the Democratic big city boss. But the governor's people deny involvement with the racially tinged material—though not necessarily because they thought it was a bad political idea.

"Some in the campaign wanted to push the Arrington thing like crazy," says Davis, "but the governor didn't want to. He didn't want to bad-mouth Blount."

"He had everything to do with it," retorts Perdue. "[James] allows minions in phony organizations to do these things while he hides. . . . Fob James is a total lying cheat."

Backlash?

In the end, James won big: a twelve-point margin that left pollsters and pundits a bit stunned. "Even the James campaign thought they would lose," claims Perdue. "Playing the race card at the end was all that worked for them."

A study of the returns suggests that while about 20,000 Birmingham blacks were persuaded to vote in the GOP contest, around 60,000 white Democrats—presumably conservatives—crossed over in rural areas, two-thirds of them voting for James. That suggests the governor picked up a net margin of 5,000 to 10,000 votes out of the Democratic crossover. That, however, does not necessarily measure the full impact of the backlash to the Arrington endorsement.

Analysis of the returns shows that James may have converted significant numbers of first-primary Blount voters in the suburbs surrounding Birmingham. The challenger managed to carry Jefferson County by only five points.

In the bitter trade of recriminations flung by rival consultants after the runoff, Montgomery mayor Emory Folmar, chairman of the James effort, claimed Blount and Perdue had been duped into pursuing Arrington's support. "We set a trap for [Perdue] with Mayor Arrington and his Democrat crossover votes," he wrote in the July 27 issue of Bill Shipp's Georgia newsletter.

The suggestion is that James only pretended to be pursuing Arrington's support to (a) lull Blount into thinking such an endorsement would be a net asset and (b) get inside information as to what Arrington and Watkins were looking for in trade.

While intricately Machiavellian, such a scheme would be consistent with James's overall campaign appeal, which seems to be pitched to the old George Wallace coalition.

Veteran campaign consultant Perdue was particularly put off by his experience in the primary and says he is leaving politics for the construction business. He qualifies his retirement statement by saying that he will still help past clients he "really believes in."

Could such a throwback campaign have a winning appeal anywhere else? Political scientist Cotter thinks it might, to a point: "Public opinion here varies little from the national norms on all the key issues—gun control, abortion, racial attitudes. Quality-of-life indicators have lagged. That may be the key difference."

13

The Squeaky Wheel(s) Make It Interesting

A GOP Star Barely Survives New Jersey Governor's Race in 1997

GOV. CHRISTINE TODD WHITMAN (R) VS.
JIM MCGREEVEY (D)

Peter Wendel

Democrat Jim McGreevey, a virtually unknown forty-year-old small-town mayor and first term state senator, came within 22,000 votes—out of 2.4 million cast—of unseating Gov. Christine Todd Whitman of New Jersey.

How did this obscure mayor of Woodbridge give such a glowing national GOP star the fight of her political life?

Through a well-orchestrated, well-disciplined media strategy, McGreevey effectively framed his message around two quintessential middle-class issues that the patrician Whitman had neglected during her first term—soaring auto insurance rates and property taxes. In doing so, McGreevey transformed himself into a middle-class populist champion sensitive to the needs of the working family.

Whitman responded slowly to McGreevey's charges that she was uncaring in her handling of New Jersey's steep auto insurance rates. And by the time she was forced to grapple with this increasingly potent issue, her young challenger, with his razor-sharp focus on rolling back rates, had eaten into her early lead. Steady attacks leveled against Whitman's auto insurance policies gradually began to overshadow the celebrated 30 percent income tax cut that she had delivered during her early days in the governor's mansion.

Through a simple, well-defined comparative message, the McGreevey camp succeeded, early on, in blunting the advantage of Whitman's deep income tax cut. In fact, McGreevey controlled the campaign dialogue to

Originally published in *Campaigns & Elections* magazine, December/January 1998.

such an extent that Whitman's own message, by default, became a passive response to McGreevey's proposals to reduce New Jersey's ballooning car-insurance rates and property taxes, both of which carried the ignoble distinction of being the highest in the nation.

Of course, McGreevey needed big issues to make a race of it. A poll taken in February 1997 by Quinnipiac College placed Whitman ahead of the suburban mayor, 58–22 percent. At the time, McGreevey was also polling a mere three points in the Democratic primary.

By early March, polls gave Whitman a 52 percent positive job rating, a 44 percent negative rating, and a reelect of 39 percent. At that time, her lead over McGreevey had narrowed but was still a healthy 53–30 percent. The Democrat who polled the best against her was Congressman Rob Andrews, but he lost the primary to McGreevey's last-minute surge.

It would be an uphill climb to topple Whitman. To do it, McGreevey assembled a professional campaign team that included Struble, Oppel and Donovan; Message & Media; and Penn + Schoen, the polling firm that worked for President Clinton's reelection.

Whitman also had an experienced consultant team in her corner that included Murphy, Pintak, Gauthier—the media firm that handled her 1993 win—and the Tarrance Group for polling.

Back at the Trough

Political analysts frequently refer to New Jersey as a traditional "trough" state. That is, a state in which incumbents must continuously "feed" voters with economic benefits. Garden State voters are known for their propensity to elect candidates based on their ability to deliver. They are often split down the middle in hotly contested partisan battles.

In 1981, moderate Republican Tom Kean defeated Democrat Jim Florio by 1,797 votes out of 2.4 million cast. The battle, and the recount, was bitter and bloody. Florio came back eight years later and won the governorship.

In 1990, a little known local official named Christine Todd Whitman took on two-term U.S. senator and "good government" icon Bill Bradley in a race that pundits handicapped as an easy incumbent win. Though Bradley started far ahead in the polls and massively outspent Whitman, $12 million to $900,000, he won with a disappointingly thin 50.4 percent of the vote.

In 1993, Whitman defeated then-incumbent Governor Florio by a slim 26,000 votes, roughly 1 percent of the 2.5 million total. That year, her campaign message centered on Florio's breaking of a no-new-taxes promise. Whitman offered a 30 percent income tax reduction—a $1.2 billion cut that was crafted with the help of publisher Steve Forbes—and voters ate it up.

Christine Todd Whitman

Jim McGreevey

This time, McGreevey followed Whitman's formula for success by promoting a rollback in auto insurance rates and property taxes.

According to GOP consultant Mark Campbell, the McGreevey campaign recognized the nature of the New Jersey voter and capitalized on it. "They ran a classic 'what have you done for me lately' campaign," he explained. "Although Whitman had a very productive first term and did some remarkable things, the voters asked, What's next? What have you done for me lately?"

The centerpiece of McGreevey's platform was an immediate 10 percent across-the-board cut in auto insurance premiums. He also called for an elected (not appointed) state insurance commissioner, and, in populist keeping, proposed the appointment of a public advocate to represent consumers.

Whitman's insurance plan, which had failed to gain legislative approval, tied a 25 percent rate reduction to consumers waiving their right to sue for accident "pain and suffering."

Despite her efforts to soften the insurance issue, polls showed that it continued to be a big drain on Whitman. A Mason-Dixon/PMR survey conducted two months before election day revealed that 41 percent of voters favored McGreevey's insurance plan, while 32 percent favored Whitman's proposal.

A *New York Times*/CBS News poll around the same time gave Whitman an anemic 17 percent approval rating on the issue with a whopping 67 percent disapproval rating. Her numbers on property taxes, which had skyrocketed after the income tax cut, were not much better: 24 percent approval and 53 percent disapproval.

McGreevey repeatedly attacked Whitman for the eleven insurance-rate hikes approved during her four-year term—a hard hit given the saliency of the issue. "We really hurt her on auto insurance," said McGreevey consultant Karl Struble. "We made it the defining issue of the campaign."

Republican Campbell agrees that the focus on insurance was a direct hit. "It was a very good challenger issue," he said. "It's always easier to focus on things that people are unhappy about."

Media Strategy

Both candidates realized that winning the election, in large part, hinged on appealing to the state's large block of independent, nonaligned voters— a constituency that is notoriously late in deciding. To this end, both McGreevey and Whitman had planned to save resources for the final push— an eleventh-hour media blitz, as well as an aggressive get-out-the-vote drive.

This late-spending strategy held up for Whitman, who, along with other New Jersey GOP candidates, enjoyed some $3 million in party committee largesse for campaign ads. The Republican National Committee alone put up $750,000. McGreevey was not as fortunate, as his party could only muster $100,000.

When Whitman kicked off her general election media campaign (she had done extensive advertising before the primaries earlier in the year) she did it on a positive note, touting her accomplishments. Her ads, however, seemed to have little impact on her standing. Her trial heat numbers hovered in the mid-40 percent range for months.

After opening positive, Whitman then aired an ad that portrayed the still undefined McGreevey as a traditional tax-and-spend liberal who had supported then-governor Jim Florio's $2.8 billion tax increase. But it fell short of the all-out multi-media attack that some Democrats feared would effectively "take out" McGreevey as a contender before he could even make his case.

It was McGreevey who kept Whitman on the defensive throughout most of the campaign, effectively neutralizing many of her advantages, which included her handling of the income tax cut, economic development, education and crime. He argued that Whitman's deep income tax cuts were nullified by sky-high property taxes and made the point that she was forced into a "fiscally irresponsible" $2.8 billion pension bond sale to compensate for her earlier tax slashing.

McGreevey and his media team defined a comparative message that translated into a rising sentiment that he cared about "people like me."

"Our message defined clear differences between the two candidates," Struble said. "And differences are what all campaigns are about."

Even though McGreevey was successful in drawing issue distinctions between himself and his opponent, his campaign never entirely succeeded in portraying McGreevey as a credible governor. As late as October, two-thirds of New Jersey voters had no particular impression of him. Campaign insiders say a lack of money was to blame for that apparent communications gap.

Complicating the equation for Whitman, though, was the abortion issue. Her strong pro-choice position, her distaste for the power held by the Religious Right in her party's organizational structure and her opposition to a ban on late-term abortions had angered social conservatives to a boil. Some openly bolted the GOP to support other candidates, particularly pro-life Libertarian Martin Sabrin and, to a lesser extent, Conservative Richard Pezzullo.

The movement of thousands of Republican-leaning voters between Whitman, Sabrin and the undecided column during the closing weeks of the election was critical to the eventual outcome. National pro-lifers such as Dan Quayle, Congressman John Kasich (R-Ohio) and Sen. Rick Santorurn (R-Penn.) were brought in to help Whitman rally the GOP faithful.

Though Whitman's moderate social policies turned off her party's right wing, her loss was offset to some extent by her appeal to some swing voters who normally voted Democratic.

Mea Culpa

A *New York Post*/Zogby poll conducted October 8–9 showed McGreevey within 4 points of Whitman, 39–35, with 22 percent undecided.

Whitman's standing had weakened to the point that she was forced to resort to a strategy other embattled incumbents have employed over the years: she ran a "Mea Culpa" spot. "I am proud of what we have done together," she said in the ad. "But I know there is more to do. You have sent me a message—auto insurance and property taxes cost too much and people are hurting. I've heard you loud and clear."

According to Struble, the "Mea Culpa" ad backfired on Whitman because it reinforced McGreevey's message and almost pushed the Democrats through to victory.

As the race wound down to the nerve-wracking last days before voters went to the polls, it became a nightmare for pundits, pollsters and election prognosticators. Televised pundits such as Mark Shields, Bob Novak, and Paul Gigot called it for McGreevey, while Kate O'Berne, Eleanor Clift, and Tim Russert projected a GOP win.

The Political Oddsmaker, the online elections handicapping service provided by *Campaigns & Elections* magazine, had the race even over the weekend before election day but then tilted a tiny advantage to Whitman on Monday, its last posting of odds. The final *Oddsmaker* gave Whitman a 50 percent chance of winning and McGreevey an 18:17 shot (a 48.6 percent chance).

Polls showed it close, too, though to differing degrees. Mason-Dixon/ PMR (October 27–29) had Whitman ahead by 3 points; the *New York Times*/CBS poll (October 25–29) gave the incumbent a larger, 11-point lead; the *Newark Star-Ledger* showed Whitman on top by an even bigger 14 points; the Zogby International Tracking poll (October 21–November 2) had the incumbent 2 points ahead of her challenger.

Turnout would be vital. Both sides invested considerable resources in get-out-the-vote drives. Whitman's campaign, along with local GOP committees, sponsored a grassroots mobilization that put thousands of volunteers to work. McGreevey was helped mightily by an extensive effort led by organized labor that included phones, mail, neighborhood canvassing, and poll workers.

In the end, Whitman held off McGreevey 47–46 percent, winning 1,107,225 votes, compared to McGreevey's 1,085,639 and Sabrin's 111,727. It was a photo-finish win, but it was still a win.

An exit poll conducted by Voter News Service revealed that McGreevey drew strong support from voters who were frustrated by Whitman's failure to control soaring insurance rates. As many as nine in ten voters identified auto insurance as "important" in making their choice for governor.

McGreevey received 83 percent of the black vote, which made up 10 percent of the total. That was 8 points higher than Florio's vote in 1993.

Whitman had received 46 percent of her votes from women in 1993. In 1997, she received 52 percent.

Though they did not quite make it, McGreevey's campaign team was happy they had come so far. "Campaigns like ours that are patient, set their strategy early and stay disciplined on their message are ultimately rewarded," Struble summed up. "We controlled the dialogue of the campaign and consequently almost won a race we had no business being in."

14

Only in Louisiana?

Populist Message Propels Republican to Governor's Mansion in Louisiana in 1995

MIKE FOSTER (R) DEFEATS SEVERAL OPPONENTS IN AN OPEN SEAT RACE

Ronald A. Faucheux

It has been said that if you want to learn how to play politics, you should go to Chicago, Boston, New York, or even Texas. But if you want the post-graduate course, you must go to Louisiana.

Louisiana elected a new governor November 18. But the real contest was held October 21, the primary election that propelled Mike Foster, a little-known white state senator with populist conservative leanings, into a runoff with an African American congressman, Cleo Fields, a tireless campaigner and an unapologetic liberal.

It was America's first major statewide election after the O. J. Simpson verdict and Louis Farrakhan's Million Man March. The election's late-blooming racial polarization was arguably caused, at least in part, by those events. But one must be careful here. This is the state, you should remember, that four years ago put a former Ku Klux Klansman into a gubernatorial runoff. And that happened long before anyone had ever heard of Johnnie Cochran.

In a more strategic sense, this election proved once again that just putting a pretty face on TV, especially for a longshot, is not enough. Foster's upset win showed that the way to bag the big ones in today's politics is with a focused message targeted to identifiable voter groups, a well-financed mix of both electronic and print paid media, and a heavy emphasis on grassroots organization.

Originally published in *Campaigns & Elections* magazine, December/January 1996.

Hot and Spicy

Not only does Louisiana's hot and spicy politics have a unique blend of Latin and Mediterranean flair, but its electoral system itself is as rare as a good gumbo in Idaho.

It was in the early 1970s that newly elected governor Edwin Edwards, exhausted after two rough Democratic primaries and an uncharacteristically competitive general election, vowed that he would never go through that ordeal again. So he got the legislature to pass the Open Elections Law.

Under this system, there is a single primary election in which all candidates run, regardless of party. If one candidate receives a majority, he or she is elected and there is no general election. If no candidate receives a majority in the primary, however, then the top two vote-getters run it off, regardless of their party affiliation, in a general election.

In addition, Louisiana elections are held on Saturdays so that, according to Gov. Earl Long, who passed this reform, it would be more convenient for working people to vote.

Louisiana is a state of rich cultural diversity and a fascinating political history dominated by strong personalities.

Once Gov. Huey Long swept out the Bourbon aristocracy in 1928 and championed the cause of share-our-wealth populism, a colorful but cynical political culture took root. Big elections in Louisiana are always spirited contests, marked by strategic sophistication and Machiavellian treachery. Until the oil bust of the mid-1980s depleted public and private coffers, Louisiana had the most expensive campaigns in America. It is a place with few pretensions about its politics.

The state's electorate has four major parts: African Americans (about 28 percent), south Louisiana whites (Cajun Catholics with an eclectic "Let the Good Times Roll!" political orientation), metro New Orleans whites (urbanites and suburbanites, some labor and liberals, but mostly Republican), and north Louisiana whites (heavily Protestant, conservative, and rural).

At the start of the 1995 campaign season, there was a long line of gubernatorial wannabees, including:

- Former governor Buddy Roemer (R), a one-termer who was elected in 1987 and lost a reelection bid in 1991
- Former governor David Treen (R), a one-termer who was elected in 1979 and lost a reelection bid in 1983
- Lt. Gov. Melinda Schwegmann (D), elected in 1991, a popular politician in her own right and the wife of a well-liked public service commissioner and grocery store magnate

- State Treasurer Mary Landrieu (D), an aggressive young reformer and daughter of former New Orleans mayor and ex–HUD secretary Moon Landrieu
- State Rep. Quentin Dastugue (R), an outspoken fiscal conservative and Edwards foe, who was the official candidate of the state Republican Party
- U.S. Rep. Cleo Fields (D), a thirty-two-year-old African American elected from a snake-shaped district that meanders through southern, central, and northern parts of the state
- U.S. Rep. William Jefferson (D), from New Orleans, dean of the state's black elected officialdom
- Former State Rep. David Duke (R), who lost a governor's race four years earlier
- Mike Foster (D), a wealthy sixty-five-year-old two-term state senator from coastal South Louisiana and grandson of a former governor, Murphy Foster
- Phil Preis (D), a rich north Louisiana lawyer who would run as a citizen-reformer with the help of high-powered Washington consultants
- Robert Adley (D), a former Roemer legislative floor leader from north Louisiana, who mounted an underfinanced, last-minute candidacy
- Harry Lee (D), the amiable sheriff of Jefferson Parish (a New Orleans suburb) and close Edwards friend; his trial balloon candidacy collapsed only two months after it began

The field was once referred to as "Noah's Ark" because of the presence of two white female Democrats, two black Democratic U.S. representatives, and two former Republican governors. But the ranks quickly thinned as the filing deadline neared.

Whatever Edwin Wants

It is impossible to set the stage for this election without first discussing Edwin Edwards, the ruling potentate at the time of the race and the man who has dominated state politics since 1971, when he was first elected governor.

In his early years, Edwards pushed through a sweeping agenda that included increased taxes on oil and gas, lower consumer sales taxes, and a new state constitution with a reorganized government.

Despite his embrace of many "good government" reforms, the quick-witted Edwards, silver in both hair and tongue, soon gained a reputation for wheeling and dealing, unabashed womanizing, and high-rolling Las Vegas gambling. Nonetheless, he was easily reelected in 1975. During his second

Mike Foster

term, he presided over a state prosperous from high energy prices. He ended his eight-year, term-limited tenure more popular than ever.

In 1979, Louisiana elected its first GOP governor since Reconstruction, Dave Treen. But after this four-year interregnum, Edwards wanted back in. As usual, he got what he wanted. He trounced Treen, winning more than 61 percent of the vote in 1983. A memorable moment in one televised debate between the two combatants was when the straight-laced Treen sternly asked the roguish Edwards why he always talked out of both sides of his mouth. Edwards, cool as a cucumber, shot back: "So that people like you with nothing between their ears can understand."

Edwards's third term was not a happy time. With declining oil prices, the state's economy had plunged into a deep recession. Edwards now had to raise taxes and make budget cuts just to stand still. He was also hit by a federal criminal indictment in 1985 involving state hospital permits. After two arduous trials, he was found not guilty. But his public standing was severely damaged.

Despite low poll ratings, Edwards sought an unprecedented fourth term in 1987. But the magic was gone. He ran second in the primary to Democrat Buddy Roemer, his first loss in thirty years.

Roemer had been elected to Congress in 1980 and quickly gained the enmity of the Democratic leadership for his independence. Even though he began his political career as an operative for Edwards, along with father Charles Roemer, a controversial and skillful political mastermind who had

The Horses, Handlers, Wagers, and Payoffs

Top Candidates	Media Consultant	Pollster	Primary Vote Percentage
Mike Foster (R)	Roy Fletcher	none	26
Cleo Fields (D)	Fenn, King, Murphy	Ron Lester	19
Mary Landrieu (D)	Greer, Margolis	Celinda Lake	18
Buddy Roemer (R)	National Media	Public Opinion	18
Phil Preis (D)	Squier, Knapp, Ochs	Garin-Hart	9
Melinda Schwegmann (D)	David Axelrod	Penn + Schoen	5

served as Edwards's commissioner of administration, young Roemer campaigned for governor in 1987 as an outsider, promising revolutionary change.

"I don't like Louisiana politics," said Roemer in one of the most effective talking-head TV spots in political campaign history, "but I love Louisiana. I love Louisiana enough to make some people angry."

Stuck in fifth place throughout a long campaign, the Harvard-educated Roemer suddenly caught fire five weeks out, fueled by his captivating TV performances and a coordinated series of newspaper endorsements. He stunned the political establishment by leading the incumbent in the primary, 33–28 percent. Edwards, who knew a bad bet when he saw one, dropped out of the runoff on election night.

Though Roemer's rhetoric was stirring, his performance as governor left many cold. An inability to work with legislators, a know-it-all attitude, and an unnecessary willingness to compromise his reform programs had dashed high expectations.

Despite a midterm party switch to the GOP designed to galvanize a conservative base, Roemer ran third in his 1991 reelection bid, falling behind not only eventual winner Edwards but also David Duke, the infamous ex–KKK wizard and white supremacist. It was a humiliating defeat for a man who once had a serious eye on the White House.

Democrat Edwards won the general election by forging a bizarre coalition of blacks, Cajuns, and labor—his usual base—together with conservative business people and mainstream Republicans who dreaded the national implications of a Duke victory.

(During his campaign against Duke, lothario Edwards quipped that he, too, was "a wizard under the sheets.")

Back in the mansion a fourth time, Edwards concentrated on passing a land-based casino in New Orleans. This legislative battle would occur only a year or two after enactment of a lottery, riverboat casinos, and video poker—all passed during the governorship of avid poker-player Buddy Roemer, who, in a display of deft political jujitsu, had allowed these new forms of gaming to become law even while opposing them.

Although Edwards had himself opposed legalized casinos during his first two terms as governor despite his own fondness for craps, he now saw it as the state's last economic resort. But the crass maneuverings that surrounded passage of the land-based casino bill without a public vote was the last straw for voters tired of unseemly political machinations. Edwards won it, but the price was high. His negative ratings shot back up.

A year and a half before the 1995 election, and fresh off his honeymoon with a new bride nearly four decades his junior, Edwards folded his hand and announced he would not seek a fifth term. That left the field wide open.

Open Field

With Edwards out, early polls had Buddy Roemer the clear frontrunner for the 1995 race, with Mary Landrieu in second place. Although two-way pairings indicated that Roemer would have a tough time winning a runoff against either Landrieu or Schwegmann, surveys showed that he maintained his 1991 base—about one-fourth of the electorate—mostly young professionals, upper income whites, and business people.

At the start of the campaign, many pundits had rated Landrieu as the favorite to pick up all the marbles. But that prediction did not fully take into account the strategic box she was in. Her record as a two-term state legislator was decidedly liberal, which pleased many elements of the Democratic coalition. But her reformist approach to the treasurer's office, and her determined efforts to reduce the influence of powerful Democrats Edwin Edwards and state AFL-CIO chieftain Victor Bussie in the awarding of lucrative state bond contracts, had drawn blood. Her expressed desire to run against Edwards while he was still considering a reelection bid had made matters worse.

The presence of Cleo Fields in the race limited Landrieu's growth potential among blacks, as Schwegmann's candidacy threatened her support among women and home-based New Orleanians.

About Yuppie reformers like Roemer and Landrieu, David Duke would remark: "There aren't enough BMWs in Louisiana to elect any of them." His acrid analysis would prove to be on target, not only as it applied to Roemer and Landrieu but also to his party's official nominee, Quentin Dastugue.

The Old In and Out

Despite a well-run effort that captured the GOP endorsement for him, a TV spot blitz produced by Washington-based media consultant Stuart Stevens, and a Lawton Chiles–like walk across the state, Dastugue's candidacy never got off the ground. Languishing in the polls and unable to shake loose big bucks, Dastugue called it quits on the eve of the September filing deadline. In exiting, he left the state party without an endorsed candidate.

About the same time, two other candidates dropped out: Democrat Jefferson, who endorsed Fields, and Republican Duke, who said he would run for the U.S. Senate in 1996 instead. (Duke made it known that he preferred Foster to the other candidates, though Foster was careful never to cozy up to the politically radioactive racial-warrior.)

Only a few weeks before, Treen also bowed out. The squeaky-clean Treen, whose on-off-on-off candidacy aggravated his image as an indecisive ponderer, had approached the race half-heartedly despite his official announcement and impressive early debate performances. This was curious behavior for a man who had previously mounted winning campaigns for both Congress and governor.

True to form, Treen's final no-go decision would prove to be something less than final. After Dastugue's withdrawal, and only minutes before the filing deadline, Treen faxed his qualification papers to election officials in a last-ditch attempt to reenter the race. But the fax did not fly. His papers were not accepted, and the Treen candidacy was, with no more options open, over.

All of this would seem to have improved Roemer's chances. With Republicans Treen, Dastugue, and Duke out of the way, he would have a clearer shot at the Republican right. With Jefferson out, leaving one black in the race, Roemer's dream scenario—a runoff with Fields—was now possible.

But in Louisiana politics, you must never count your chickens before they are hatched, raised, plucked, and fried.

In the days leading up to filing deadline, more shoes were dropped in this race than in Imelda Marcos's closet. But there was one more to go, and it was dropped in the final hours, improbably and unexpectedly, by a long-shot contender most local pols still discounted: Mike Foster.

After campaigning for governor for over a year as a Democrat, the independent-minded Foster abruptly switched parties and filed for governor as a Republican, attempting to fill the void on the right.

It was also a void that Roemer was trying to fill. He campaigned this time as a tough, law-and-order, antiwelfare, pro-term-limits conservative. His TV spots featured proposals to put prisoners in chain gangs and to drug test welfare recipients. But true-believers were still distrustful. They remembered only too well when Roemer only too recently called himself a "John

Kennedy Democrat." Pro-lifers remembered his veto of antiabortion legislation (the only gubernatorial veto to be overridden this century). Party loyalists remembered how he brushed them off even after he joined their ranks and how his administration raised taxes and spending and allowed gambling to seep in.

Roemer's sharpened rightist rhetoric did not impress populist conservatives. But Foster's record and rhetoric, and now his new party label, did.

Foster quietly built a coalition of grassroots conservatives unhappy with liberals and slick reformers. While his opponents were spending heavily on TV spots, he ran a long series of newspaper ads that were sized and formatted as opinion columns, expressing self-made, Ross Perot–like populist viewpoints. Although Foster had voted with Edwards and Senate Democratic leaders on a number of key issues and was neither photogenic nor a polished TV performer, he emerged as the clear favorite of the populist right.

Christian conservatives rallied behind Foster, seeing him as their best chance to defeat pro-choicers Landrieu, Schwegmann, and Fields while avoiding an unwanted alliance with the quirky Roemer.

Foster also had the early support of gun owners. His sponsorship of a bill that would have allowed the carrying of concealed weapons (passed by the legislature, vetoed by Edwards) and his steadfast support for the Second Amendment had attracted NRA members, a powerful voter bloc in a state that calls itself a "sportsman's paradise."

The NRA launched a major grassroots effort on Foster's behalf under the direction of its national lobbying and PAC chief, Tanya Metaksa. Interestingly, gun owners began their early drive on behalf of Foster while he was still a Democrat, thus rejecting plenty of big-name Republican possibilities (Roemer, Treen, Duke, and Dastugue) in the process.

In the last two weeks before the election, the NRA Institute for Legislative Action sent out tens of thousands of direct-mail pieces. They also organized a massive "phone tree" to turn out their supporters.

In assessing the victory, Metaksa said the coalition effort that was mounted to defeat former U.S. House speaker Tom Foley in 1994 showed how grassroots "can be instrumental in defeating a candidate," while Foster's election showed how it "can be instrumental in electing one."

Many small business activists also sided with Foster because of his strong advocacy of tort reform and his opposition to big government.

Together, this grassroots coalition provided this still largely unknown longshot with the best support network of any candidate in the race. That, together with Foster's ability to write large checks out of his own bank account, made the difference.

Foster also won endorsements from Treen, Sheriff Harry Lee, and GOP presidential candidate Pat Buchanan.

Into a Tailspin

In the middle of the gubernatorial race, state politics were thrown into a tailspin by news stories of an ongoing FBI investigation into gambling and, in particular, video poker regulation. Transcripts of tape recordings implicated powerful state legislators.

These reports made corruption a top issue. Candidates now tripped over one another in their attempts to appeal to increasing public dissatisfaction with politics as usual.

Even though Democrats were generally the targets of the FBI probe, both Democrats and conservative Republicans saw the investigation as an opportunity to undermine Roemer, who had allowed video poker and riverboat casinos to become law.

Foster's media consultant, Baton Rouge–based Roy Fletcher, produced a TV spot recalling that his candidate's grandfather, who had been governor in the 1890s, had run gambling out of the state, drawing an obvious but unstated parallel to what his grandson would also do if he became governor. The spot, of course, did not mention that Foster had voted for some gambling authorization bills.

For months, polls showed the top-tier candidates to be Roemer, Landrieu, and Schwegmann, with Fields close behind. But as the campaign entered its last several weeks, the worm turned.

Roemer's vote began to slowly dissipate as Schwegmann's lackluster campaign was taking its toll and her numbers were slipping, freeing up thousands of voters to other candidates. Landrieu, viewed as the most electable Democrat in a runoff, showed limited upward movement. Fields was busy consolidating his base among African Americans with the help of Rev. Jesse Jackson; his prospects hinged on turnout. Preis's TV spots pushed an appealing outsider message (his slogan: "Preis is Right"), but he still was far behind. Only Foster had real momentum.

As New Orleans–based pollster Joe Walker said, "Voters took a long time finding a candidate they liked in this unsettled field. That's why for six months the polls fluctuated anytime anybody went on TV. It only came together at the end."

Of course, as the end neared, the hatchets came out.

With three weeks to go, Schwegmann went up with a TV ad attacking Landrieu for taking contributions from gaming interests. But the tactic, which displeased pro-choice women and Democrats who had always feared the possibility of these two canceling each other out, backfired.

The state Democratic Party unloaded a TV attack produced by media consultant Deno Seder against Roemer, challenging his claim to have run a scandal-free administration. An independent radio expenditure by Newt

Gingrich's GOPAC pushed the message that the ruling Democrats were corrupt.

Another independent expenditure directed at Roemer was financed by wealthy businessman Jack Kent, who believed Roemer had treated his company unfairly over environmental permits. This was the second time Kent had gone after Roemer. In the 1991 race, he spent over $500,000 for TV ads that savaged the then-incumbent and played a key role in Roemer's defeat that year. This time, Kent spent over $300,000 on TV, newspaper, and radio ads hitting Roemer's history of failed business dealings and his inability to manage money, asking voters to "make Roemer history."

Roemer attacked Foster in the final days, questioning his credentials as a reformer. He used news clips of a private luncheon attended by Foster, Sheriff Harry Lee, and a number of Lee backers who were also close to Edwin Edwards and gaming interests.

The endorsement of New Orleans mayor Marc Morial was seen as critical in the bitter, eleventh-hour struggle between Landrieu and Fields for the city's large African American vote. So when Morial split the difference and endorsed both of them, it denied Landrieu the knock-out punch she needed.

On primary day, October 21, the electorate polarized around two grassroots underdogs representing far different philosophies and constituencies: Mike Foster on the right and Cleo Fields on the left. Early frontrunners Roemer, Landrieu, and Schwegmann ran, respectively, fourth, third, and sixth. Preis came in fifth. White voters broke in favor of Foster, with Roemer and Landrieu trailing. Over 70 percent of blacks voted for Fields, with Landrieu a distant second.

To win the runoff, Fields needed a massive black turnout and a third of the white vote. A tough task, indeed.

Fields proved himself to be a resourceful campaigner, with superb stump skills, but he was unable to overcome the Foster juggernaut to become the state's first black governor since Reconstruction.

On November 18, Foster picked up all the marbles. In so doing, he taught us more than a thing or two about grassroots politics and what an underdog needs to do to get elected in the face of stiff, diverse opposition.

Only in Louisiana? Maybe not.

15

The Unsinkable Willie Brown

Local Forces Elect Controversial Politician Mayor of San Francisco in 1995

WILLIE BROWN (D) BEATS MAYOR FRANK JORDAN (D) AND ROBERTA ACHTENBERG (D)

David Beiler

San Francisco may not be the most typical constituency in America, but it probably has the nation's most entertaining politics west of the Mississippi. The 1995 mayor's race did not disappoint, as the most powerful African American elected official in the country—a colorful master of state legislative wheeling and dealing and world-class partisan fundraising—took the temple of high-minded liberalism by sheer force of personality.

One might fairly wonder why the legendary Willie Brown would even stoop to such a task, grubbing for votes on the street for a job he once described as only "dog-doo and potholes." After all, this is the man who has made the California General Assembly his personal playground during fifteen years of skillful rule as speaker. By always knowing exactly what he needed to move legislation—and how to get it—Brown became the driving wheel in state government, the man every knowledgeable capitol operative needed to know to make things click.

White Boys Get Taken

Term-limited by California's Prop 140, Brown faced this year's legislature as a lame duck with both wings clipped. Due to exit the chamber for good at the end of the term, he now faced a Republican caucus that had the forty-one-member majority necessary to finally vote him out of the speaker's chair. For the California GOP, it would be an accomplishment akin

---

Originally published in *Campaigns & Elections* magazine, February 1996.

to finding the Holy Grail. But this was Willie Brown they were taking on; and with Willie Brown, all political permutations are possible.

Using his hypnotic wiles, awe-inspiring reputation, and genius for finding the win-win deal, Brown persuaded GOP assemblyman Paul Horcher to cross party lines and support his reelection as speaker. That deadlocked the Assembly, but now-independent Horcher then voted with the Democrats to oust Richard Mountjoy (R) from the chamber, an Assembly member who had also been elected to the Senate. That gave Democrats a 40–39 edge and Brown a new lease on the speaker's gavel.

This course of events was not as crazy as it looked: term limits have given the legislature a "get it while you can" attitude that works against the system of party loyalty. Given the symbol of "good ole boy" corruption that Brown has become for most white Californians, Horcher must have known he was compromising his popularity with his constituents. But then, he would not be serving much longer anyway. At least now he had two years to enjoy Brown's blandishments, or so he thought: no California elected official had been recalled in more than eighty years.

Nevertheless, angry Assembly Republicans set out to do just that: they quickly filed enough recall signatures to put the question to a May 16 vote. As the noose began to slip around Horcher's neck, Brown began to eye the San Francisco mayor's race as a possible escape hatch for his political career. Nine days after the renegade ex-Republican went down by a 5:3 count and a reliable GOPer had simultaneously been elected in his stead, Brown filed preliminary papers for a mayoral candidacy, announcing he would be vacating the speakership "as soon as Republicans unify to find a replacement." Two vacancies had kept Republicans from voting him out of power immediately, but both were in heavily GOP districts; by the time the second one was filled on June 6, Speaker Brown would be no more

Recognizing his reign had come to an end, Brown finished filing for mayor on June 3.

But Willie's control over the lower chamber was dying harder than Harold Stassen's presidential ambitions. Two days later—on the eve of his imminent ouster—Brown delivered all thirty-nine Democrat votes in the Assembly to disgruntled GOP moderate Doris Allen, who added her own vote and won the speakership 40–39.

Republicans went into apoplectic fits as Democrats were awarded control of the key committees and Brown was given the new title "speaker emeritus." Once again tripped up on his ascension to the throne, GOP leader Jim Brulte found his office effects in the hall: Brown had taken over his office, as the new "minority leader." There was little solace offered by the new tenant: "Those white boys got taken, fair and square," Brown gloated.

Now foaming at the mouth, Republicans were not content to start a recall campaign against Allen alone: they went after moderate Democrat Michael Machado as well, whose only crime had been to vote for the speaker candidate of his party. "This is politics," GOP senator Rob Hurtt explained to the *Los Angeles Times*. "This is for control of the state of California. . . . We think he's vulnerable. We're going to go after him, pure and simple."

As Brown campaigned for the mayoralty, the Assembly soap opera continued. Horcher got a new job as a political consultant to the state Democratic Party. Machado overwhelmingly defeated the effort to recall him. Allen resigned the speakership in September to defend herself against the recall, but Brown then engineered the election of her lone GOP ally—freshman assemblyman Brian Sentencich—to the post. Two days before, Allen had dismissed GOP critics as "power-mongering men with short penises," without identifying the source of her information. She was recalled by a 71 percent majority in November.

Bit Players

Brown's interest in the mayor's race caught many city politicos off guard. Liberal ex-mayor Art Agnos had laid the groundwork for an attempted comeback, but he quickly stepped aside for the speaker emeritus. That left three principal opponents between Brown and City Hall:

- Frank Jordan, the incumbent; a former police chief with thirty years on the force; gained a runoff berth in 1991 by being the only moderate in an otherwise liberal field, then got elected as the alternative to the unpopular Agnos; an inarticulate political novice with an "everyman" image; struggled with the mayor's job the first two years—ironically running through four chiefs of police—but could now point to a declining crime rate and an improving local economy.
- Roberta Achtenberg, a former city supervisor who became undersecretary of housing and urban development under President Clinton; a wonkish, thoughtful reformer, she is also a lesbian.
- Angela Alioto, city supervisor, daughter of ex-mayor Joe Alioto, sometime girlfriend of ex-governor Jerry Brown; a plain-spoken, emotional, and warm-hearted liberal.

Although Brown started as a slight favorite, he had Achilles' heels up to his knees, all centered on the popular perception of him as an arrogant high-flyer. "As Brown's method enshrined a system of moneyed access,"

Around the Track: Following the Race with Media Tracking Polls
(figures represent percentages of total vote)

	Mid-September	Late October	Early November	November 7 results
Brown	43	51	56	57
Jordan	30	36	29	43
Undecided	22	13	15	—

SOURCES: September, David Binder Research poll of 500 likely voters (margin of error ± 5 percent) for the *San Francisco Examiner*. October and November, Mark Baldassare & Associates, poll of 600 registered voters (margin of error ± 4 percent) for *San Francisco Chronicle*/KRON.

Note Mayor Jordan's Halloween shower stumble between the second and third polls.

wrote Democratic analyst Bill Bradley in the *Los Angeles Times*, "his ideological bent and desire for continued control led him to ignore emerging constituencies and growing demand for a radically reconfigured government."

Brown had long maintained a big campaign war chest, fueled by interest group infusions. Holding a balance of $800,000 at the time of his entry into the mayor's race, the fund was usually doled out to friendly Assembly Democrats. Brown had raised millions for himself and fellow Democrats over the years, including $700,000 from tobacco companies alone.

That record would not help him now: San Francisco may be the most inhospitable venue in the country for smoking, and its strict campaign-finance laws limit all donations to $500 in the primary and $250 in the runoff. Nor would the ex-speaker be permitted to dip into his Assembly war chest for the mayoral campaign.

There was also the matter of Brown's outside income from his law practice (about $250,000), mostly from wealthy corporate clients. Add to that his recent tax returns, which featured controversial deductions such as fancy cars he had sold off from his collection.

Connected to all the money was a widely held impression that Brown had grown out of touch after more than three decades in Sacramento. There was plenty of evidence to support the theory: "San Francisco has really changed!" Brown marveled on the first publicized walking tour of his campaign. "Uh, Mr. Speaker," an accompanying reporter reminded, "this is your district." To which an unfazed Brown replied, "That's right." Two weeks later, at his formal announcement, it was a different story: "I've watched this city change for thirty years," insisted the returned prodigal son.

When asked about losing the quarter million in income from legal fees that would not be permitted him as mayor, Brown complained, "I can't expect the members of my immediate family to make that kind of sacrifice for what is essentially my hobby." In the case of the mayor's post, that "hobby" would pay a paltry $139,000.

Knave of Clubs

Mayor Jordan immediately sought to capitalize on Brown's lucrative moonlighting, declaring he would do no work for city contractors for five years after leaving office.

The implicit challenge was never in danger of being taken up, though Brown conceded he "most likely" would no longer be able to represent backers of the Mission Bay Project—a $2 billion development on three hundred acres near downtown San Francisco—who had been trying to wring concessions out of the city government.

A local columnist wondered why Brown did not turn the influence-peddling issue back on Jordan, citing lobbying done by the mayor's 1991 campaign manager in behalf of a $40 million no-bid city contract for Motorola. But then, the man in question—consultant Jack Davis—was now running Brown's campaign. The best he could do was accuse Hizzoner of using a city fax machine to send out a campaign press release.

As the campaign wore on, however, Jordan and Brown exchanged numerous broadsides over ethics, though the mayor invariably was supplied with more ammunition. In a typical example, it was suggested Brown had engineered a deal whereby PG&E—a powerful San Francisco utility with valuable city contracts—bought $3 million in energy from Catenaga Corp., a Brown client partially owned by Los Angeles attorney Johnnie Cochran. Legislative hearings on how PG&E would pay for $53 million in cost overruns at a nuclear power plant were canceled, and the state Public Utilities Commission soon settled the entire matter to PG&E's satisfaction.

Jordan, in turn, was hit with several allegations revolving around James Fang—a former campaign aide and scion to a powerful local family—whom Jordan had appointed to a $65,000 job. Fang was kept on the city payroll even after it was learned that he had fudged his resume; his family was awarded a city advertising contract even though a competitor had bid $200,000 lower; and Fang eventually admitted he had funneled shady contributions to Jordan's 1991 campaign.

Backed by virtually no organizations beyond the environmental community, the far less known Achtenberg began impressing liberal professionals in debates, and she eventually convinced them they need not settle for Brown as the "progressive" alternative to Jordan: whichever liberal made it into the runoff would win. She gradually climbed in the polls and began raising substantial funds, thanks in part to the efforts of Jim Hormel, meat packing heir and liberal financial angel.

The Horses, Handlers, Wagers, and Payoffs

	Willie Brown (D)	Frank Jordan (D)
Media	Paul Kinney	Clint Reilly
Pollster	Corey, Canapary	Fairbank, Maslin, Maullin
Spending	$2.5 million (est.)	$1.8 million (est.)
Votes	104,902 (57 percent)	79,257 (43 percent)
Amount spent per vote	$23.82	$22.71

"It was almost a generational thing," elaborates Achtenberg manager Eric Jaye. "If you were over forty-five you remembered Willie Brown as this fearless antiwar progressive. If you were under thirty-five, you saw him as a venal politician in Armani suits and fancy cars. Starting late and basically building from the ground up, we ultimately had three thousand volunteers by primary day and moved 600,000 pieces of literature by hand."

Achtenberg got a big boost three weeks before the primary: strapped for cash and mired in the polls at single digits, Alioto withdrew. Midway through her announcement, Achtenberg dramatically entered the room to accept her former colleague's endorsement. Alioto's father, however, soon backed Jordan, joining two other ex-mayors: Republican George Christopher and U.S. Sen. Dianne Feinstein (D).

The endorsement champ, however, was Brown. Strongly backed by organized labor, he eventually won the support of forty-eight local Democratic clubs—an accomplishment that proved critical to his success.

"Getting those clubs on board was a tedious, time-consuming task," recalls Brown political director Gale Kaufman. "You have to go to two or three meetings per endorsement and fill out lengthy questionnaires just to be considered. But it put to rest the feeling that Willie had been in Sacramento too long, that he was out of touch, and it gave him the ground organization he lacked, after thirty years of automatic reelections."

Even the Police Officers' Association—unimpressed with Jordan's thirty-year career as one of their own—backed Brown. "The rank-and-file cops have long considered him an empty holster," explains *San Francisco Chronicle* reporter Phil Matier.

Rub-a-Dub-Dub . . .

The mayor's stodgy, lackluster image was not complemented by public perceptions of his wife, widely considered an imperious Nancy Reagan clone. Wanting to soften her public persona, Wendy Jordan turned to a family friend (and campaign finance officer), who then contacted the public relations firm used by his own company. The PR folks had just the thing on tap: a chatty tour of local radio stations. It just so happened that one of their clients was a Los Angeles–based radio program that was about to be syndicated onto San Francisco's KRQR. And so the convenient match was made: Mrs. Jordan would go trick-or-treating with a couple of L.A. shock jocks on a Halloween night remote, photographer in tow.

Jordan's strategist Clint Reilly had nixed the initial radio tour and would have gone into convulsions had he known about the unfolding hobgoblin caper, but Mrs. Jordan was not to be denied her makeover. The tricksters rang the Jordan doorbell on Halloween night and were treated to a tour of the place by Hizzoner himself.

When the bizarre tour group got to the master bath, the jock, known for outrageous antics, suggested they all take a shower together. Mrs. Jordan declined but reportedly goaded her husband into lathering up with the boys while the photographer clicked away. The pix were soon picked up by the *San Francisco Examiner* and splashed across the Associated Press wire.

Heretofore gathering momentum with Brown-bashing, the Jordan campaign saw its numbers begin swirling down the drain, a week before the primary. Reilly—who had privately acknowledged his client would have to poll at least five points ahead of the field to have a shot at winning the runoff—now claims that the incident cost Jordan an immediate four-to-five points and a first-place primary showing.

"It reinforced his image of incompetence," explains *Chronicle* reporter Andrew Ross. "He had bungled his way through the first two years of his term, and this brought it all back."

Events appeared to be breaking Achtenberg's way. With their doubts about Jordan's leadership qualities renewed, white middle-class voters began drifting into her camp. Just before the November 7 vote, it was revealed Brown had signed the order that terminated two legislative employees who had charged their boss—a San Diego assemblyman—with sexual harassment. The city's well-liberated women's vote began turning to the lesbian candidate in outraged reaction, even though Brown had won endorsements from the National Organization for Women and the National Women's Political Caucus.

But by primary day, massive Brown and Jordan direct-mail spending submerged Achtenberg's message in the critical final hours. Jordan stumbled across the tape on Brown's heels, 34 to 32 percent, with Achtenberg five points behind.

Waning Daze

Personalities aside, Jordan's prospects looked promising on paper. On the basis of standard crosstabs, the Achtenberg vote was not fertile ground for an old-style machine pol like Willie Brown. Predominantly white, well-educated, and female, this constituency was strong on good government reform and intolerant of greasy-palmed public servants. But it was also heavily gay and liberal. The gay vote makes up about 16 percent of the city's electorate.

"Brown had a long history of support for gay causes," recounts Ross, "and while Jordan would be considered pretty liberal anywhere else, this is San Francisco. Here, he was always the conservative candidate. The fluke coalition that elected him was non-ideological; a lot of those people never figured they'd stick with him."

One such group may have been Asian Americans, a strong Jordan cohort in 1991. This time around, they were largely in Brown's corner, led by Supervisor Mabel Tang and two prominent Jordan defectors: the Fang publishing family and Public Utilities Commissioner E. Dennis Normandy, a Filipino leader whose son had been fired from the police force.

Achtenberg endorsed Brown on primary night, and polls indicated three-quarters of her voters would follow suit. Jordan snared the endorsement of the Log Cabin Club—an alliance of gay Republicans—but for the most part swing voters believed in activist government, and they found no assurance in the mayor's proposed spending cuts or his seemingly disengaged persona.

Worried and edgy in the primary campaign, a buoyant Brown now cut the confident figure voters were looking for. "If I'm mayor," he was fond of saying, "the buses will run on time, the potholes will be filled . . . the streets are going to be safe and clean if I have to sweep them myself." He became dismissive of the incumbent: "We must treat these five weeks like sudden death overtime. Let's stop this turkey by Thanksgiving."

Jordan's poor poll numbers undercut the financial pull of his incumbency; by primary day, he was already in debt. There would be no money for broadcast ads in the runoff; by the end, tens of thousands of Jordan mail pieces reportedly remained unsent, the postmaster being unwilling to accept credit.

"I was surprised Frank ran out of money," Brown consultant John Whitehurst concedes, "but I wasn't surprised he never ran broadcast [spots]. TV is the least effective communications medium for municipal campaigns in San Francisco. Street signs are the broadcast medium of choice here."

A good example was the teaser signs put up by Jordan workers bearing the simple word, "Trust." Two weeks later they were replaced with pictures of Brown labeled "Mistrust." But this election would turn on something else.

"It wasn't about ideology, it wasn't about character," Whitehurst insists. "It was about effectiveness, about getting things done. . . . That was Willie's theme, and the shower incident made sure Jordan couldn't escape it."

Jordan clearly could not move off the gaffe, first explaining it as "a Halloween trick in a moment of levity," then admitting "in retrospect . . . I would rather have not done it." Finally, he was reduced to calling up reporters: "Some people feel I had let them down, that I let the city down," he told one. "I do apologize."

When Brown heard of the contrite calls, he quipped: "He isn't calling them into the shower, is he?" The challenger's campaign plastered the city with ninety-two thousand posters with the famed "Three Men in a Tub" photo.

Ironically, the mayor's last hope centered on showers—the meteorological kind. It rained in San Francisco on election day—hard. Turnout plunged to 40 percent, giving Jordan backers hope that their older, more affluent constituency would carry the day. But the massive Brown ground operation stood at the ready, with one thousand umbrellas, eight hundred ponchos, and flashlights, leading the candidate to declare it would use "every single technique of delivering a warm body to the polls."

By that time, the incumbent had fallen short of such qualifications.

PART IV
Referenda and Initiatives

16

Gun Play

How the NRA Defeated Initiative 676 in Washington State in 1997

Ronald A. Faucheux

It was a classic duel. On one side stood supporters of gun control. On the other, opponents. Initiative 676 in Washington State would have required that trigger locks accompany all gun sales and transfers. It would have also mandated that all handgun owners get a gun-safety license after either passing a test or completing a gun-safety course.

The campaign to win over voters in this public referendum was seen as a do-or-die shootout by both sides of this extremely emotional, controversial issue.

The scene was set for serious combat by the national news media. "Here in the state of Washington," reported NBC's Tom Brokaw on location, "the front lines have been drawn in the deadly battle over gun control. . . . It's now a full-blown political war."

Three weeks before the November 4 election day, the *New York Times* declared the referendum a "crucial test for NRA's lobbying prowess," pointing out that "polls show that if the vote were taken today, the measure would very likely pass by a wide margin."

An Associated Press dispatch surmised that voter approval of the proposition would "mark a costly setback for the gun lobby, particularly the NRA."

From the perspective of gun-control advocates, this looked like a great opportunity to shoot down the gun lobby at a time and place that could give their cause "big mo" going into the 1998 elections. It was also a chance to test the muscle of a supposedly cash-strapped, divided NRA. An invita-

Originally published in *Campaigns & Elections* magazine, February 1998.

tion sent out to a pro-676 fundraiser in Washington, D.C., had as its theme, "Bankrupt the NRA."

"We have a tremendous opportunity to take a giant leap forward in our fight to require gun licensing in this country," wrote Sarah Brady in a fundraising letter produced by her group, Handgun Control, Inc. "If Initiative 676 succeeds, there's no question but that we will have created enormous momentum for a national gun licensing law."

If Washington passed Initiative 676, it would serve as a powerful impetus for supporters of gun control to expand their efforts. The NRA was trapped. They had to fight. The line had been drawn in the dust not only by gun-control advocates but by the press. With polls showing considerable voter sentiment for more gun restrictions, gun-control opponents were about to walk into what looked like a massacre in the making.

Competitive Battleground

Washington State was an interesting laboratory for this type of high-stakes gun play. Although Washington voters elected a slew of conservative Republicans to Congress in 1994, overall the state has been a competitive partisan and ideological battleground with national importance in recent years.

Washington voters went for Michael Dukakis in 1988 when most states supported George Bush. Bill Clinton captured its eleven electoral votes in both 1992 and 1996—the last time defeating Bob Dole by a solid thirteen points.

In 1996 some of the GOP gains that had been won two years earlier were eroded. Conservative Randy Tate (R), elected to Congress in 1994, lost his seat in 1996 to Democrat Adam Smith, 50–47 percent. Four other Republicans had close calls. In the same election, Democrat Gary Locke won the governorship, trouncing conservative Ellen Craswell by an eighteen-point margin.

In the U.S. Senate, Washington has one Democrat (Patty Murray) and one Republican (Slade Gorton).

Polls taken as late as September showed that 676 was supported by nearly two-thirds of the state's voters. But that was before the public campaign began.

The "Yes on 676" campaign was captained by two respected and experienced Washington State political consultants: Diane McDade, who had worked on the gun issue for a number of years and who coordinated the strategy and media team; and Blair Butterworth, a Democrat whose firm, FDR Services, had handled Locke's successful gubernatorial campaign. Tom Wales, an assistant U.S. Attorney from Seattle, served as spokesperson for Washington Citizens for Handgun Safety.

Thirty-Second TV Spot

"Keep Them Safe"

Pro–Initiative 676

Produced by: FDR Services/
McDade Consulting

ANNOUNCER: We do so much to keep our children safe. Yet in the last five years, 241 of our kids were killed or injured by an unlocked gun. Let's get smarter about kids and guns. Initiative 676 requires hand-gun owners to purchase a child safety trigger lock and take a safety class. Oh sure, it's a little inconve-nient, but what would you rather do: Buy a lock and attend a class or buy a coffin and attend a funeral?

Paid for by Washington Citizens for Handgun Safety.

The anti-676 campaign was spearheaded by the NRA's Tanya Metaksa, a tough political operator and seasoned campaign strategist who commands the organization's lobbying arm, the Institute for Legislative Action (NRA-ILA). She also directs the Political Victory Fund, the NRA's political action committee. The campaign was managed by Fred Myers, a political consul-tant based in Mississippi. Doing the media was Tom Edmonds, of the Wash-ington, D.C.-based firm Edmonds Associates, and Ackerman-McQueen, an ad agency located in Oklahoma City. Bob Moore, of Moore Information, Inc., a national Republican survey research firm, did the polling. Joe Wal-

Thirty-Second TV Spot

"Bad Law"

Anti–Initiative 676

Produced by: Edmonds Associates, Inc.

ANNOUNCER: The truth is in the volumes of fine print. Initiative 676 is not about safety. 676 requires release of your private medical records, simply for exercising a right guaranteed in our state constitution. It puts stalking victims at even greater risk by making them wait for permission to protect themselves. That's why thousands of law enforcement officers, responsible parents, and citizens are opposing 676.

Paid for by Washington Citizens Against Regulatory Excess. No on 676.

dron chaired the pro–gun rights coalition, which sponsored campaign activity through the statewide committee set up by opponents called Washington Citizens Against Regulatory Excess, or WeCARE. Another key organizational and fundraising player was Allen Gottlieb, who chairs Citizens for the Right to Keep and Bear Arms and is based in Washington State.

Clear the Goal Post

Early in 1997, proponents of 676 decided they would go for it in November. According to Butterworth, this represented a decision "to prospect the

Thirty-Second TV Spot
"Good for You, Dad"
Pro–Initiative 676

Produced by: FDR Services/
McDade Consulting

WOMAN: To every one of you Dads out there who owns a handgun and feels you really need it for your family's safety, good for you. If it doesn't have a child safety trigger lock, shame on you. Because in the past five years unlocked guns have killed or injured 241 of our children. I-676 will require you to buy a trigger lock and attend a safety class. Sure, it's a little inconvenient, but not as much as buying a coffin and attending a funeral.

ANNOUNCER: Paid for by Washington Citizens for Handgun Safety.

state" to determine the extent to which they could use the initiative and referendum process to make gun laws that the legislature had refused to pass. "From the get-go," he admits, "it was clear that our side would be mismatched against the NRA's organization in terms of field and ground people."

The first step was to secure the required 180,000 valid signatures to put the issue on the ballot. To make sure they cleared the goal post, they aimed for 230,000 signatures, which they eventually exceeded by nearly 20,000 names. It is estimated that about 110,000 signatures were gathered by volunteers, and the rest, 140,000, were collected through paid petition circulators.

After getting the measure on the ballot in July, Butterworth says, "reality began to sink in that, despite the enthusiasm the issue generated and despite the efforts of many dedicated supporters, it would be tough to maintain a high level of voter support." He said news coverage surrounding "tragic situations"—such as publicized shootings and gun accidents by children—would produce "flurries of voter interest" that would quickly diminish once the stories were off the front pages.

Nevertheless, polls at the time were still showing that over 60 percent of the state's electorate supported the proposition, at least in general terms.

"The big unknown was to what extent the NRA would play. If they spent a million or two, we figured we could still win. But if they spent four or five or six million, it would be too much to overcome," says Butterworth, who, along with McDade, prepared a campaign plan that included that harsh assessment. "There was no way we could match a four to six million dollar campaign. The NRA was successful at tapping vast resources across the country; we were not. Our side does not have the kind of organization in place that the NRA has."

While proponents were pleased with the number of volunteers and big-name political endorsements they received, many of them expressed disappointment at the lack of deeply committed, emotional support they were able to find. "Polls show most voters favor gun controls. But they also show that they do not think gun controls really work," says one Democratic pollster who did not participate in the 676 campaign. "It's easier for the pro-gun people to stir up money and activism."

Proponents had hoped that gun controllers from nearby California, who planned to push for a similar proposition in their state, would provide help as a way to spark momentum. But for a few exceptions, that help never came.

Butterworth, regarded as a skilled strategist who has worked in a wide variety of campaigns, said it was difficult to find productive lists to use to mine money and volunteers. He said his side targeted lists of people who had supported prominent, pro–gun control Democrats—such as Sen. Patty Murray and Seattle mayor Norm Rice, a former gubernatorial candidate—but with meager results. They found that it was difficult to translate party and candidate propensities into activism for 676.

Even a fundraising letter signed by the governor's father, which provided a personal account of how he had been shot by a robber while working in his store, did not produce substantial gain. Their best list, Butterworth says, was the membership roster of Handgun Control, Inc. "Voters got involved based on personal experiences, not on the basis of past partisan involvement. And that made it harder for our side to build a support base with the resources we had. We just did not have the juice."

Grassroots Model

Proponents of the measure estimate that their side spent about $1.2 million (opponents say it was closer to $1.5 million), of which $350,000 was used during the petition-gathering process, with the remainder for the referendum-campaign phase. Most of their money went to pay for TV spots, although small amounts were put into newspaper and radio ads. Their spending strategy stressed persuasion as opposed to mobilization of grassroots support for election day. Though they mailed out 200,000 tabloids to the voters they targeted as the most favorable and made extensive use of volunteer phone banks, the proponents of the measure were clearly outorganized and out-worked by the opponents.

Estimates of opposition campaign spending range between $2.5 million and $4 million. Proponents claim that these anti-676 spending estimates, high or low, do not fully take into account all of the in-kind resources generated by the NRA's vast membership and grassroots contact network.

Apart from money for advertising, Metaksa says the primary chore of the NRA's campaign was the activation of their 80,000 members across the state. Their mobilization was a model of grassroots politics at its most effective. They put up 100,000 yard signs, raised thousands of small contributions in the $10 to $20 range, deluged newspapers with letters to the editor, and made a million phone calls. Yard signs were in such demand, NRA members would compete with one another to grab them. With obvious satisfaction, Metaksa heaps extravagant praise on her group's membership: "The winning NRA team has never done it this well, this massively, and this creatively—ever."

The strategy behind the anti-676 ad campaign, says consultant Tom Edmonds, was to drive home the message that "this election is not about safety." Targeting specific pitches to women, farmers, and gun owners in various parts of the state, their strategy was to "expose the details of the proposal" and to use its complexity and length to raise public doubt about what it would do.

One of their tactics was heavy use of talk radio. "The more discussion, the more debate, the better we did," says Edmonds.

Conceding Nothing

The timing of the pro-676 effort was determined, in large measure, by state election law. It was difficult for any November ballot measure to attract much attention before the late September primary was over. The primary campaign centered on a number of important local races including the Seattle mayoral race. The state's large number of "permanent absentee" voters were also a factor. In fact, more people voted by mail in the Seattle mayoral primary than at the polls on election day.

Because absentee ballots were mailed out in mid-October, issue campaigners would have to reach most voters before that time. So, both sides began their advertising around October 1, much of it targeted to older, more conservative voters who tend to vote absentee.

The pro-676 side aired TV ads first. Their initial media flight targeted the Spokane market, an area expected to be one of the least favorable to the proposition. "When they went up in Spokane," remembers Edmonds, "that sent a signal to us that they were conceding nothing, that they were running a Pickett's charge and coming at us in our strong areas."

Although the NRA fielded a far superior ground effort and had more money to spend on ads and billboards, proponents were able to draw heavy-duty support from a wide array of powerful politicians—including Governor Locke—as well as all of the state's living first ladies, Democrats and Republicans. Even software billionaire Bill Gates, who lives and works in Washington State, contributed $35,000. Gates's father, a Republican who has long championed gun-control issues, coughed up $150,000.

While supporters of 676 said that it would save the lives of children by preventing accidental shootings, the NRA drove home the message that it was an unconstitutional attempt to expand government power and would create a licensing bureaucracy that would not be effective in terms of child safety or reducing crime. Parents, not government, should protect the safety of their children in their own homes.

Opponents of 676 argued that law-abiding citizens need accessible guns for protection and, therefore, would have to keep keys to trigger locks accessible. If a child can find a gun that's been put away, the child could also find a trigger lock key, they explained. They also said that passage of 676 would mean stalking victims would lose special protections because of the measure's licensing provisions, and that gun owners would give up confidentiality of some of their medical records. The specter of gun registration and confiscation was raised.

Butterworth called it a "classic NRA campaign—they keep throwing out messages, true or untrue, until something sticks." Metaksa, of course, has a different view: "Our advertising message succeeded only because it resonated with the voices of our grassroots membership—that gun-owner licensing meant no safety, no self-defense, and no privacy."

Edmonds was critical of the tone of the pro-676 media. "It was snotty and over the edge. They overreached on the facts and overplayed their basic premise that children were being killed right and left in gun accidents."

Turning Point

According to most surveys, voters often look to law enforcement authorities for information and opinions about public safety and gun issues. That meant the endorsement of police groups would be prized possessions. As you would expect, both sides went after those endorsements with fierce determination.

After a bloody meeting, the state troopers' association voted for neutrality. The organization representing sheriffs and police chiefs officially kept out, although the NRA was able to win over most of their individual leaders. That left the rank-and-file local police officers' associations. Proponents knew there was little chance to get their endorsements, so they fought hard to neutralize them. They failed.

"The turning point in the campaign was when the cops went against us," says Butterworth. "Even though quite a few of their leaders wanted to stay neutral, the NRA did a great job whipping up the rank-and-file. That made the difference—and it gave opponents credible spokespersons for their ads and in the media."

Anti-676 signs would proclaim: "Vote NO . . . 7,539 police officers can't be wrong." That number represented about 80 percent of the state's law enforcement community.

Nearing election day, thirty-three of the state's thirty-nine sheriffs had also climbed aboard the increasingly rapid anti-676 train.

By mid-October, according to polls, opposition nibbling had whittled support for the initiative from 67 percent down to 46 percent and had driven up opposition to 49 percent.

Not taking any chances, anti-676 forces under Fred Myers's direction mobilized a sophisticated, computer-driven turnout operation that tracked friendly voters to the polls. Their phone, mail, and personal contacts with "favorables" during the mail-in ballot period and on election day were ceaseless.

Like a Rock

On November 4, Initiative 676, the hope of gun-control advocates nationwide, went down in a fiery blaze: 71 percent of the voters, 899,176 to 371,914, said no. In the end, reported the *Seattle Post-Intelligencer,* it "sank like a rock," losing every county in the state.

Opposition to the referendum motivated election-day turnout to an extent unusual for a single ballot proposition. Many people cast only one vote—against 676. "Some 100,000 Washington voters went to the polls Tuesday, drew the curtain, voted 'no' on 676, and left the voting booth,

Thirty-Second TV Spot

"Home Alone"

Anti–Initiative 676

Produced by: Edmonds Associates, Inc.

ANNOUNCER: Paid for by Washington Citizens Against Regulatory Excess . . . Are you ever home alone? If 676 passes, you could be a criminal subject to prosecution and not know it. Because 676 would require a license to own or possess a handgun, even if your spouse had a permit and you never use a handgun, you would be required to take an eight-hour course, pass a test or . . . risk being a criminal in your own home.

Vote No on 676.

declining to vote on any other issue or any other candidate," said John Carlson, a radio talk show host at KIRO in Seattle.

Ballots cast on 676 exceeded those on other controversial measures voted on the same day, such as measures about the legalization of marijuana for medical purposes, homosexual job discrimination, and health insurance portability. It was reported in the local press that opposition to 676 had "lured droves of conservatives out to vote, which helped defeat a number of other liberal proposals."

According to polls, the turnaround brought about by the NRA's campaign was stunning, especially among women. Reportedly, a month before

Thirty-Second TV Spot

"Cops"

Anti–Initiative 676

Produced by: Edmonds Associates, Inc.

ANNOUNCER: Law enforcement opposes 676.

DETECTIVE RON OULES: If it was about safety, law enforcement would whole-heartedly endorse it. But it's not about safety.

EXEC. DIR. OF "COPS" MIKE PATRICK: To tell a parent that if they have a trigger lock on the gun, on their gun, that their child is going to be safe is absolutely false.

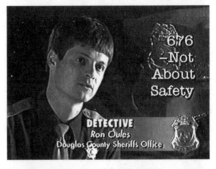

CHIEF OF POLICE TERRY MANGAN: It will jeopardize more people because of the false hope of safety than it actually will help protect.

ANNOUNCER: Support our police, vote NO . . . Paid for by Washington Citizens Against Regulatory Excess.

the election, Seattle women supported the proposition 85–15 percent. On election day, they voted against it 60–40 percent.

Proponents of 676 attributed the magnitude of their loss to the amount of money spent by their enemies. But NRA executives were quick to dispute that claim. "Money alone cannot achieve that measure of trust. Only people can. And people did," says Metaksa.

Tom Wyld, spokesperson for the NRA, pointed out that his side attracted eleven thousand small donors. He chided the pro-676 campaign for raising "their million from about one thousand people, with the bulk coming from about fifty wealthy individuals, such as Bill Gates." To sharpen his populist point, Wyld went on to say that the largest group of anti-676 donors came from the Microsoft Gun Club, a none-too-subtle shot at Gates, Microsoft's chief executive.

Standing in front of a banner that read "Fight For It," Metaksa toasted her troops on election night and called their victory "the political story of the year." Wayne LaPierre, the NRA's CEO and executive vice president, said it was the group's biggest win since it defeated a similar California referendum in 1982.

"The Washington drama was more than the rejection of a particular licensing proposal," says Metaksa. "It was the rejection of the gun ban movement's theory that NRA influence is limited to legislatures. In fact, our influence only ends there; it begins in grassroots America."

"I hope this does not make people give up," lamented gun control advocate Daniel Gross to the press after defeat of 676 became apparent on November 4.

"It just reaffirms the power of the NRA." That's something both sides can probably agree on.

17
Political Football

How the San Francisco 49ers Won a New Stadium and Shopping Mall in 1997

Noah Wepman

When the San Francisco 49ers football team decided it needed a new stadium to replace the aging Candlestick Park and wanted the city to finance part of it, they faced an uphill political battle. But, even with the full backing of San Francisco mayor Willie Brown (D), the 49ers had no idea what a monumental effort it would take to convince the city's voters they needed a new stadium and shopping mall/entertainment complex.

Passage of Propositions D and F at the June 3, 1997, special election would permit the city to sell $100 million in lease revenue bonds to help finance the new stadium. It would also change zoning laws to allow for a larger stadium and the 1.4 million square foot shopping center—a $525 million project. Sales tax revenue from the new mall would help finance construction of the stadium.

The new stadium complex would prove to be a hard sell to the voters, even with all the money the 49ers were willing to sink into the campaign. Many voters looked across the bay to Oakland and saw the potential disaster awaiting them.

The city of Oakland and Alameda County had cut the L.A. Raiders a sweet deal to move back to Oakland. Under the new management, taxpayers could end up paying for renovations to the Raiders' stadium out of the city's general fund if the intended revenue streams fail to bring in the projected amounts.

But the 49ers were not about to let what the Raiders had done stop them. Eddie DeBartolo, Jr., owner of the 49ers, put together the same cam-

Originally published in *Campaigns & Elections* magazine, October/November 1997.

paign team that had just helped the Giants (San Francisco's major league baseball team) win approval for a new stadium of their own. With early poll numbers showing that only 39 percent of voters supported the team's plan, the five-time Super Bowl champs had their work cut out for them.

Starting Early

There was organized opposition even before Propositions D and F were placed on the ballot. The Committee to Stop the Giveaway, which formed in 1992 to fight the Giants' new ballpark, quickly reorganized to take on San Francisco's other major sports team. But the Committee to Stop the Giveaway was not the 49ers' primary opposition.

The group leading the fight against the proposal was an umbrella organization that encompassed various neighborhood groups, the League of Conservation Voters, and the Sierra Club. Opponents of the Candlestick Mall was principally bankrolled by Clinton Reilly, a semiretired political consultant and mentor to political pro Jack Davis, the 49ers' campaign manager. This alleged friendship-gone-sour story was played up in the press. But, according to Davis, "This story was embellished by the press. I have the utmost respect for Clint Reilly, and there are no bad feelings between us."

The main reason Reilly got involved, according to Davis, was because Reilly may have wanted to establish himself as a possible candidate for mayor. "There are bad feelings between Reilly and Brown that go back a long way," says Davis. This aside, Opponents of the Candlestick Mall was against the stadium proposal because it believed the 49ers would be getting a new stadium at the expense of San Francisco taxpayers. Budget analyst Harvey Rose predicted the 49ers' proposal could drain several million dollars annually from the city's general fund.

The environmental community joined with Opponents of the Candlestick Mall because the proposal would put the complex next to the 155-acre Candlestick Point State Recreation Area. Environmentalists feared this juxtaposition would result in a degradation of the recreation area.

The 49ers had an uphill fight from the beginning. A poll conducted March 10 by Mark Baldassare for the *San Francisco Chronicle* showed that 47 percent of voters opposed the 49ers' plan, 39 percent supported it, and 14 percent were undecided. But the 49ers were ready to face the fray.

Owner DeBartolo had already hired Jack Davis, ex-consultant to Mayor Willie Brown, to manage the campaign. Paul Kinney, a media consultant based in Sacramento, began shooting the television spots in December 1996 —a full two months before the measures were even placed on the ballot.

The 49ers' camp began its campaign by explaining in detail what the proposal meant: The bonds would be paid back out of revenues from the new stadium, money that was already budgeted for maintenance at old

Candlestick Park, and money out of the city's sales tax revenue from the mall that would be built.

According to numbers from Brown's office, the new complex would generate a $1.8 million annual gain; however, many voters had trouble getting past the fact that the city's general fund would have to be tapped to pay off the bonds if revenues generated were not sufficient. This fear would resonate to the very end of the campaign.

Unfortunately, the more numbers the 49ers fed the public in their attempt to explain how the complex would pay for itself, the more confused people became. Opponents of the Candlestick Mall, led by campaign manager Jim Ross, fed off of this chaos.

"From the beginning we wanted to create an environment where debate happened in the newspapers," Ross said. Gaining media interest was key to Ross's organization. It was clear from day one that the opposition would not have the kind of money the 49ers had to sink into their campaign; therefore, getting all the free media possible would be vital.

On May 3 a shock wave rocked the 49ers' camp and the city of San Francisco. Davis, the 49ers' campaign chief, had thrown himself a fiftieth birthday party that reportedly included strippers, prostitutes, a three-hundred-pound sado-masochist performing live sex acts on his partner, and a dominatrix who carved a satanic star into a man's back and then urinated on him. This party quickly made network news, and soon all eyes were on Davis, the 49ers, and San Francisco.

While the party was a huge embarrassment for Davis and the football team, it did not appear to have a lasting effect on the campaign. Paul Kinney, the 49ers media consultant, said, "The party was a seven- to ten-day distraction to the campaign, but ultimately voters did not care."

A poll conducted by David Binder for KPIX Channel 5 shortly after the strange shindig showed that little had changed from the March 10 poll—39 percent were in favor of the stadium, 43 percent were opposed, and 18 percent were undecided. The only change was reflected in the increase in the number of those undecided.

Fine Tuning the Message

Three weeks before the election, many people were saying the 49ers needed a miracle. They had the endorsement of Senators Barbara Boxer (D) and Dianne Feinstein (D), the Democratic and Republican parties of San Francisco, the local chapter of NOW, the NAACP, the Alice B. Toklas Lesbian Gay Democratic Club, and most of the local labor unions, but nothing seemed to move the poll numbers in the right direction.

As a result, the campaign team decided to change its message. They decided to concentrate on their base, who from the beginning supported the team's proposal, because they would never win over the majority of undecideds.

The original message the campaign used—the proposal relied on no new taxes, would not dip into the general funds, and would use funds already budgeted for Candlestick Park—tested at about 54 percent before the campaign started. Nevertheless, the 49ers' consultant team decided to switch its message.

The message that finally hit home was that if San Franciscans voted "No" on the two propositions, the 49ers would pick up and leave town. The final direct-mail pieces and television spots focused on what it would cost San Francisco if the 49ers left town. They came up with the tag line, "Because there's too much to lose."

According to Eric Jaye, a partner in the San Francisco-based direct-mail firm Terris & Jaye, "This didn't just mean losing the 49ers organization, but also jobs and other revenue streams." According to the 49ers, a new stadium and shopping center would bring ten thousand jobs to San Francisco, which would help move people from welfare to work and bring in millions of dollars for public schools and affordable housing.

The End Is the Beginning

According to Jaye, "Many voters, when they made their decision, focused on a cost/benefit analysis of the proposal." Some voters concluded they simply did not want to run the risk of tapping into the city's general fund. The 49ers and Mayor Brown took the ultimate step to quash this fear when they announced on May 19 that the city and the 49ers had taken out an insurance policy with Morgan Stanley investment bankers and Financial Security Assurance, Inc.

Under the policy, FSA would provide insurance for the city's proposed $100 million bond issue. The insurance would safeguard San Francisco's general fund if the new mall failed to generate enough money to repay the bonds, indemnifying voters against the possibility of dipping into the general fund.

This policy was later seen as one of the factors that ultimately helped the 49ers win; however, it did not have the desired immediate effect. On May 25, the *San Francisco Examiner* released the results of a poll showing 55 percent against the measure, 32 percent in favor, and 13 percent undecided. The results were terribly disappointing and showed that the insurance policy did not raise the "Yes" votes and that, in fact, the 49ers were slipping in the polls.

Two weeks out, the 49ers knew that it was do-or-die. The campaign began airing two new ads that followed the "Because there's too much to

Two separate pro–initiative 676 mailers are pictured above. The mailer on the top stresses the need for a strong voter turnout and includes a message from Sen. Dianne Feinstein, while the mailer below it is targeted to Republicans.

lose" theme. The first one showed a crumbling Candlestick Park, a disappearing Muni (San Francisco's local bus system), and an evaporating Super Bowl. The second featured future Hall of Fame defensive back Ronnie Lott and quarterback Steve Young discussing why the team and the city needed a new stadium. Both ads attempted to demonstrate what the city stood to lose if the 49ers left.

In one of the top five media markets in the country, direct mail became a very important targeting tool to reach the 410,000 registered voters in San Francisco. This is the reason the 49ers sent out so much mail and why

The mailer above is targeted to the city's large gay community. Cover, above left; inside, above right.

the Opponents of the Candlestick Mall, working with limited funds, used only direct mail and no television commercials to get their message out.

During the last two weeks of the campaign, the 49ers' direct-mail team blanketed the city with eighteen mailers targeted to nine different demographic groups. One, targeted to Republicans, showed two sets of feet—one wearing cleats, the other dress shoes—dangling above flames. "We put their feet to the fire," it says, advising Republicans that there are "written guarantees that San Francisco taxpayers can't get burned" (see previous page). Another piece, targeted to women, asked, "What will bring shoppers to a new mall in the Bayview?" The answer—in five-inch-high red type—"50% Off" on prices. A third, with a cover photo of two African American female riveters taken at the Hunters Point shipyards during World War II, saying "Never Forget," exhorted voters to "Bring the jobs back to the Bayview."

In addition to the mail and TV spots, the 49ers had the celebrity advantage. Popular players were sent around the city to meet with voters in behalf of the new stadium. Opponents did not have the celebrities or funds needed to keep up with their adversaries. They did manage, however, to send out three direct-mail pieces.

With one week until the election, another hurdle was put in the way of the 49ers. This one came from state senator Quentin Kopp (I), an opponent, who unveiled an alternative proposal for a new stadium built with monies produced by a surcharge on season ticket holders. The proposal was appealing: the city would donate the land, and the users would pay for the stadium, with no risk to the city treasury. The Sunday before the election, Brown and Kopp went on television and debated the two proposals.

Finally, on June 3, the 49ers came out on top. Proposition D passed with 50.4 percent of the vote (87,560 to 86,948), and Proposition F passed with 50.3 percent (87,094 to 85,898). The team would remain in the city.

Proponents were able to pull a victory from the jaws of defeat largely because they had $2.2 million—much of it supplied by the DeBartolo family—to spend on the campaign, which equates to $26.54 for each "yes" vote.

Polling showed that the winning margin was attributable to the insurance policy to protect public investments, the strong appeal to women, the vigorous pitch to bring the Super Bowl to San Francisco, and the massive get-out-the-vote effort. Unlike the sophisticated proponent campaign, the antistadium camp had a volunteer-driven GOTV effort and spent only $102,959. "It was beyond David versus Goliath," said Ross. "David at least had a sling. We were throwing rocks with our hands."

Ultimately, though, the major voter concern was that the five-time Super Bowl champs would leave if they didn't get a new stadium. "In the end, the message that moved voters was that San Francisco would lose the 49ers if they voted No," Kinney explained.

Despite continued opposition, most local observers predict that the new stadium and mall will be open by 2000. And when it is, more than a few members of the press will sit back and watch to see what kind of victory party Jack Davis throws.

18

Using Conservative Values to Support Gay Rights

How Opponents Defeated Oregon's Anti–Gay Rights Referendum in 1994

Bob Meadow, Dawn Laguens, Heidi Von Szeliski, and Michael Terris

Interpretations of the 1994 Republican landslide abound. Some analysts say it was a wholesale rejection of Bill Clinton; others say it was a thirst for change that was not slaked in the 1992 election. Regardless, most analyses entail at least one common theme: The electorate is more focused on "traditional family values."

State ballot measures ranging from term limits to tax reductions to restrictions on immigrant services were successful, further reinforcing the notion that, on social issues at least, the country is moving rightward.

However, amid the electorate's broad conservative tilt, a few candidates and measures bucked the trend. One notable example was Measure 13 in Oregon, an antigay initiative that was rejected by a margin of 52 to 48 percent. The successful campaign to defeat this measure provides a dramatic example of how a disciplined campaign can channel the conservative values of the electorate against a right-leaning measure.

The "No on 13" victory demonstrates that campaigns based on fundamental values are not necessarily the sole province of the right; they can be harnessed by others as well.

Consensus Language

In 1992, the Christian Coalition–inspired "Oregon Citizens' Alliance" (OCA) qualified Measure 9 for the Oregon ballot. The harshly worded measure (it referred to gays as "pedophiles" and "sodomists") was defeated, 56 to

Originally published in *Campaigns & Elections* magazine, March 1995.

44 percent. Despite its defeat, the OCA concluded that opponents had grown complacent and their funding had dried up. Measure 13 was the OCA's third attempt in six years to place a gay-related measure on the ballot.

Between 1992 and 1993, the OCA focused its energies on local antigay ordinances, with twenty-six initiatives passing and only one being defeated throughout the state. Emboldened by local victories, the OCA once again turned its attention to a statewide measure.

Assuming that its perceived harshness was the reason for its defeat in 1992, the Oregon Citizens' Alliance returned in 1994 with what it claimed was a kinder, gentler measure to amend the Oregon constitution, titled "The Minority Status and Child Protection Act." In reality, the new measure was tougher to defeat because it employed consensus language that tapped into voters' fiscal conservatism.

For example, the measure would have banned antidiscrimination ordinances based on sexual orientation and prohibited the use of public funds to "promote" homosexuality in schools. In addition, the measure would have prohibited any minority status based on sexual orientation, banned any discussion of homosexuality in school curricula, prohibited partner benefits, and established censorship boards or limited library access to books and materials that referred to homosexuality.

Nevertheless, the OCA's new focus on "child protection" suggested that the OCA would be shifting its campaign message away from antigay rhetoric to the more broadly appealing notion of child protection. It also signaled the group's intention to seek the support of parents, and especially suburban women voters, who data and previous voting patterns have shown to be the strongest opponents of antigay measures.

The statewide organization previously formed to fight local antigay measures—the Support Our Communities Political Action Committee (SOC-PAC)—emerged as the No on 13 Committee. This committee mobilized a broad base of business and community groups to fight the measure. Julie Davis, executive director of SOCPAC and the No on 13 campaign manager, fought the measure in conjunction with the professional campaign team of Dawn Laguens (Seder/Laguens, general and electronic media consultants); Bob Meadow and Heidi Von Szeliski (Decision Research, polling and focus group research); and Michael Terris (Terris & Jaye, direct mail).

Benchmark polling in late July showed dead-even sentiment on the measure, at 45 percent for each side. Clearly, passions were high on the issue, with only 10 percent of voters undecided four months before the election. Given the 13 percent gap separating the "yes' and "no" sides in 1992 for Measure 9, these benchmark findings suggested to the campaign team that the OCA's new approach in recrafting Measure 9 was meeting some success.

Four Key Elements

The polling, as well as follow-up gender-separated focus groups held in two different media markets, revealed four key elements that ultimately drove the campaign:

- The data showed that across demographic groups, voters do not want to discriminate. This held true regardless of whether the voters were supportive of gay rights or opposed to a so-called gay agenda.
- There was strong agreement that people, regardless of their sexual orientation, have certain basic rights such as housing, earning a living, or being free from harassment. (Other arguments that have worked elsewhere, such as the cost of implementing the measure, fear of boycotts, or creating a new bureaucracy, were less compelling to Oregon voters.)
- Parents of school children—especially women between the ages of thirty and fifty, who were most likely to have school-age children—would be a key group for the No on 13 campaign because these women were most susceptible to the OCA's arguments concerning the protection of children.
- Given the shift of the electorate toward Republicans and the key role that independent and Perot voters would play, it was important to portray Measure 13 as a nonpartisan issue. Thus, the key to defeating the measure was to maintain a high margin of "no" votes among Democratic women, break even among independent women, and minimize the margin of victory for the "yes" vote among Republican women, who, like their male counterparts, favored the measure. At the same time, it was important to make sure that the gender gap on the issue did not widen.

Staying on Message

The first step in the campaign was to frame a coordinated message strategy between day-to-day campaign activities and earned media, the electronic media, and direct mail, to ensure that voters saw the campaign in terms of discrimination, not providing "special" rights for gays and lesbians.

Promoting the idea that Measure 13 was about discrimination, however, was a challenging task for the No on 13 campaign because initial survey and focus group data showed that voters did not think the measure was discriminatory. Keeping the message focused on discrimination tapped into mainstream voter values and minimized the prospects that the measure would turn into a referendum on what the OCA called the "gay lifestyle."

In daily earned media activities and in editorial board meetings with newspapers throughout the state, voters were carried through the logic of our core message: Discrimination is wrong; Measure 13 would permanently legalize discrimination; therefore, Measure 13 is wrong.

Second, we needed to be certain that voters saw Measure 13 as an assault on basic rights, thus tapping into another conservative voter value— opposition to expanded and intrusive government. We wanted people to perceive Measure 13 as a threat to everyone regardless of sexual orientation, rather than to accept the OCA's view that Measure 13 would stop the expansion of special rights to the gay minority.

Among the most difficult tasks facing the No on 13 campaign was to reassure voters that a "no" vote was a vote against discrimination—not necessarily a vote on their personal feelings about homosexuality. Not unexpectedly, this created tension between the electoral imperative of gaining support from a group much broader than our base, and the urge to use our paid media to address and change attitudes about gays and lesbians.

Mindful of how attempts to educate voters during high-visibility campaigns had failed and diverted campaigns from their primary task of winning, the consultant team recommended a course that hewed closely to such universal values as opposition to discrimination. The "educational" aspect would have to wait until after the election.

The OCA believed it could convince voters by presenting radical views and creating fears based on stereotypes. The OCA's campaign was rooted in its belief that voters would want to take a stand against an "immoral" lifestyle. In addition to phone-bank calling and fundamentalist church leafleting, the OCA focused its public campaign on two elements.

First, the OCA believed that voters would want to stop the expansion of special rights which, wrongly or not, voters increasingly saw as taxpayer-funded gifts to minorities in the form of quotas, set-asides, programs, and so forth. Second, the OCA's media campaign was based on fear, underscoring the need to protect children by publicizing isolated examples of school materials and teachers who advocated homosexuality—even associating child molestation with homosexuality.

For opponents of the measure, coordinating the use of media was a key element in ensuring the communication of core messages. We knew from polling and focus group data that some of the opposition to 1992's Measure 9 was based on the extreme language of the measure, so the potential appeal of a less strident version that highlighted "special rights" and the use of tax dollars to "promote or approve" of homosexuality was a real danger for the No campaign.

Mom and Apple Pie

The No campaign's initial television spot was designed to quickly regroup the anti–Measure 9 voters by noting the similarities between Measures 9 and 13. It took a humorous look at Measure 13 as a "dressed up, better looking and smoother version" of its evil twin, Measure 9. We limited the media buy for this spot to the media markets where Measure 9 was most soundly defeated, because elsewhere in the state, voters were likely to think that a measure similar to Measure 9 would be a good idea.

The initial brochure carried through on this theme, with a magnifying glass showing that on close examination Measure 13 was just like Measure 9. This mailer also reprinted and annotated the measure's text, to familiarize voters with the measure.

The second TV spot was targeted to women with school-age children. The narrative message was delivered by "Mom" (a professional actress who was also a mother, an Oregon voter, and an opponent of Measure 13), dressed in ordinary clothes and with little make-up, speaking sincerely to the camera. Two versions—thirty and sixty seconds—were produced.

"Mom" noted that she teaches her children that discrimination is wrong. Indirectly responding to the OCA's reasoning, she also indicated that even if there was a problem with what children were being taught in school, she would rather take it up with the local school board than write discrimination into the constitution.

The cumulative effect of these messages was clear in the tracking poll data, which showed that electronic and direct-mail efforts were expanding the "no" vote among Democratic and independent women, while the deficit among Republican women decreased. Open-ended comments revealed that the notions we were pushing—Measure 13 was discriminatory and it would not protect children—were penetrating among all voting groups.

As the election neared, a phone-bank effort from Don Powell of Telemark, Inc. and a get-out-the-vote assault from the No on 13 field organization helped guarantee the defeat of Measure 13. All evidence pointed to the importance of a consistent, value-driven, antidiscrimination message across television, cable, radio, direct mail, phone banks, and earned media, as well as the relentless pursuit of voting groups targeted through the survey research.

In a year when the conservative political climate made the passage of Measure 13 seem almost inevitable, the No on 13 effort ultimately prevailed because it was able to define the issues. Voters were persuaded that voting "no" protected inalienable rights and did not create new ones.

19

Bay State Class Warfare

How a "Guaranteed" Income Tax Cut Proposition Was Defeated in Massachusetts in 1994

Phyliss Johnston

"Tax the rich. Vote yourself a tax break." This was the rallying cry used to promote a graduated state personal income tax on the 1994 Massachusetts ballot. There was no mistaking the class warfare strategy underlying the call for "tax fairness": force the wealthiest 8 percent to pay more while "guaranteeing" tax relief for the 92 percent of low- and middle-income taxpayers.

What was not immediately clear was how measures promising tax cuts for nine out of ten taxpayers could be defeated. An examination of the campaign—and the aftermath of a class warfare implosion—raises interesting implications for Massachusetts and the country.

Battle Lines

At issue were two related measures. Question 6, a two-sentence constitutional amendment, would have required that the state's existing flat income tax be replaced with a graduated system. Question 7, a tax-rate law proposed by initiative, would have set new personal income tax rates beginning in 1995 if both measures were approved by voters.

The principal sponsor and author of Questions 6 and 7 was the Tax Equity Alliance of Massachusetts (TEAM), a Massachusetts lobbying group supported by public employee unions and headed by talk show host Jim Braude. The coalition formed under the banner of the Campaign for Guaranteed Tax Relief included the stalwarts of the state's liberal tradition—the

Originally published in *Campaigns & Elections* magazine, April 1995.

state AFL-CIO, the Massachusetts Teachers Association, and U.S. Rep. Joe Kennedy (D)—along with the American Association of Retired Persons and the League of Women Voters.

The opposition read like a "who's who" of the state's business community. At the forefront of the NO on 6 & 7 coalition stood the Massachusetts High Technology Council, Massachusetts Taxpayers Foundation, Massachusetts Bankers Association, National Federation of Independent Business, Associated Industries of Massachusetts, and Massachusetts Business Roundtable. The coalition hired Winner/Wagner & Mandabach, a national political consulting firm specializing in ballot questions, to direct the campaign.

Early polling, based on the ballot wording, showed the measures leading by a 2 to 1 margin. A survey of six hundred registered voters conducted by Opinion Dynamics for the opposition found that 71 percent favored Question 6, with only 21 percent opposing and 8 percent not sure. Public opinion on Question 7 was also positive: 62 percent in favor; 26 percent opposed; and 12 percent not sure.

Research showed that, overall, the pro-grad-tax arguments were more powerful than those raised by the opponents. The claim of tax fairness and equity (included in the actual ballot wording) was extremely effective with voters, particularly when linked to the offer of a tax break for nine out of ten Massachusetts taxpayers.

Conversely, several anti-grad-tax arguments were effective in firming up "no" voters and swaying persuadable voters. Question 6 would give the legislature the power to change the tax rates proposed in Question 7. In addition, passage of the two measures would immediately increase personal tax rates for small business owners and entrepreneurs. Although each could be a powerful argument, neither was regarded as a "silver bullet."

According to consultant Paul Mandabach, the research presented a three-pronged creative challenge: (1) simplify the complex tax arguments into cogent campaign messages; (2) combine the two measures into one package; and (3) unify all the messages through one central theme or metaphor. "Unifying the messages through a pejorative metaphor was the most difficult and important challenge we faced," Mandabach points out.

With the battle lines drawn and the odds posted, the grad-tax measures captured early and continuing media coverage. Of the nine questions on the November ballot, the showdown between labor and business, Democrats and Republicans, "the rich and the rest" was the hot issue.

The early months of the campaign reinforced this public perception. Democratic gubernatorial primary candidates aligned with the unions. Republican governor William Weld stood with the business community.

Fat Cat Attack

The yes campaign opened up on the attack. The group fired on potential corporate contributors to the no campaign during the Boston Marathon. Ironically, the race coincides with Patriot's Day, the fateful April day in 1775 when Massachusetts militiamen discharged the "shot heard round the world." The grad-tax proponents were taking aim at a sponsor of the historic race, the John Hancock Mutual Life Insurance Company. The imagery used in the *Boston Globe* account of a plane flying a banner proclaiming "Cut your taxes? Does Hancock say no?" over the company headquarters presaged the ultimate role reversal of the pro and anti campaigns. The pro-grad-tax guerrilla squad struck.

In the following months, the yes campaign escalated its attacks on executives of leading banks and high tech companies who contributed corporate dollars to the NO on 6 & 7 Committee. Grad-tax supporters distributed leaflets to employees at the targeted firms. The message was delivered in "shoot 'em up style." One "wanted poster"–style leaflet bore a photo of a corporate contributor surrounded by the question "Why does this man want to kill your tax cut?" A second handout, headlined "A Holdup is in Progress! of employees, customers, and shareholders," listed the anti-grad-tax "crimes" of the company "suspects" (AKA three executives) along with their respective salaries and stock options.

In early September, the grad-tax proponents ignited a firestorm with their first radio ad. The sixty-second spot singled out one corporate CEO as a "big spender" who was using "corporate funds to help his own bottom line . . . while his company lost $2 billion and is laying off 20,000 workers." Listeners were urged to call an "800" number to hear a hypothetical discussion, recorded by actors portraying a seemingly befuddled CEO and his assistant, on the merits of the grad tax.

Former U.S. senator Paul Tsongas (D-Mass.) led the counterattack, slamming the ad as "business bashing." Democratic state senator and former gubernatorial candidate Michael Barrett quickly added his denouncement of the anti-business tactics. Although a grad-tax proponent, Barrett said, "I think it creates the kind of class warfare that makes business people hate the Democrats. That doesn't get us anywhere."

The leader of the pro-grad-tax campaign responded with an emphatic "no" when asked if the leafleting and radio strategy backfired. According to Braude, the intent was not to stir up public outrage against targeted CEOs. The strategy was aimed at increasing the motivation of pro-grad-tax activists and decreasing the number of potential corporate contributors to the opponents' campaign.

"It had a wonderful impact on our active supporters," said Braude. "You'd have to ask the businesspeople what impact it had on them."

Kevin Kiley, executive vice president of the Massachusetts Bankers Association, believes the personal attack strategy had a dual impact. "The public assaults on CEOs encouraged some of the highly visible coalition members to take a more public position against the grad tax," he said. "For others, the tactics acted as a stimulus to step up to the plate."

Tax Cut or Tax Trap?

With the airing of the attack radio spot, both campaigns moved squarely into the limelight. The first NO on 6 & 7 radio ad laid the groundwork for framing the issue by employing "tax trap" as a strong metaphor for the measures that would ensnare small business employers and individual taxpayers.

The first round of TV ads quickly followed. The reality-based tack taken in the proponents' ad sharply contrasted with the metaphoric approach of the opponents'.

The yes campaign's thirty-second spot featured photos of people displayed in rapid succession along with the amount each would save on state taxes if Questions 6 and 7 passed. The MTV-style montage ends with a stretch limousine moving along a city street as a narrator says, "Of course some people's taxes will go up a little, but they can afford it."

In the first opposition ad, the camera remains fixed as a hand sets a chunk of cheese in a mouse trap, labeled only with the numbers "6 & 7." The message delivered visually and verbally—"It's a tax trap!"—was simple and straightforward. It conveyed the easily grasped metaphor the no campaign used to frame all its messages.

As the research showed, the images used should vary. Whether shown a mouse trap, bear trap, or lobster trap, voters would grasp the meaning. Moreover, the no campaign hoped that the imagery would affect the perception of the yes campaign's promises of tax relief as bait for the tax trap.

After the first week of head-to-head ads, in which both sides had about equal TV exposure, voter attitudes shifted. A tracking poll conducted by Opinion Dynamics in late September showed a twenty-point drop in the "yes" vote on both questions. This increased the "no" and "undecided" vote by ten points each.

The NO on 6 & 7 campaign continued on the air for eight weeks, reinforcing its tax trap frame with thirty-second production spots and credible spokesperson ads. The yes campaign temporarily pulled its ad off TV, concentrating instead on free media and grassroots activities.

At this juncture the yes campaign appeared to move from the offense to the defense. Its personal attacks had raised more public criticism of its tactics than press coverage of its staged protests. The new topic for its press releases and events was countering the opponents' argument that small business owners would be damaged by the grad tax. However, this shift to the opposition's turf did little to undercut the small business message that the no side had been delivering since the onset of the campaign.

Role Reversal

In the closing weeks of the campaign, the NO on 6 & 7 Committee drove home its message that the tax proposition would hurt all taxpayers, sooner or later. The immediate impacts on small business employers would ultimately be felt by everyone. Voters were warned not to be tempted by the bait—a thinly veiled appeal to short-term greed. After all, the lure of a tax cut for 92 percent sounded too good to be true. And, as the adage goes. . . .

The credibility of these messages was bolstered by the campaign's volunteer TV spokespeople. A local fisherman and a recycler explained to voters that the grad tax would raise tax rates on many small business owners like themselves. Senator Tsongas urged voters to "put the grad tax behind us and work together to create jobs."

The final salvos of the yes campaign consisted of two TV ads aimed at discrediting the opponents' claim that the measures would grant the legislature new taxing powers. A howling wolf was the image used in one spot, while the favorable ballot wording of Question 6 appeared in the second ad. Both ended with the admonition to "vote yourself a tax break." Neither served to reverse the campaign's downward spiral tracked in private and public polls.

As compelling as the tax fairness and tax break arguments were, neither made a decisive impact on the majority of voters. They failed where the tax trap metaphor succeeded.

A newspaper reporter captured the situation best when he described a casual conversation with his mother, an apolitical Somerville resident, a week before election day. He asked her what she was going to do on 6 and 7, and she said she was voting no because it was a "tax trap." He asked her what that meant, and she answered, "I don't know, I just know that it's a tax trap."

Implications

On election day, the grad tax was overwhelmingly defeated by 70 to 30 percent (Question 6) and 71 to 29 percent (Question 7). Voters clearly did not rally around the class warfare banner.

At first blush, Massachusetts may have looked ripe for a graduated state income tax. Traditionally pro-labor and liberal, the Bay State has long been—and still remains—Kennedy country and a stronghold for President Clinton. On closer inspection, the state's electorate widely supported a second term for its pro-business Republican governor. More important, the region is home to working people still bruised from the worst recession to hit the state since the Great Depression.

The fact that Massachusetts voters would not fall for a political trap like these two ballot initiatives has larger implications for other states that may face similar questions in the future.

Index

Abortion, 3–4
  Boxer vs. Fong, 32, 35, 37–38
  D'Amato vs. Schumer, 33, 36, 40
  Dornan vs. Sanchez, 104
  EMILY's list, 10, 85, 89
  Feingold vs. Neumann, 47–48, 50–52
  Foster primary/runoff victory, 163
  Hagel vs. Nelson, 58
  James vs. Blount, 149
  Lewis vs. Prather, 112
  Ventura vs. Coleman vs. Humphrey, 123–124, 129
  Whitman vs. McGreevey, 154
Abrams, Robert, 31
Abramson, Paul, 27n. 24
Achtenberg, Roberta, 25, 166–174
Adley, Robert, 158
Advertising. *See also* Television and radio advertising consultants, 9
  GOP funding advantage, 12
  issue advocacy, 8–9
  lawn signs, 18
  media, 8–10
  newspapers, 18, 96–97
  phone banks and phone lists, 18–19, 90
  soft money use, 8–9
Affiliation, party. *See* Parties and party funds
AFL-CIO, 8, 130, 202
African American voters
  Boxer vs. Fong, 43
  D'Amato vs. Schumer, 33
  Dornan vs. Sanchez, 101
  Feingold vs. Neumann, 51, 53
  Foster primary/runoff victory, 165
  James vs. Blount, 140–141, 145, 148–149
  Lewis vs. Prather, 116
  Louisiana electorate, 157, 165
  McKinney primary victory, 107–111
  redistricting, 107–108
  Whitman vs. McGreevey, 155
Agriculture, 3, 127, 129
Alabama, James vs. Blount, 24, 137–149
Aldrich, John, 27n. 24
Alesina, Alberto, 28n. 35
Allen, Doris, 167–168
Armed forces, 5
Asian American voters, 35–36, 42–43, 101, 173
Auto insurance, 150–155

Balanced budget, 5
Baldwin, Tammy, 23, 50, 83–92
Ballot initiatives. *See* Referenda and ballot initiatives

Barkley, Dean, 121–124, 125, 127, 129, 133
Barrett, Michael, 203
Beck, Paul Allen, 27n. 27
Behr, Roy L., 28n. 38
Beyle, Thad, 27nn. 13, 14, 28n. 50
Bibby, John F., 27n. 34
Biersack, Robert, 27nn. 18, 23
Big government, 4
Black voters. *See* African American voters
Blount, Winton, 24, 137–149
Bolger, Glen, 56
Bowler, Shaun, 28n. 49
Box-Steffensmeier, Janet M., 27n. 21
Boxer, Barbara, 22, 31–44
Bradley, Bill, 168–169
Brady, David, 26n. 11
Braude, Jim, 201, 204
Brody, Richard, 26n. 8
Brown, Willie, 25, 166–174
Bryant, Ted, 139, 141
Bush, George, 4
Butterworth, Blair, 178, 180–182, 184–185
Byrd, Robert, 15–16

California
  Boxer vs. Fong, 22, 31–44
  Brown vs. Jordan vs. Achtenberg, 25, 166–174
  Dornan vs. Sanchez, 19, 23, 100–105
  referenda, 20–21, 25, 189–195
  San Francisco football stadium, 25, 189–195
  term limits, 166–167
Campaign committees, national, 13–14
  Feingold vs. Neumann, 49, 51
  Lewis vs. Prather, 113–115
  Pressler vs. Johnson, 67
  Whitman vs. McGreevey, 153
Campaign financing, 5, 7–12
  advertising spending on, 8–10, 18
  Baldwin vs. Musser, 85–86, 89, 91
  campaign committees, role of, 13–14
  competitive campaigns, costs of, 10–11
  consultants, 9
  corporate donors, 8
  D'Amato vs. Schumer, 32
  direct mail appeals, 9, 18
  disclosure requirements, 8
  Feingold vs. Neumann, reform of as issue in, 45–46, 50–51, 54
  hard money, 8–12
  individual donors, 8–9
  interest groups, 8–11
  issue advocacy spending, 8–9
  message, connecting money to, 19–20

Campaign financing *(continued)*
  need to raise large sums, 10
  networks and network building, 9, 16
  open seat contests, 11
  parties and party funds, 8–15. *See also* Parties and party funds
  personal funds of candidates, 8–10
  political action committees, 8–11. *See also* Political action committees (PACs)
  polls and pollsters, 9
  public funding of state and local campaigns, 7–8
  San Francisco, 169
  seed money, 9–10
  soft money, 8–9, 12, 45, 50–51
  sources, 8–12
  state and local campaigns, 7–8
  television and radio advertising, 9–10, 15, 18
  Ventura vs. Coleman vs. Humphrey, 123, 131
  volunteers, 9–10
  war chests, 11
Campaign strategies and tactics, 18–20, 21–26
  communications strategies, 18–20, 36–39
  credibility, 19–20
  message as central to, 19–20
  personal character, 55–70, 94–98
  targeting messages to specific groups, 19
  television and radio ads. *See* Television and radio advertising
Campbell, Angus, 27n. 29
Campbell, Mark, 152–153
Castellanos, Alex, 74, 77
Center for Responsive Politics, 28n. 44
Challengers, obstacles faced by, 9–11, 12–15, 17–18
Checchi, Al, 19, 34
Christian Coalition, 48, 51, 58, 116, 142, 196–200
Christian groups, 8–9, 24–25
Claxton, Donny, 141
Clinton, Bill, 4–6, 14, 23, 113, 115, 116-117
Cogan, John, 26n. 11
Coleman, Norm, and race for Minnesota governorship, 14, 24, 121–134
Communications strategies, 18–20, 36–39
Consultants, 9, 13–14, 147
"Contract with America," 4–5
Contributions. *See* Campaign financing
Converse, Philip E., 27n. 29
Cook, Charles, 93
Cooper, Jim, 22, 71–79
Corporate donations to campaigns, 8–9
Cotter, Pat, 140–141, 149
Crime, 4, 6. *See also* Gun control
  Baldwin vs. Musser, 90
  Boxer vs. Fong, 33, 35
  D'Amato vs. Schumer, 39
  Dornan vs. Sanchez, 103–104
  James vs. Blount, 144, 147
  Thompson vs. Cooper, 77
Czar, Kathy, 121, 131, 136

D'Amato, Al, 22, 31–44
Dastugue, Quentin, 158, 161–163

Davis, Fred, 146–148
Davis, Jack, 170, 190–191
Davis, Julie, 197
Death penalty, 33, 36
Democratic party, 3–7. *See also* Parties and party funds
Devlin, Paul, 87
Direct mail appeals. *See* Mailings and leaflets
Disclosure of campaign contributions, 8, 54
DiVall, Linda, 74
Dole, Robert, 5
Donovan, Todd, 28n. 49
Dornan, Bob, 23, 100–105
Duffy, Jennifer, 36
Dukakis, Michael, 4
Duke, David, 158, 160–163

Edmonds, Tom, 179, 183–184
Education, 3–4, 6–7
  Baldwin vs. Musser, 86–87
  Boxer vs. Fong, 32
  D'Amato vs. Schumer, 36
  Dornan vs. Sanchez, 103–104
  Hagel vs. Nelson, 60
  James vs. Blount, 137, 141–144, 147
  Ventura vs. Coleman vs. Humphrey, 127
Edwards, Edwin, 157–162
Eichenbaum, Steve, 48, 50–51
Elderly voters, 4
  Baldwin vs. Musser, 90
  Dornan vs. Sanchez, 103–104
  Massachusetts progressive income tax referendum, 202
  McKinney primary victory, 108–110
EMILY's list, 10, 85, 89
Environment, 3, 7–9
  Baldwin vs. Musser, 89
  Boxer vs. Fong, 37–39
  Feingold vs. Neumann, 51
  San Francisco football stadium referendum, 190
  Ventura vs. Coleman vs. Humphrey, 122

Fang, James, 170
Faucheux, Ron, 28n. 43
Federal Election Commission (FEC), 8
Feingold, Russell, 22, 45–54
Feinstein, Dianne, 31
Ferraro, Geraldine, 35
Fields, Cleo, 156, 158, 160–165
Financing. *See* Campaign financing
Finkelstein, Arthur, 19, 39, 66–67, 70
Fiorina, Morris, 28n. 36
Flag salute, 4
Flake, Floyd, 33
Fletcher, Bill, 106, 109
Foley, Tom, 5
Fong, Matt, 22, 31–44
Football stadium referendum, San Francisco, 25, 189–195
Foster, Mike, 25, 156–165

Franking privilege, 15
Funding and fundraising. *See* Campaign financing

Gambling, 164
Gay rights and gay voters
    Baldwin vs. Musser, 87–89
    Boxer vs. Fong, 35, 38
    Brown vs. Jordan vs. Achtenberg, 172–173
    Clinton views, 5
    Oregon referenda, 26, 196–200
    San Francisco football stadium referendum, 194
    Ventura vs. Coleman vs. Humphrey, 130
Georgia, McKinney primary victory in, 23,
    106–111
Gephardt, Dick, 20
Get-out-the-vote drives. *See* Voter registration,
    mobilization, and turnout
Gierzynski, Anthony, 27n. 33
Gimpel, James G., 26n. 10
Gingrich, Newt, 5–6, 38, 164–165
Goodin, Robert, 28n. 48
GOP. *See* Republican party
GOPAC, 164–165
Gottlieb, Allen, 180
Green, John, 27n. 23, 28n. 39
Green, Mark, 35
Green Party, 14, 23, 93–99
Gubernatorial elections
    costs of competitive campaigns, 10
    and incumbency, in 1996–1998, 7
    James vs. Blount, 137–149
    Ventura vs. Coleman vs. Humphrey, 14, 24,
        121–134
    Whitman vs. McGreevey, 150–155
Gun control, 3, 5, 7
    Boxer vs. Fong, 32, 35, 37–39
    D'Amato vs. Schumer, 33, 36
    Foster primary/runoff victory, 163
    Hagel vs. Nelson, 58
    James vs. Blount, 149
    Lewis vs. Prather, 116
    Thompson vs. Cooper, 78–79
    Ventura vs. Coleman vs. Humphrey, 126
    Washington referendum, 25, 177–188

Hagel, Chuck, 22, 55–61
Handgun Control Inc., 178, 182
Hard money, 8–12, 12
Hart, Peter, 3
Health care, 3–4, 6
    Baldwin vs. Musser, 86–87, 90
    Boxer vs. Fong, 32, 39
    Clinton reform plan, 5
    D'Amato vs. Schumer, 33
    Thompson vs. Cooper, 72–73, 75
Herrnson, Paul S., 27n. 18, 27n. 23, 28n. 39
Hillsman, Bill, 128–129, 131–132
Hispanic voters, 43, 101
Homosexuality. *See* Gay rights and gay voters
Horcher, Paul, 167
House of Representatives elections, 22–23, 81–118

Baldwin vs. Musser, 22, 83–92
    campaign committees, role of, 13–14
    costs of competitive campaigns, 10–11
    incumbency advantage, 10–11, 15–18, 21
    individual donation limits, 8
    Lewis vs. Prather, 112–117
    McKinney primary victory, 106–111
    national vs. local issues, 2–7, 15–16
    reelection rates, 15–18, 21
    Redmond vs. Serna vs. Miller, 93–99
Huffington, Michael, 31
Humphrey, Skip, 14, 24, 121–134
Hurtt, Rob, 168

Income tax. *See* Taxation
Incumbency
    campaign financing advantages, strategies, and
        trends, 9–11, 15–18
    franking privilege, 15
    PAC donations, 1996, 16
    partisanship decline, effect on, 12–15
    reelection rates, 15–16, 21
    state and local elections, 7, 16–17
Independent expenditures of PACs, 8
Independent parties, 13. *See also* Third-party
    candidates
Independent voters, 12–15, 153, 198
Individual donations to campaigns, 8–9, 12–15
Initiatives, ballot. *See* Referenda and ballot initiatives
Interest groups. *See* Political action committees
    (PACs)
Issa, Darrell, 34
Issue advocacy, 8–9, 12, 14, 46, 89

James, Fob, 24, 137–149
Jaye, Eric, 171, 192
Jefferson, William, 158
Jewish voters, 33, 43
Johnson, R. J., 50, 52–53
Johnson, Tim, 22, 62–70
Jordan, Frank, 25, 166–174

Kent, Jack, 165
Kentucky, Lewis vs. Prather, 23, 112–117
Kiley, Kevin, 204
Kinney, Paul, 190–191, 195
Klingermann, Hans-Dieter, 28n. 48
Ku Klux Klan, 156, 160

Labor unions, 8–9, 12, 130
Lacy, Bill, 74
Ladd, Everett Carll, 26nn. 5, 6, 28n. 37
Laguens, Dawn, 197
Landrieu, Mary, 158–165
Lazarus, Edward H., 28n. 38
Leaflets. *See* Mailings and leaflets
League of Conservation Voters, 51, 54, 190
League of Women Voters, 130
Lee, Harry, 158, 161
Lesbian rights. *See* Gay rights and gay voters
Lewinsky scandal, 5–6

Lewis, Ron, 23, 112–117
Linehan, Lou Ann, 57
Local elections, 24-25, 166–174
  campaign committees, role of, 13–14
  financing, 7–8
  incumbency, 11, 16–17
  individual donation limits, 8
  national issues, overview, 6–7
  term limits, 17
Local issues in national elections, 2–7, 15–16
Loomis, Burdette, 28n. 47
Lotteries, state, 7
Louisiana
  African American voters, 157, 165
  Foster primary/runoff victory, 156–165
  primary election system, 157
Lungren, Dan, 36, 42

Machado, Michael, 168
Madsen, Phil, 134
Mailings and leaflets, 9, 18
  Brown vs. Jordan vs. Achtenberg, 172–173
  Dornan vs. Sanchez, 102–105
  Foster primary/runoff victory, 163
  franking privilege, 15
  James vs. Blount, 148
  Massachusetts progressive income tax referendum, 203
  McKinney primary victory, 110
  Oregon gay rights referenda, 198–200
  Redmond vs. Serna vs. Miller, 95–98
  San Francisco football stadium referendum, 192–195
  Washington gun control referendum, 183
Malbin, Michael, 28n. 52
Mann, Thomas E., 28n. 52
Margolis, Jim, 19–20, 37–38
Massachusetts, 4
  progressive income tax referendum, 25–26, 201–206
Mayhew, David, 26n. 3
McConnell, Mitch, 23, 47, 113–15
McDade, Diane, 178, 182
McGreevey, Jim, 24–25, 150–155
McKinney, Cynthia, primary victory of, 23, 106–111
McLoughlin, John, 146
McWilliams, Carey, 27n. 26
Media, advertising. See Advertising, Television and radio advertising
Medicare, 4–5
Metaksa, Tanya, 179, 183, 187–188
Midterm elections, 6
Miller, Carol, 23, 93–99. See also Third-party candidates
Miller, Warren, 27nn. 25, 29
Minnesota, Ventura vs. Coleman vs. Humphrey, 14, 24, 121–134
Minor-party candidates, 14–15
Moncrief, Gary F., 27n. 19
Money. See Campaign financing

Moore, Dennis, 20
Morris, Dick, 5
Morris, Hank, 35, 39
Murray, Patty, 9
Musser, Josephine, 22, 83–92

National Election Studies, 27n. 30
National issues affecting local elections, 2–7
National Organization for Women, 85
National Rifle Association (NRA), 25, 52, 78–79, 116, 163, 177–188
Nebraska, Hagel vs. Nelson, 22, 55–61
Neimi, Richard A., 27n. 27
Nelson, Ben, 22, 55–61
Networks and network building, 9, 16
Neumann, Mark, 22, 45–54
New Jersey, Whitman vs. McGreevey, 24–25, 150–155
New Mexico, Redmond vs. Serna vs. Miller, 23, 93–99
New York, D'Amato vs. Schumer, 22, 31–44
Newspaper advertising, 18, 96–97, 165
Newspaper endorsements, 106–107, 122
North Dakota referenda, 20
NRA. See National Rifle Association

O'Neill, Tip, 3, 26n. 4, 102
Open seat contests, 11
  Baldwin vs. Musser, 83–92
  Lewis vs. Prather, 112–117
  Thompson vs. Cooper, 71–79
Oregon referenda, 20
  Gay rights, 26, 196–200
Ornstein, Norman J., 28n. 52

PACs. See Political action committees
Parties and party funds, 8–15
  advertising and issue advocacy, 9
  Baldwin vs. Musser, 89
  campaign committees, role of, 13–14
  coordination with individual campaigns, 9
  decline of personal identification with party, 12–15
  Feingold vs. Neumann, 51
  Foster primary/runoff victory, 164
  GOP advantage, 11–12
  Hagel vs. Nelson, 58
  independent voters, rise of, 12–15
  individual donation limits, 8
  Lewis vs. Prather, 113–116
  split ticket voters, 14
  state restrictions, 9
  Ventura vs. Coleman vs. Humphrey, 133
  Whitman vs. McGreevey, 153
Partisanship, decline of, 12–15
Patriotism, 4
Pearson, Dave, 95
Perdue, Tom, 143–144, 146–149
Perot, Ross, 14–15, 122–123, 130
Personal character, focus on, 55–61, 62–70
Personal funds of candidates, 8–10

Peterson, Paul, 28n. 36
Petition drives, 181
Phone banks and phone lists, 18–19
  Baldwin vs. Musser, 90
  McKinney primary victory, 109–110
  Oregon gay rights referenda, 199–200
  Redmond vs. Serna vs. Miller, 95–96, 98
  Ventura vs. Coleman vs. Humphrey, 130
  Washington gun control referendum, 183
Pledge of Allegiance, 4
Political action committees (PACs), 8–11
  Baldwin vs. Musser, 89
  campaign committees, role of, 13–14
  EMILY's list, 10, 85, 89
  Feingold vs. Neumann, 45
  Foster primary/runoff victory, 164–165
  GOP advantage in PAC donations, 11
  incumbents, 1996 donations to, 16
  independent expenditures, 8
  individual donation limits, 8
  Lewis vs. Prather, 115
  Thompson vs. Cooper, 72, 78
Political parties. See Parties and party funds
Polls and pollsters, 9, 94, 97–98, 144. See also
  Consultants
Popkin, Samuel, 26n. 7
Powell, Lynda, 27n. 23
Prather, Joe, 23, 112–117
Prayer in schools, 137, 141–144, 147
Preis, Phil, 158, 164
Pressler, Larry, 22, 62–70
Proxmire, William, 27n. 16, 49
Public funding of state and local elections, 7–8,
  128, 136

Raymond, Allen, 51
Reelection to House and Senate, 15–18, 21
Redmond, Bill, 23, 93–99
Reed, Ralph, 24, 140, 147
Referenda and ballot initiatives, 20–21, 25–26,
  175–206
  Massachusetts progressive income tax proposi-
    tion, 25–26, 201–206
  Oregon gay rights referendum, 26, 196–200
  San Francisco football stadium propositions, 25,
    189–195
  Washington gun control initiative, 25, 177–188
Reform Party, 14, 24, 121–134
Reilly, Clinton, 172, 190
Religious right, 137, 139, 141–142, 147. See also
  Christian Coalition
Republican party, 3–7. See also Parties and party
  funds
Republican revolution, in 1994, 4–5
Retirements, impact on 1996 congressional elec-
  tions, 5
Rivers, Doug, 26n. 11
Roemer, Buddy, 157–165
Rohde, David, 27n. 24
Rosenstone, Steven J., 27n. 30, 28n. 38
Rosenthal, Howard, 28n. 35

Ross, Andrew, 172
Ross, Jim, 191, 195
Rostenkowski, Dan, 5
Rozell, Mark, 26n. 12, 27n. 22

Sabato, Larry, 27n. 13
San Francisco
  Brown vs. Jordan vs. Achtenberg, 25, 166–174
  football stadium referendum, 25, 189–195
Sanchez, Loretta, 23, 100–105
Sanders, Bernard, 14
Sapiro, Virginia, 27n. 30
Schumer, Charles, 22, 31–44
Schwegmann, Melinda, 157, 160–165
Scott, Sonny, 143–144
Seder, Deno, 164
Seed money, 9–10
Senate elections, 21–22, 29–80
  Boxer vs. Fong, 31–44
  campaign committees, role of, 13–14
  costs of competitive campaigns, 10–11
  D'Amato vs. Schumer, 31–44
  Feingold vs. Neumann, 45–54
  Hagel vs. Nelson, 55–61
  incumbency advantage, 11, 15–18, 21
  individual donation limits, 8
  national vs. local issues, 2–7, 15–16
  Pressler vs. Johnson, 62–70
  reelection rates, 15–16, 21
  Thompson vs. Cooper, 71–79
Senior citizens. See Elderly voters
Serna, Eric, 23, 93–99
Shallman, John, 102, 105
Shanks, J. Merrill, 27n. 25
Shutdown of government, 5, 6
Sierra Club, 39, 51, 89, 190
Smith, Linda, 9
Sniderman, Paul, 26n. 8
Snowbarger, Vince, 20
Social Security, 6, 36, 87, 90
Soft money, 8–9, 12, 45, 50–51
Sonner, Molly, 26n. 12
Soraul, Frank J., 27n. 28
South Dakota, Pressler vs. Johnson, 22, 62–70
Spano, Wy, 128–129, 130, 136
Split ticket voters, 14
Spring, Terri, 83–84
State elections, 7, 24–25, 119–165
  campaign committees, role of, 13–14
  financing, 7–8, 10–11
  incumbency, 7, 11, 16–17
  individual donation limits, 8
  national elections, difference from, 6–7
  national issues, influence on, 6–7
  party funds, restrictions on, 9
  referenda and ballot initiatives, 20–21
  term limits, 17
  volunteers, campaign, 9–10
Steeper, Fred, 121, 130
Stenberg, Don, 56–59
Stimson, James, 26n. 9

Stokes, Donald E., 27n. 29
Strategies. *See* Campaign strategies and tactics
Struble, Karl, 153–155
Student voters, 87–88, 90–92, 127, 134

Tactics. *See* Campaign strategies and tactics
Taxation, 3–4, 6
    Baldwin vs. Musser, 86, 90
    Boxer vs. Fong, 33, 35
    Hagel vs. Nelson, 59–61
    James vs. Blount, 144
    Massachusetts progressive income tax referendum, 25–26, 201–206
    San Francisco football stadium referendum, 189–195
    Ventura vs. Coleman vs. Humphrey, 126, 130
    Whitman vs. McGreevey, 150–154
Television and radio advertising, 9–10, 15, 18
    Baldwin vs. Musser, 86–88, 90–92
    Boxer vs. Fong, 38–39, 42
    Brown vs. Jordan vs. Achtenberg, 173
    D'Amato vs. Schumer, 37, 39–41
    Dornan vs. Sanchez, 103–104
    Feingold vs. Neumann, 48–52
    Foster primary/runoff victory, 164–165
    Hagel vs. Nelson, 58–61
    James vs. Blount, 139, 142–143, 146–147
    Lewis vs. Prather, 115–116
    Masachusetts progressive income tax referendum, 203–205
    McKinney primary victory, 106–109
    Oregon gay rights referendum, 198–200
    Pressler vs. Johnson, 66–69
    Redmond vs. Serna vs. Miller, 95
    San Francisco football stadium referendum, 190–195
    Thompson vs. Cooper, 74–79
    Ventura vs. Coleman vs. Humphrey, 129–135
    Washington gun control referendum, 179–187
    Whitman vs. McGreevey, 153–154
Tennessee, Thompson vs. Cooper, 22, 71–79
Term limits, 5, 17, 166–167
Terris, Michael, 197
Tetlock, Philip, 26n. 8
Third-party candidates, 14–15, 23, 24, 93–99, 121–134
Thompson, Fred, 22, 71–79
Thompson, Joel A., 27n. 19
Thompson, Tommy, 53
Tort reform, 140, 144, 152, 163
Trade policy, 73
Treen, David, 157, 159, 162–163
Tsongas, Paul, 203, 205

Ulm, Gene, 47, 53
U.S. House of Representatives. *See* House of Representatives elections
U.S. Senate. *See* Senate elections

Ventura, Jesse, 14, 24, 121–134
Volunteers, campaign, 9–10, 90–91
Von Szeliski, Heidi, 197
Voter registration, mobilization, and turnout
    1998 elections, effect of voter turnout on, 5–6
    Baldwin vs. Musser, 87–88, 90–92
    Brown vs. Jordan vs. Achtenberg, 174
    campaign committees, role of, 14
    Dornan vs. Sanchez, 103–104
    Feingold vs. Neumann, 52–53
    McKinney primary victory, 110
    party spending, 9, 12
    Redmond vs. Serna vs. Miller, 98–99
    San Francisco football stadium referendum, 195
    soft money use, 8
    Ventura vs. Coleman vs. Humphrey, 134–136
    Washington gun control referendum, 183
    Whitman vs. McGreevey, 155

Waldron, Joe, 179–180
Wales, Tom, 178
War chests, 11
Washington referenda, 20
    gun control, 25, 177–188
Web sites, 87, 90, 128, 134, 135
Weicker, Lowell, 14
Weingast, Barry, 28n. 48
Weisberg, Herbert F., 27n. 27
Welfare reform, 5
Whitman, Christine Todd, 24–25, 150–155
Wilcox, Clyde, 26n. 12, 27nn. 15, 18, 22, 23, 28n. 51
Wisconsin
    Baldwin vs. Musser, 22, 83–92
    Feingold vs. Neumann, 22, 45–54
Women voters, 4
    Baldwin vs. Musser, 85
    Brown vs. Jordan vs. Achtenberg, 172
    D'Amato vs. Schumer, 33
    Lewis vs. Prather, 112
    Mass. progressive income tax referendum, 202
    McKinney primary victory, 110
    Oregon gay rights referenda, 198–200
    Redmond vs. Serna vs. Miller, 97–98
    Ventura vs. Coleman vs. Humphrey, 128–131, 134
    Washington gun control referendum, 183, 186–187
Wyld, Tom, 187